Investigating Work, Unemployment and Leisure

Nick Madry & Mark Kirby

306 ~~JOR~~ MAD

Collins Educational
An Imprint of HarperCollins*Publishers*

Published by Collins Educational
An imprint of HarperCollins*Publishers*
77–85 Fulham Palace Road
Hammersmith, London W6 8JB

First published in 1996

ISBN 0–00-322404–X

For Julie, James and Anna
N.J.M.

**For my brother Julian, my sister Melanie as well as for Andrew and Benjamin Waters.
I would also like to dedicate this book to the memory of my uncle, Norman Joseph Williams,
who sadly died shortly before its publication**
M.A.K.

Commissioned by Emma Dunlop
Edited by Kay Wright
Production by Jane Bressloff
Cover artwork and design by Derek Lee
Illustrations by Julia Osorno
Typeset by Harper Phototypesetters Ltd, Northampton
Printed and bound by Scotprint Ltd, Musselburgh

Contents

Acknowledgements

We would like to take this opportunity to thank all those people who have provided help, support and encouragement while we were writing this book and in particular: John Clossick, John Cosby, Julian Dean, Jan Derry, Richard Dunn, John Hazlewood, Rachel Hek, Lesley Hoggart, Alison Kirton, Francine Koubel, Costas Lapavitsas, Chris LeBlond, Maria Lenn, Sarah Marks, Eddie Sanderson, Helen Tucker, Mary Waterhouse and The Computer Unit at Amersham & Wycombe College.

The Library Staff at Amersham & Wycombe College as always provided an excellent service as they do for us and our students all-year round. Thanks in particular to Bill, Anne, Maggie and Céline.

Pat McNeill always remained positive and encouraging even when faced with things which were likely to turn his hair grey.

Emma Dunlop , Jim Ryan, Louise Wilson and Kay Wright had the unenviable task of turning our rambled scribblings into something which could be published and the final appearance of this book owes everything to their skills and forebearance.

Finally, we would like to thank our A-level sociology students at Amersham & Wycombe College and our colleagues in the General Education section for putting up with us.

None of these people bears any responsibility for any stupidities which remain within this book. Responsibility for these resides with the two authors named on the cover.

Nick Madry
Mark Kirby

The authors and publisher are indebted to the following:

For permission to reproduce text extracts:

4th Estate (*Rivethead*, pp52–3); Blackwell Publishers (Chp5, Item C, p132; Chp5, Item C, p145; Chp9, Item A, p212); Cassell Academic (Chp2, Item B, p46–7; Chp6, Item A, p146); Causeway Press (Chp7, Item A, p174); Community Care (Chp6, Item D, p145–6); Department of Employment (Chp2, Item A, Fig 2.9, p46); Equal Opportunities Commission (Chp3, Item B, p75–6); Guardian News Services (Chp4, Item E, p105); Philip Allan Publishers (Chp2, Item C, p47; Chp3, Item A, p75; Chp4, Item D, p104; Chp5, Item B, p132; Chp9, Item B, p212–3); Laurence Pollinger Ltd. and the Estate of Frieda Lawrence Ravagli (Wages, p10); Macmillan Press Ltd. (Chp5, Item D, p132); Oxford University Press (Chp1, p12); Sage Publications (Chp7, Item B, p174).

For permission to reproduce photographs, cartoons and illustrations:
Biff Products, Mick Kidd (Fig 8.1, p189); Blackwell Publishers (Figs 2.1, 4.3, pp24, 86; Tables 2.3, 3.2, 5.5, 7.4, pp40, 60, 113, 155; Blackwell Science (Fig 2.6. p41); Peter Brooks (Fig 1.3, p10); Policy Studies Unit, Cambridge NEC (Fig 3.6, p73; Table 1.3, p5); Cartoonists & Writers Syndi-

cate (Fig 1.4, p18); Central Statistical Office (Tables 1.2, 3.4, 7.1, 7.2, 7.6, 7.7, 7.9, pp3, 71, 150, 151, 159, 160, 170; Figs 2.5, 5.2, 5.3, 5.4, 7.4, 8.2, pp39, 114, 115, 165, 190); Chapman & Hall (Table 7.5, p158); Department of Employment (Fig 2.9, p46); *The Economist* (Fig 3.4, p65); Equal Opportunities Commission (Fig 3.7, p76); Phil Evans Cartoons (Figs 1.1, .1.2, 2.4, 4.4, 4.8, pp5, 8, 36, 87, 98); Ewan McNaughton Associates, Daily Telegraph (Table 1.1, p3); John Gorman (Fig 4.2, p84); Gower Publishing Ltd (Fig 3.3, p56); Guardian Media Group Plc. (Figs 2.2, 5.1, 5.5, 9.1, 9.2, pp31, 110, 117, 196, 198); Table 5.10, 6.4, pp127, 140); Heinemann/Reed Educational (Fig 5.8, p128); HMSO (Tables 4.1, 4.4, 5.2, 5.4, p80, 101, 109, 112; Figs 2.7, 4.5, 5.7, 5.8, pp42, 91, 124, 125); Leeds Postcards (Figs 1.5, 3.5, pp19, 66); Macmillan Press Ltd (Fig 2.2, p31); MCB University Press (Table 3.3, p63); John Sturrock, Network Photographers (Fig 4.6, p93); New Left Review (Table 9.1, p210); New Scientist (Fig 2.8, p45); News Line, Workers' Revolutionary Party (Fig 4.7, p94); New Statesman and Society (Fig 6.1, 7.1, pp144, 162; Table 4.2, 6.6, pp89–90, 144); OPCS (Table 6.1, p136); Open University Press (Figs 7.2, 7.3, pp163, 164; Table 7.8. p166); Oxford University Press (Table 6.1, 6.2, 6.3, 6.5, pp136, 137, 139, 142); Philip Allen Publishers Ltd. (Table 1.4, 3.1, pp16, 57; Fig 2.5, p39); Policy Studies Institute (Table 4.3, p97); Rex Features (Fig 3.1, p53); Rough Guides Ltd. (Fig 9.4, p206); David Simmonds (Fig 3.2, p55); Stanley Thornes Publishing (Fig 7.5, p169; Table 7.10, p173); Thomas Nelson Ltd. (Table 3.5, p72); Times Newspapers Ltd. (Fig 9.3, p199; Table 4.5, p103); Unemployment Unit (Tables 5.1, 5.3, pp108, 111).

While every effort has been made to contact copyright-holders, this has not proved possible in every case. The Publishers would be pleased to hear from any copyright-holders not acknowledged.

Preface

The Sociology in Action series aims to provide readers with an interesting up-to-date account of the main themes in the areas covered. The series has been written primarily for students following the sociology 'A' and 'AS' level syllabuses. However, it is also designed to be helpful to those entering for GCSE examinations in sociology as well as related disciplines. The series will also prove valuable for those preparing for the certificate qualifications in social work and General National Vocational Qualifications, and for undergraduates following sociology subsidiary courses. To this end, each book relates the issues specific to its subject area to the broader concerns of social science and the humanities. The philosophy underlying the series has been to encourage students to deepen their understanding of the subject by engaging in short exercises and larger-scale projects as they progress through the books. The authors have followed the student-centred approach which provided the impetus for the establishment of the GCSE syllabus and such innovative courses as the AEBs 'A' level syllabus developed by the InterBoard consortium.

Investigating Work, Unemployment & Leisure provides a picture of the social organisation of work and leisure and how these have changed through time. We believe that in order to understand contemporary events it is necessary to have some historical perspective and this book therefore delves back into history to provide a context for exploring sociological debates about work, unemployment and leisure in contemporary society. It seems to us important to state that we feel these remain important areas of study and an arena for a blurring of the boundaries between sociology and the other social sciences which is a very welcome contemporary trend.

The book includes exercises and suggestions for coursework which it is hoped will be developed and modified according to the aims and needs of the students and the facilities available.

We hope you find the book interesting and useful in your studies. We thank you for searching this book out and apologise for any stupidities which remain despite the efforts of others.

Nick Madry
Mark Kirby

1

Sociological approaches to work and production

'Who first invented work?'

Charles Lamb, Letter to Barton, September 1822

Had Lamb been a sociologist he might have asked the question, 'Who first socially constructed "work"?'. In either case the underlying assumption is the same – that the nature of work is problematic. According to Keith Grint (1991), 'no unambiguous or objective definition of work is possible'. He adopts the view that work is a social construction, meaning that there is nothing natural, inevitable or permanent about what is deemed to constitute 'work'. What counts as 'work' and the significance attached to it can vary tremendously in human societies as it is a 'phenomenon without fixed or universal meaning across space and time . . . some cultures do not distinguish between work and non-work; others distinguish between work and leisure; still others by reference to employment as a particular category of work'. The meaning of work at any particular time or place is a reflection of cultural evaluations and power relations, as can be seen for instance in the subordinate and gendered status of domestic labour and its popular classification as non-work.

This chapter begins with an investigation of the difficulties involved in distinguishing between the spheres of work and non-work. It discusses the ambiguous character of work by considering wider alternatives to formal paid labour and looks at the links between the formal sphere and the informal domestic sphere. The chapter then explores the classical approaches of Karl Marx, Emile Durkheim and Max Weber, and while it demonstrates the primary importance they attached to work over other forms of activity and discourse, it also illustrate the continuing relevance of their theories for contemporary society.

Work and non-work

In the complex relationship between work, unemployment and leisure, work is the pivotal concept, for without the concept of work itself the other two would be meaningless. It is only by reference to work that we come to understand the meaning of unemployment and leisure. This is true even during a period when, it is argued, work is becoming relatively less central for many people, whether by choice in the sense that greater emphasis is placed on leisure, or involuntarily as a result of long-term unemployment. As Paul Thompson (1993) says:

> Even at a time of inexorably rising unemployment work matters. Not only is it the means of securing a reasonable standard of living, for those who are

employed, our experience of work also continues to shape among other things, politics, class and leisure. How work motivates or fails to gain our commitment helps determine the performance of companies and countries. It is important, therefore, that sociologists understand the changing nature of work.

But what exactly is work?

Try to write a brief definition of work in your own words.

For many years the definition of work was not an issue in sociology. Work meant paid employment, the selling of labour in the context of an employee–employer contract. A number of changes have complicated the picture in recent years, for instance the changing perception of unemployment as numbers in this category have risen, the redefinition of domestic labour as a result of changing perceptions of gender roles, and the growth in leisure as a result of changing patterns of work and consumption. As the future of paid employment has become more problematic, sociologists have taken a new interest in what has been termed the 'informal economy', meaning work that occurs outside the traditional and official category of paid employment.

The three economies

Gershuny and Pahl (1980) were among the first sociologists to explore this area. They distinguished between the formal and informal economies. The *formal economy* is that which is done overtly and is officially recognized as contributing to the Gross National Product. The *informal economy*, they argued, could be divided into three parts:

* the *hidden* or *'black'* economy (from the term 'black market'). This refers to work which should be part of the formal economy but is done for 'cash in hand' or 'off the books', in other words without the Inland Revenue knowing about it. This sector is small and illegal;

* the *household* economy (including housework);

* the *communal* economy.

Sociologists refer to a number of aspects of society which are 'hidden'. Give an example of one such area and explain what it has in common with the concept of the 'hidden economy'.

The last two constitute what is known as the 'grey economy', which consists of work done for free. This sector is large and legal and involves almost all adults but it is difficult to measure. Some estimates have suggested that the grey economy might account for as much as 51 per cent of all labour hours.

1) Give an example of 'work' in each of these categories.
2) If the informal economy is hidden, suggest how it might be possible to measure it.

The analysis of the informal economy has been taken a stage further by Deem (1988). She subdivides the hidden or black economy into three parts:

* utilitarian crime, which involves time, effort and material gain;

* work whose proceeds are not declared to the state, undertaken by the

unemployed, those with a second job (moonlighting), pensioners or others supplementing their other sources of income;

- pilfering from employers, making financial gain through illicit activities associated with a job.

Deem further divides work in the informal economy into domestic work and work in the community. Domestic work involves the production of goods or services by members of a household for members of that household which otherwise would have to be purchased. Traditionally much of this work has been done by women and has often been undervalued in financial terms. Some feminists have argued that housework should be paid. Table 1.1 suggests that they may have a point.

Table 1.1   How it adds up: the average housewife's weekly timetable

	Hours	*£*
Nanny	17.9	105.61
Cook	12.2	65.27
Cleaner	12.2	65.27
Laundress	9.3	35.34
Shopper	6.4	24.32
Dishwasher	5.7	21.66
Driver	2.6	11.70
Gardener	1.4	8.26
Seamstress	1.7	6.12
Other	1.3	5.20
Total	70.7	348.75

Hourly rates from employment agencies across the country.

Source: *Daily Telegraph,* 3 February 1993

Table 1.2   Time used in a typical week, by employment status and sex, 1992–3

	Full-time employees		*Part-time female*		*Retired*	
	Males	*Females*	*employees*	*Housewives*	*Males*	*Females*
Weekly hours spent on:						
Employment and travel	47.1	42.2	20.8	0.4	0.5	0.6
Essential cooking, shopping and housework	13.0	25.5	32.5	38.1	17.0	33.0
Essential childcare, personal hygiene and other shopping	13.2	20.0	25.2	29.4	10.0	14.0
Sleep	49.0	49.0	49.0	49.0	49.0	49.0
Free time	45.7	31.4	40.6	51.1	91.5	71.4
Free time per weekday	5.0	3.0	4.7	6.6	12.8	9.7
Free time per wekend day	10.3	8.2	8.5	9.0	13.8	11.5

Source: *Social Trends 24,* London: HMSO (1994)

1) *Which group of people have the least leisure time, according to Table 1.2? What are the reasons for this?*

2) *It is evident that the amount of time spent on housework has not declined in the last 50 years despite the increased availability of 'labour-saving' devices. Why might this be so?*

3) *Some feminists have argued for many years that housework should be paid. Using the information from these two items, how far do you think this argument is justified?*

4) *Other feminists oppose the idea that housework should be a paid activity. Suggest one possible reason for adopting such a view.*

5) *Suggest reasons why payment for housework has not yet come about. Feminists have a number of theories on this. You will find a good summary of this debate in Abbott and Wallace (1990).*

6) *In what sense, if any, could housewives or househusbands be 'paid' if their partner is in paid employment?*

Work in the community is either done on a casual basis, such as when helping a neighbour, or systematically such as by regular work for a charity. This work would otherwise be paid and is a growing area of the hidden economy due to the Conservative government's policy of transferring work from the formal sector to the informal. The 'Care in the Community' programme is one example of this.

Deem argues that many of the features of work in the formal economy are mirrored in the informal economy: in both sectors working conditions, discretion and opportunities are influenced by class, race and gender, by the state and by power relations and ideologies.

Construct a table with two columns, one headed 'Work in the formal economy' and the other 'Work in the informal economy'. Then, using the categories social class, ethnicity, gender, state policy, power relations and ideology, write a brief explanation of how each of these factors might affect the nature of the work experience and opportunities in the formal and informal sectors respectively.

Produce a report which profiles the contemporary labour market. Consider differences in employment patterns according to social class, ethnicity and gender in terms of pay, terms and conditions (e.g. full-time, part-time, temporary, etc.), and distribution across sectors of industry. Write a summary of your findings and suggest how different sociological theories might explain them.

An obvious starting point would be the latest copy of Social Trends. *Also try to obtain copies of material produced by the organization Labour Research. Newspapers frequently contain reports on changes in patterns of employment. Back issues of* Sociology Review *would also be helpful, particularly with the theoretical explanations.*

1) *What effect would you expect an increase in unemployment to have on the amount of activity in (a) the household economy, and (b) the black economy?*

2) *Would a fall in unemployment be likely to result in more or less DIY work?*

Operationalizing the concepts of work and non-work

Roger Gomm (1992), following Deem's suggestion, extends the attempt to classify work and non-work in an exercise which has been adapted here.

Figure 1.1 Work: going full-time!

Source: Evans (1986), p. 17

1) *Copy out the following table and then complete it by ticking the appropriate columns according to the sectors of the economy in which that type of 'work' might take place, as in the first example. Add six further examples of your own.*

Table 1.3   Work and non-work

	Sphere of economy			
	Formal	Informal		
		Black	Grey	
Activity		Hidden	Household	Communal
Mending cars for money	✔			
Using office word-processor to type a novel for a friend		✔		
Making home-made wine				
Taxi driving for money				
Taxi driving for free				

Source: Adapted from Gomm (1992)

2) *Are there any forms of work which could not be considered part of the formal economy even when a cash transaction is involved?*
3) *Are there any which are confined to just one sector of the economy?*
4) *Do the jobs carried out in the household economy share any distinctive characteristics?*
5) *Ask some people to think of all the sorts of work they do in a week that are not part of a regular paid job. Ask them to include 'unofficial paid work', emphasizing the confidentiality of the exercise!*

6) *Try comparing the lists of men and women. Describe any marked differences?*

7) *Compare the lists you have compiled from questioning other people with the one you made earlier when completing Table 1.3. What do their lists include that yours did not? Identify any form of 'work' that does not fit in any of the economic spheres in Table 1.3*

8) *Now go back to your own definition of work. How adequate is that definition in the light of what you have just read? Rewrite it by incorporating the points discussed above.*

Keep a diary for two days; write down as accurately as possible everything you do, and try to allocate each activity to one of the categories in Table 1.3. (You could use a similar technique to that used by Sue Glyptis; which appears on pages 159–61 of this book.) Prepare a blank table for your own use. Divide the left-hand column into units of time, and write the activity in the appropriate box or boxes. Add another category, namely 'non-work', as an extra column on the right-hand side of the table. Allocate to this column every activity that you cannot fit into the categories of work.

This is one way of trying to find out the balance between work, non-work and leisure. Are there any disadvantages with this method? Did you deliberately leave some things out? Would it be possible to do two things at the same time? Did you record them in two boxes?

Devise a way of classifying the activities that you listed in the 'non-work' category. Why can they not simply all be classified as leisure? For example, is travelling to work leisure? Having arrived at a classification, you can be said to have operationalized the concept of 'non-work'.

Ask an equal number (not too many!) of males and females, some of whom work full time, some part time and some of whom are 'economically inactive' through choice (housewives/househusbands), to provide a record of their work and non-work activities for a period of one week using the table you have developed. Analyse the results and discuss any patterns that emerge. Who tends to have most free time? How does this compare with the findings presented in Table 1.2? This technique could be used to compare differences between other social groups. It could also be used in conjunction with the coursework suggestions on page 20.

Ultimately the distinction between work and non-work is problematic. Gershuny and Pahl (1980) say that society must take a very broad view of what work is. There is already a spontaneous process whereby working for money in 'formal employment' is replaced by a less formal pattern, so we need to enlarge our notion of work.

The notion of work that has traditionally been seen as the remit of 'the sociology of work' has been the experience of work in paid employment, usually 'men's work' in factories. Perhaps this is not surprising as it can be traced back to the concerns of the founders of sociology – Marx, Durkheim and Weber – with the effects of industrialization.

Karl Marx: exploitation and alienation

Exploited labour

Marx began from the premise that humans must eat to live and therefore they must engage in some form of production. Because work is a social activity, of necessity this involves the establishment of relations of production. In all societies beyond the most primitive, these relations are based on ownership or non-ownership of the means of production. One group (or class) owns the materials used in the production process; the others do not, and survive to the extent that their labour power can be sold in an unequal system of exchange. The group owning and controlling the means of production is in a superordinate position to the rest by virtue of this ownership. Its members are in a position to take control of the surplus produced (beyond what is needed for subsistence) in the form of profit. This is the basis of the exploitation of labour. Marx declared in *The Communist Manifesto* (1848): 'The history of all hitherto existing society is the history of class struggles.'

> *Suggest ways in which it is possible to gain an income without working in a capitalist society. As we saw in the last section, this will involve your making decisions as to what is and is not work.*

Marx is described as a materialist, which means that he viewed the material needs of human beings and the ways they have sought to meet these needs, essentially through the emergence of forms of production, as the crucial basis for explaining social relationships and the social structures of society as a whole. Critics of this view maintain that it leads to economic determinism, meaning that they feel Marxist explanations attempt to explain all social phenomena on the basis of economic activities. This criticism is reflected, for example, in Weber's argument that there were many different bases for domination in society, not just those associated with production and social classes.

In capitalist society Marx saw the relationship between labour and capital as essentially one of conflict over economic exploitation. According to the theory of surplus value, workers do not receive in wages the true value of what they produce. The conflict over this is intensified by the fact that the workers, or proletariat, are wage labourers whose primary attachment to work is via the cash nexus. In relations between capital and labour, the primary aim of capital is to minimize wages while the primary goal of labour is the reverse. However, the balance of power favours capital because capitalists have the power to hire and fire workers, but workers are subject to the vagaries of the market economy. Members of the proletariat have little choice but to sell their labour power in return for wages, and will only continue to be employed for as long as their labour power produces profit for capital. In this context labour itself becomes a commodity, and each worker has a worth measured in money terms. Workers who are not worth the wage will not be employed.

> *How is the balance of power between capital and labour related to the level of unemployment at any given time?*

The following letter was published in New Society magazine:

> Surely one of the points that underlies Marx's arguments [is] that the divisions arising from a society based on property are bound to cause economic and social instability based on intense feelings of insecurity and

Figure 1.2 Labour as a commodity

Source: Phil Evans, in Foot (1977), p. 44

anxiety. No amount of proselytizing, either on religious grounds through the puritan work ethic with its promise of monetary gain or status, disguised as the grace of god, or its modern secular equivalent – the snobbery of a graded meritocracy – will ever pacify these pressures . . .

Democracy in Britain, as in a lot of countries, is more a matter of ritual than any real capacity to have control over our own lives. It is a myth, in reality a civil war without arms and circumscribed by law. Democracy, as we normally understand it, is belied by the fact that we still have to sell our freedom in order to survive. In short, we remain the slaves of capital and those who own and control it.

A.A. Deane, *New Society*, 27 October 1983

1) *How does the author express support for a Marxist view of society?*
2) *Identify and explain the two factors referred to which might be seen by some as ways of legitimizing the capitalist system.*
3) *Try to locate contemporary newspaper articles (CD-ROM versions would be a convenient source) about the controversial pit closure programme that was sanctioned by The President of the Board of Trade, Michael Heseltine in 1992–3.*

Outline the arguments that were made for and against the closure of 'uneconomic pits' at the time. What was the outcome?

Assess the extent to which the outcome either supports or rejects the view that workers in a capitalist society 'remain the slaves of Capital and those who own and control it'.

Do the same exercise for any more recent industrial dispute with which you are familiar, or one which is currently in the news.

Alienated labour

According to Marx, work has become a means to an end, rather than an end in itself, something that is done for wages subject to the control of the employers. He believed that whenever human beings are coerced to perform an activity they will experience a sense of 'alienation'. In capitalist society, where people have to work for wages, alienation can be seen as an endemic feature of working life.

Marx's discussion of alienation was based on an explicit notion of human nature which sets us apart from other species. He wrote of 'species-specific powers', by virtue of which human beings:

- have a limitless range of creative potential;

- require reciprocal, 'truly human' relationships;

- must not be physically or mentally constrained, because humans manipulate nature whereas animals merely respond to it. The uniqueness of the human species lies in the fact that it alone produces its own means of subsistence, the very activity through which individuals can realize their full potential as humans.

- need to engage in all-round personal development.

So humans have the capacity to work creatively and express their individuality as well as their humanity by satisfying individual needs and those of others; yet for most people work is not like this at all.

The term 'alienated' literally means to be 'separated or cut off from something', in this case, from work. How is this experienced?

Whereas in craft production people can see in what they make something which is distinctively theirs, employees working for a wage do not control or own the things they produce, which are mere commodities. Humans become slaves to the object and cannot enjoy the product of their labour.

As workers are alienated from the product of their labour they are also alienated from the act of production itself, unable to find satisfaction in the performance of work. Because people cannot express their true nature in work it is no longer a means of self-expression but a means of 'self-estrangement'. So in work people feel they are a stranger to their 'true self'.

The final element of alienation is related to the wider economic conditions prevailing in capitalist society. Because it is a system based on self-interest, all human relationships are reduced to the workings of the market to the extent that self-interest becomes more important than concern for the community. When fellow humans are seen as competitors, exploiters or commodities that cost money, people are alienated from one another.

Alienation for Marx was therefore made up of four components:

1) *Alienation from the product of labour.* Workers cannot identify with an end product of labour they do not control; it is not their own.

2) *Alienation from the act of production.* Workers do not feel involved in the production process; work has become a dehumanized process and the worker is merely 'a cog in the system'.

3) *Alienation from the self (self-estrangement).* Work is not a source of pride and achievement, so workers are denied the opportunity to realize their true self.

4) *Alienation from fellow human beings.* Workers are divorced from 'truly human relationships'.

Blauner (1964) revised Marx's terminology and described the components as powerlessness, meaninglessness, self-estrangement and isolation. His application of the definition of alienation will be considered in Chapter 2 page 29.

The concept of alienation can be used to describe the experience of groups other than just workers in paid employment. Describe how the experience of school or housework might be seen in terms of these four aspects of alienation. How useful do you find the concept for this purpose?

For further development of these ideas see Bowles and Gintis, Schooling in Capitalist America, *or Oakley,* The Sociology of Housework.

Wages

The wages of work is cash.
The wages of cash is want more cash.
The wages of want more cash is vicious competition.
The wages of vicious competition – is the world we live in.

The work-cash-want circle is the viciousest circle
    that ever turned men into fiends.

Earning a wage is a prison occupation
    and a wage earner is a sort of gaol-bird.

Earning a salary is a prison overseer's job
A gaoler instead of a gaol-bird.
Living on our income is strolling grandly outside the prison
    in terror lest you have to go in.
And since the work-prison covers almost every scrap of the living
    earth, you stroll up and down on a narrow beat, about the same
    as a prisoner taking exercise.

This is called universal freedom.

D.H. Lawrence

Figure 1.3 A is for Alienation

Source: Slattery (1990), p. 2

is for

ALIENATION

▸ *Explain the relevance of the poem Wages to Marx's views of the nature of work in capitalist society.*

Explain how the illustrator of Figure 1.3 has tried to communicate each of Marx's four components of alienation.

Two features of the way in which work tends to be organized in capitalist industrial society heighten the experience of alienation for most workers, according to Marxists. These are the mechanization of production and a highly specialized division of labour. They are quintessentially expressed in the system of production known as 'Fordism' (see Chapter 3, pp. 48–77).

Increasing mechanization, and more recently automation, of the production process have the effect of deskilling workers, since work becomes fragmented into a number of very simple tasks. They also tend to result in greater managerial control over work. This line of argument was pursued most notably by Braverman (see Chapter 2, p. 31–37). Marx saw the division of labour as a form of enslavement in the sense that people become trapped in boring, repetitious work to which they are tied for their entire working life.

▸ *Explain the difference between mechanization and automation.*

It is becoming increasingly common for people to have more than one job in their lifetimes. Read the following section of this book: Chapter 3, pp 57–70 and then answer the following questions:

1) Why do you think this is happening?
2) To what extent does the evidence suggest that a reversal of the division of labour is occurring in the way that post-Fordist writers claim?

For Marx alienation existed at two levels. First, it is a subjective feeling which individuals experience; in these terms we might describe somebody as lacking job satisfaction. But, second, it also has a much deeper significance because it is an objective feature of an economic system based on exploitative class relations. It characterizes the malaise at the heart of capitalist society and extends far beyond the workplace, colouring every aspect of social life. According to this notion, people are alienated within the capitalist system whether they are aware of it or not.

Thus the term 'alienation' might be used to describe the general feeling of discontent, powerlessness and impersonality felt by many in today's 'mass society'. It has certainly been seen as one of the main causes of industrial action, absenteeism and other strategies used by labour to combat the effects of exploitative and coercive work.

The following comments from assembly line workers talking about their work, taken from Beynon's classic study, *Working for Ford* (1973), illustrate what alienation can mean:

> 'You don't achieve anything here. A robot could do it. The line here is made for morons. It doesn't need any thought. They tell you that. "We don't pay you for thinking," they say. Everyone comes to realize that they're not doing a worthwhile job. They're just on the line. For the money. Nobody likes to think that they're a failure. It's bad when you know that you're just a little cog. You just look at your pay packet – you look at what it does for your wife and kids. That's the only answer.'
>
> 'I place the car off the hoist, I've been doing that for three years now. With the line you've got to adapt yourself to speed. Some rush and get a

break. I used to do that but the job got out of hand. I just amble along now. Thirty seems a lot when you're working here. Some jobs you're on you can't talk or you'll lose concentration. When I came here first I couldn't talk at all. Now I can manage a few words with the man opposite me.'

'It's a relief when you get off the moving line. It's such a tremendous relief. I can't put it into words. When you're on the line it's on top of you all the time. You may feel ill, not one hundred per cent, but that line will be one hundred per cent. Being on sub-assembly is like getting off the roundabout. Y'know . . . day in day out . . . never stopping. I still have nightmares about it. I couldn't go back on that line. Not for anything.'

Which of the four components of alienation discussed earlier can be identified in these extracts? Refer to the extracts to illustrate your answer.

The concept has also been applied to white-collar work. C. Wright Mills's highly readable account of the changing face of white-collar work in post-war USA contains a vivid portrayal of alienation in the 'salesroom' that is America.

The personality market, the most decisive effect and symptom of the great salesroom, underlies the all-pervasive distrust and self-alienation so characteristic of metropolitan people. Without common values and mutual trust, the cash nexus that links one man to another in transient contact has been made subtle in a dozen ways and made to bite deeper into all areas of social life and relations. People are required by the salesman ethic and convention to pretend interest in others in order to manipulate them. In the course of time and as this ethic spreads, it is got on to. Still it is conformed to as part of one's job and one's style of life, but now with a winking eye, for one knows that manipulation is inherent in every human contact. Men are estranged from one another as each secretly tries to make an instrument of the other, and in time a full circle is made: one makes an instrument of himself, and is estranged from it also.

Mills (1951), p. 187

1) *Explain this passage in your own words.*
2) *How far do you agree with Mills's view of alienation in the 'personality market'?*
3) *To what extent is it still valid?*

Marx's concept of alienation has been criticized on the grounds that it is too ideologically biased, that is to say that it is too bound up with the wider Marxist critique of the capitalist system and the radical solution of a proletarian revolution. Marx was also criticized on the grounds that he was naive to believe that a communist society would produce conditions conducive to non-alienated labour. Finally, it has been said that the whole concept of alienation rests on the less than scientific notion of human nature.

Nevertheless, as Slattery (1991) states, 'when used as Marx originally intended – as an analysis of work, of human nature and of the subjective effect of class exploitation – it still wields considerable moral, if not sociological force'. It is still commonly used to describe the nature of the work experience for many people, even if it is often in terms of the watered-down version of 'low job satisfaction'.

Emile Durkheim: anomie and the division of labour

The economic division of labour

The concept of the totally self-sufficient individual conjures up images of someone struggling to provide for themselves all the basic necessities of life. In other words, the work that is involved in this process is not divided between people. In practice in an advanced industrial society it is very difficult to be totally self-sufficient even when somebody wants to be.

As soon as tasks are allocated between people on a regular basis, a division of labour occurs. At its simplest, then, the division of labour is an economic concept that refers to the division of work into a number of specialized tasks. On a wider level it also refers to the nature of the social relationships based on interdependence between individuals in such an economic system.

A rudimentary form of the division of labour tends to exist in even the least developed societies. This is usually based on a simple differentiation by age or gender. However, the economic advantages of specialization are such that as societies become more complex people tend to specialize in particular occupations.

The advantages of this industrial division of labour were evident in terms of raised living standards and cheap consumer goods. However, as we have already seen, there are negative implications to this type of work.

The division of labour was taken to new heights by 'scientific management' and the 'Fordist' method of assembly-line production based on attempts to increase the efficiency of every worker. There is a considerable debate in sociology as to whether or not this trend has been replaced by 'post-Fordism', which implies a multiplicity of skills and capacities on the part of each worker (see Chapter 3, pp. 50–9). However, most people in paid employment in advanced industrial societies clearly still earn a living by specializing in a particular trade or occupation.

The social division of labour

Durkheim saw the division of labour as the key feature distinguishing traditional societies from modern ones. He saw it as the basis of two different types of social order, according to the type of social solidarity it produced.

In traditional society the bonds that unite people are based on their essential similarity; they are held together by 'bonds of similitude'. With a very simple division of labour most people are engaged in the same occupations, and this tends to give rise to a common lifestyle and a common value system which Durkheim called the 'collective conscience'. The strength of the 'collective conscience' is that there is very little individuality and deviations are easily noticed and severely punished *'pour encourager les autres'*; in other words, the 'collective conscience' is reaffirmed and the bonds uniting people are reinforced. In such societies people are produced from the same mould, and have a high degree of homogeneity. By virtue of the low division of labour, people's experience of life is similar and the opportunities for individuality just do not exist. Durkheim described this form of social solidarity as a mechanical form of bonding. Traditional society was therefore characterized by *mechanical solidarity*.

As society becomes more complex, the division of labour increases to such an extent that the existing basis of social order is undermined. Different occupational specialisms mean that the experiences of individuals can differ greatly and the essential similarity is lost. Homogeneity gives way to heterogeneity, collectivism to individualism. People just do not have as much in common as they used to, and the result is the emergence of different sub-cultures with their own values which may diverge from those of the 'collective conscience'. The basis of social order is threatened and it is necessary for a new form of social solidarity to develop which can successfully combine social order and individual freedom.

This new form of social solidarity, which Durkheim called *organic solidarity,* was the logical consequence of a highly specialized division of labour. When no individual is totally self-sufficient, people depend on others for the provision of essential goods and services. Economic interdependency, reciprocity and cooperation for mutual benefit form the basis for order in modern, organic societies.

However, Durkheim was aware that this order might be precarious if individuality and economic self-interest were allowed to dominate at the expense of the common good. Self-interest could lead to chaos and conflict, and the survival of society would be under threat. Durkheim talked of the duality of human nature, by which he meant that we all have two consciences – the personal (based on self-interest) and the social (reflecting the interests of society). In mechanical societies these tend to be one and the same, but in organic society they do not automatically coincide. He thus saw the need for the economic relationships between individuals to be underpinned by an ethical code of moral principals, norms and values. This would be backed by a formal system of justice with the power to administer legal sanctions.

> Make a list of all the goods and services that you have consumed in the last 24 hours which you did not produce yourself, and another list of those you provided for yourself. How dependent are you on the work of others?

Anomie and problems of modern society

Durkheim was not centrally concerned with the economic effects of the changed division of labour, but instead with its moral effects. Although in economic terms the increasing division of labour was progressive, Durkheim also identified problems that may occur, and in this respect he differed substantially from thinkers such as Adam Smith and the sociologist Herbert Spencer (whose ideas have inspired the contemporary New Right). The danger of untrammelled individualism is neatly illustrated in this extract from Joseph Heller's novel, *Catch 22:*

> 'From now on I'm thinking only of me.'
> Major Danby replied indulgently with a superior smile: 'But, Yossarian, suppose everyone felt that way.'
> 'Then,' said Yossarian, 'I'd certainly be a damned fool to feel any other way, wouldn't I?'

How did Durkheim propose that society could overcome the tendency towards individualism?

- He argued that societies could not be organized simply on the basis of contracts between individuals, as Smith and Spencer envisaged, for the simple reason that there must be a framework of commonly understood assumptions to enable people to engage in contracts. This social element underlies economic transactions. A society based simply on individuals contracting with each other would be inherently unstable, because such contracts would potentially be unjust.

- The only way in which social cohesion could be combined with the notion of individuality was through a system of universally shared morals enshrined in enforceable laws. The law also provided Durkheim (as a positivist) with some overt measure of the form and degree of solidarity existing in society.

- He viewed the transformation of society as being from ones with undifferentiated tasks with a highly repressive form of law to the differentiated modern society in which the law is primarily restitutive. His conception of this change was evolutionary, and sometimes it appears that Durkheim viewed it as almost automatic. This has led to the criticism that he did not really provide a thorough theory of social change.

- He was, however, clear that problems could emerge in this process, particularly if the level of individuality was too high. Here again Durkheim contrasts strongly with the predecessors of the contemporary New Right.

- He suggested that if the process of transition is forced (the forced division of labour) then problems might emerge. The name he gave to this phenomenon was *anomie*.

- He believed that if societies operated on extremely individualistic lines, unequal and unjust contracts would be established due to the inequalities of wealth and income in society. He therefore opposed inherited wealth and argued for a meritocratic society.

- He argued that extremes of individualism would lead to *anomie* because people would be insufficiently tied into the moral order of society. Important examples of *anomie* included industrial conflict and strikes, as well as crime and suicide.

- However, his faith in the evolution of societies led him to believe that such phenomena were purely temporary manifestations that occurred during transitional periods. Thus *anomie* could be overcome without the need for a total transformation of society.

Durkheim later revised his views due to the rise of authoritarianism and the outbreak of the First World War. He now argued that there was a need to develop greater forms of democratization. His notion of democracy was based on the idea that there needed to be the greatest possible level of communication between state officials and the mass of the population. Secondary associations, modelled on the medieval guilds, were to act as the key intermediaries between the state and the people; in modern times this role was best provided by professional associations and possibly trade unions. In this way people would be involved in debate and represented by their occupational groups. Durkheim's conception of democracy and society was therefore crucially centred on the arena of work.

> *There is a debate in sociology over the extent to which the 'professional status' of certain occupational groups is based on a commitment to serving the community according to a self-regulated ethical code of practice, or whether it is more accurate to see their control over selection and recruitment procedures and restrictive practices, not to mention the high rewards often associated with such professions, as a self-interested strategy.*
>
> *1) Give an example of an occupation that is normally seen as one of the professions. What distinguishes it from other occupations that lack professional status?*

2) *How far do you agree that either professional associations or trade unions can be seen as prototypes of a future social order of the type envisaged by Durkheim?*

Information on the professions can be found in Haralambos and Holborn, 1995, pp. 301–4.

Durkheim's vision of the role of secondary associations may have provided the model for the forms of industrial democracy proposed in the 1970s and the method of national decision making known as tripartism or corporatism, involving representatives of employers, employees and the government, which were prominent in the UK in the 1950s and 1960s.

Durkheim has been criticized for his belief that the problems he identified and saw as manifestations of *anomie* were abnormal and purely temporary. Marxists have argued that he misidentified a fundamental aspect of modern society as a temporary aberration.

His evolutionary views on how societies change have also been criticized as simplistic, ignoring divisions and inequalities of power in society and overlooking the importance of the use of violence (the First World War being a prime example). It is clear that these developments in the world around him (including the death of his son in the war) did cause him to modify his views somewhat and to develop his views on democracy.

Table 1.4 Popular perceptions of social justice (by voting choice)

Percentages of respondents agreeing strongly or somewhat with the propositions	Con	Lab	Lib Dem	All
Equality of opportunity				
1. It's fair if people have more money or wealth but only if there are equal opportunities.	80	74	84	78
2. It is just that disadvantaged groups are given extra help so that they can have equal opportunities in life.	84	80	84	80
3. In Britain, people have equal opportunities to get ahead.	58	34	35	42
Equality				
4. The fairest way to distribute wealth and income is to give everyone equal shares.	18	41	21	29
Desert				
5. People who work hard deserve to earn more than those who do not.	97	94	95	95
6. It is simply luck if some people are more intelligent than others, so they don't deserve to earn more money.	15	21	16	16
7. In Britain, people get rewarded for their effort.	56	39	48	47
8. In Britain, people get rewarded for their intelligence and skill.	65	50	52	56
Functional inequality				
9. There is incentive for individual effort only if income differences are large enough.	73	64	66	66
10. People would not want to take extra responsibility at work unless they were paid extra for it.	83	83	84	84
11. It's alright if businessmen make good profits because everybody benefits in the end.	55	33	43	42
12. Income differences in Britain today are just, because they encourage hard work, so that everyone benefits in the end.	60	29	35	40

Source: Swift, Marshall and Burgoyne (1992), p. 29

However, he never really explained the way bureaucracy in modern society can operate to undermine democratic processes, unlike his contemporary Max Weber.

His concept of *anomie* nonetheless remains important as an attempt to consider the social and cultural underpinnings of modern society, and was influential in the later development of functionalist analysis, which centres on cultural consensus. In more recent times it has inspired social-democratic ideas on the need for a sense of community and has supported the rejection of New Right individualism.

1) *Explain how the information in Table 1.4 relates to Durkheim's ideas about the nature of organic solidarity.*

2) *To what extent does this information suggest that British society is anomic?*

Max Weber: bureaucratization and rationality

According to Weber, complex societies based on an extensive division of labour are not self-regulating systems but ultimately require regulation by the state. He believed the twentieth century was more likely to witness a bureaucratic revolution than a proletarian one. He connected the process of bureaucratization with two more fundamental and interrelated trends – the growing rationality of societies in the West, and the decline of enchantment (disenchantment) and magic (demystification). Rationalization refers to logical, calculating modes of thought, action and planning. This mode of thinking replaces belief systems based on magic, faith or superstition, notably religious belief of various types.

Weber noted that in modern Western capitalism there were various spheres in which rationalization had proceeded to an extent that was unknown in any previous type of society. Two areas in which this was particularly apparent were science and rational calculation (or book-keeping). Scientific knowledge was demystifying the world as it provided explanations for the previously inexplicable. According to Weber, this has had the effect of reducing the level of uncertainty and risk in life, which as a consequence have become more amenable to bureaucratic control, which he saw as more technically efficient.

The spread of science made possible the progressive implementation of rational technology in production. This together with rational calculation promoted the rational conduct of the entrepreneurial activity so distinctive of capitalism.

Unlike Marx, who explained the rise of capitalism on the basis of changes in the forces and relations of production, Weber was much more concerned to examine the development of the ideas of rationality and efficiency that he saw as characteristic of the modern world. In his famous study *The Protestant Ethic and the Spirit of Capitalism* (1901) he argues that some of the values of ascetic Protestantism, which made a virtue out of hard work, discouraged pleasure and encouraged self-discipline and an austere lifestyle (often referred to as 'the work ethic'), contributed to the development of capitalism. He considered Protestantism to be a much more sceptical, 'rational' religion than Roman Catholicism, and therefore the development of Protestantism was a move towards more 'rational' ways of thinking, which later encouraged the emergence of capitalism. Weber thus emphasized changes in ideas much more than changes in the material factors of production as determinants of social development.

Figure 1.4 The Iron Cage
of Bureaucracy

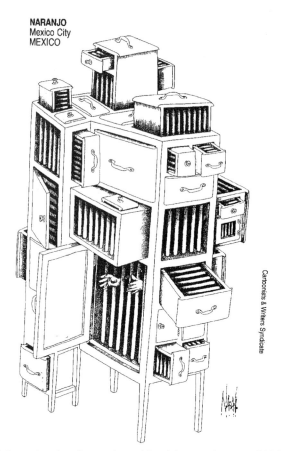

NARANJO
Mexico City
MEXICO

Cartoonists & Writers Syndicate

Though he celebrated rationality as the spirit of the modern age, Weber saw a danger that the growth of a bureaucracy (to administer society rationally) could lead to bureaucratic domination, which he considered a nightmarish prospect. He argued that society could become ensnared in an 'iron cage' of bureaucracy, a prospect that led him to make some critical comments on rationality in general.

These negative views of the rational aspect of modern society have been taken up by a number of contemporary writers who can be described as 'postmodernist' in their rejection of the ideas of rationality and science and their promotion instead of the importance of artistic and aesthetic values as the basis on which we should live. This leads them to stress the importance of the sphere of consumption much more than the sphere of production.

Weber's concept of rationality is therefore central to the sociology of work and leisure, not only because it provides an alternative account of the motions of capitalist society to the Marxist materialist analysis, but also because it has offered an opening for the reaction to the values of rationality, efficiency and increasing production that is gaining in popularity in contemporary sociology.

1) (a) *Explain the message of the postcard on the opposite page.*
   (b) *To what extent does it contrast with Weber's views on the 'spirit of the modern age'?*
2) (a) *How important do you think the 'work ethic' is in contemporary Britain?*

Figure 1.5 'Resist the work ethic'

Source: Jannie Oosthuisen, Leeds Postcards

Consider the lilies of the field
how they grow
They toil not,
neither do they spin
And yet I say unto you
That even Solomon in all his glory
was not arrayed like one of these

resist the work ethic

    (b)   *How might sociologists attempt to measure it?*

  3) (a)   *What advantages did Weber believe a rational approach provided?*

    (b)   *What criticisms might be made of the notion of rationality?*

    (c)   *How might people's reactions against rationality be manifested in the sphere of work and leisure?*

Conclusion

This chapter has attempted to link some of the key ideas of the three writers who are generally viewed as the 'fathers of modern sociology', showing how their theories were crucially influenced by the changes in the world around them. We have also noted the centrality in their thinking of the world of work, production, industry, industrial relations and capitalism. Their contrasting views provide starting points for analysis of the modern (or possibly postmodern?) world we live in today.

 Which of the three writers outlined above do you think provides the most important starting point for an analysis of contemporary trends in work and leisure? Which concepts do you feel are most useful/least useful?

One criticism that might be made of the content of this chapter is in relation to its choice of writers to consider. These are all male, all white and all dead. It could therefore be suggested that they do not provide an appropriate selection. We have included them because we think they have important things to say, but we are also aware of this potential criticism.

1) How valid do you think this criticism might be?

2) Investigate the origins of feminist writing on work and leisure, and write a short report of 500 words explaining how the concepts developed by feminist writers might inform and provide a background to an investigation of work and leisure.

3) Consider what other writers (if any) you might include in a list of early sociologists who offer important insights into the world of work and leisure. Discuss your choices with your colleagues/classmates.

Essay Questions

1) In the view of some conflict theorists, social stratification originates in the economic relations of a society, and it results in *exploitation, domination* and *conflict*. Thus it has been argued that society can be divided into two main classes in antagonism to one another.

A) Give brief definitions of the three terms shown in italics above.

B) Choose one society and show how these terms can be applied.

C) Name and illustrate two other concepts drawn from within the conflict approach which you would use to bring out the nature and consequences of social stratification. (JMB, June 1986, Paper 2)

2) What is meant by the term 'increasing complexity of the division of labour'? Using comparative examples, what do you consider to be either the main causes or the main consequences of this? (London University, 1988, Paper 3)

3) 'All institutions in the modern world are becoming increasingly bureaucratic.' Discuss. (Cambridge Local Examinations Syndicate, June 1987)

4) 'Regardless of the type of society, as long as women are allocated domestic roles they will continue to have lower status than men.' To what extent do you agree with this statement? (London University, 1988, Paper 3)

Coursework suggestions

Carry out an investigation into the relationship between the various aspects of the formal and informal economies referred to earlier in this chapter. You might consider replicating or modifying the investigation by Pahl and Wallace (1985). Pahl's original schedule of 41 services (1984, pp. 218–19) is reproduced in Abercrombie and Warde (1994, pp. 98–9). You could perhaps try to discover if there is the same degree of polarization between households that have the benefit of regular income from paid employment and those that do not. To what extent do the findings vary according to age and ethnicity?

Bibliography

Abercrombie, N. and Warde, A. et al (1994) *Contemporary British Society,* 2nd edition Cambridge: Polity

Abbott, P. and Wallace, C. (1990) *An Introduction to Sociology: Feminist Perspectives,* London: Routledge

Beynon, H. (1973) *Working for Ford,* Harmondsworth: Allen Lane

Deem, R. (1988) *Work, Unemployment and Leisure,* London: Tavistock

Durkheim, E. (1893) *The Division of Labour in Society,* 1960 edn, New York: Free Press

Evans, P. (1986) *The Labours and Researches of Evans,* London: Labour Research Department

Foot, P. (1977) *Why You Should Be a Socialist,* London: Socialist Workers Party

Gershuny, J. and Pahl, R. (1980) 'Britain in the decade of the three economies', *New Society,* 3 January

Gomm, R. (1991) *Sociology 'A' Level,* Cambridge: NEC
—— (1992) *Sociology Resource Bank,* Cambridge: NEC

Grint, K. (1993) *The Sociology of Work,* Cambridge: Polity

Haralambos, M. and Holborn, M. (1995) *Sociology: Themes and Perspectives,* 4th edition, London: Collins Educational

Heller, J. (1961) *Catch 22,* London: Transworld

Lawrence, D.H. (1972) *Selected Poems,* Harmondsworth: Penguin

Marx, K. and Engels, F. (1846) *The German Ideology,* 1970 edn, London: Lawrence & Wishart

—— and Engels, F. (1848) *The Communist Manifesto,* 1965 edn, Moscow: Progress Publishers

Mills, C. W. (1951) *White Collar: The American Middle Classes,* New York: Oxford University Press

Pahl, R. (1984) *Divisions of Labour,* Oxford: Blackwell

Pahl, R. and Wallace, C. (1985) 'Household work strategies in the recession', in Redclift, N. and Mingione, E. (eds) *Beyond Employment,* Oxford: Blackwell

Slattery, M. (1990) *The ABC of Sociology,* Basingstoke: Macmillan

—— (1991) *Key Ideas in Sociology,* Basingstoke: Macmillan

Smith, A. (1776) *The Wealth of Nations,* 1982 edn, Harmondsworth: Penguin

Spencer, H. (1891) *The Study of Sociology,* New York: Appleton

Swift, A., Marshall, G. and Burgoyne, C. (1992) 'Which road to social justice?', *Sociology Review,* Vol. 2, No. 2

Thompson, P. (1993) 'The labour process: changing theory, changing practice', *Sociology Review,* Vol. 3, No. 2, November

Weber, M. (1901) *The Protestant Ethic and the Spirit of Capitalism,* 1976 edn, London: Allen & Unwin

2

Changing patterns of work: pre-industrial to post-industrial?

> 'Work is of two kinds: first altering the position of matter at or near the earth's surface relatively to other such matter; second, telling other people to do so. The first kind is unpleasant and ill paid, the second is pleasant and highly paid.'
>
> Bertrand Russell, *In Praise of Idleness*

There is a tendency within sociology to classify society on the basis of the predominant economic mode of production. Work in any society is embedded within a particular mode of production which shapes its distinctive character. Changes in the mode of production have profound effects both for individuals and for the social structure.

It was a concern to explain the social changes brought about by industrialization that exercised Marx, Durkheim and Weber. More recently it has been argued that, due to technological change in the nature of production and the concomitant changes in social relationships, capitalism is entering a new, 'post-industrial' phase, with equally pervasive and increasingly global social effects.

This chapter will examine the main features of work in industrial society and evaluate how far changing patterns of work in advanced capitalist countries now justify the use of the term 'post-industrial society'.

Industrial society

The aim here is to examine the archetypal features of work in highly industrialized societies. However, this is not to underestimate the importance of the historical legacy of the birth pains of industrialization for an understanding of contemporary work. As Keith Grint (1993, p. 89) says in reference to the brutality of work down the years, 'Work today is not a prisoner of the past but it is a bruised descendant.'

Occupational change

Industrialization and the growth of the factory system had the following effects on patterns of employment:

- the decline of agricultural work;
- the decline of most rural industry;
- the decline of multiple occupations and sources of income;

- the decline of the family as a collective work unit;

- the polarization of work opportunities for men and women.

The picture was of course much more complex than this. The idea that pre-industrial Britain consisted of a homogeneous workforce of skilled craft workers which industrialization proceeded to fragment into a myriad of occupational specialisms is as much an oversimplification as the idea that jobs in agricultural production were replaced en masse by employment in industrial manufacturing.

It is generally assumed that industrialization had the effect of separating work and home life, placing men in the former (public) domain while consigning women to the latter (private) domain. Prior to industrialization it does appear that women were involved in a wide variety of jobs, often working alongside men, though a gendered division of labour has always existed. Women were disproportionately represented in the most menial, poorly paid and domestically related jobs. Patriarchal control also tended to determine the ranking of occupations by status and skill; in this hierarchy women were placed somewhere between men and children, skill being considered by men as exclusively their possession.

Prior to industrialization, work was a collective activity centred on the household economy, which depended on multiple incomes. From the end of the eighteenth century, however, men came to be associated with occupational identities outside the domestic sphere, and the ideology of 'the male as breadwinner' began to take hold. The need for a married woman to work to contribute to the family income became a symbol of poverty, and the idea of married women working became less respectable as it became less common.

1) To what extent do contemporary attitudes to the idea of married women working differ from the one outlined here?

2) Identify the two occupational categories in Figure 2.1 that consistently show the biggest difference between the employment of men and women during the period 1841–1921. How might sociologists account for this difference?

Figure 2.1 clearly illustrates the historical extent of sex differences in occupational distribution. Women are noticeable by their absence from the labour force except in the areas of domestic service, textiles, and in later periods commercial employment. For instance, according to the Census of 1841 only 6 per cent of factory workers were women and throughout the whole period of the industrial revolution the largest source of employment for women was domestic service, reflecting the lack of opportunities elsewhere, partly as a result of legislation such as the succession of Factory Acts of 1802, 1819 and 1847, and the related 1867 Agricultural Act, all of which placed restrictions on the types and hours of employment permitted for both women and children.

 Try to locate details of these Acts and assess the extent to which they reflect the values of patriarchal ideology.

Ann Oakley's *Housewife* (1974) contains an account of the changing status of women resulting from industrialization. According to her it had the following effects on the role of women:

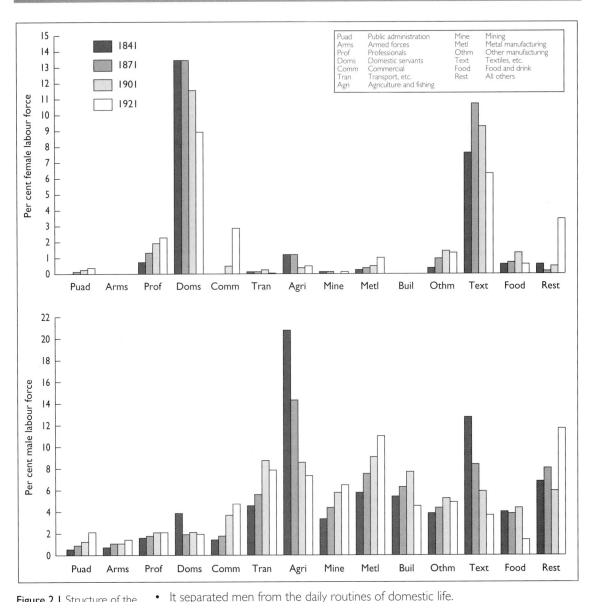

Figure 2.1 Structure of the male and female labour force, 1841–1921 (%)

Source: Grint (1993), pp. 67,68

- It separated men from the daily routines of domestic life.

- It created the economic dependence of women and children on men.

- Housework and childcare became isolated from other work.

The net result was that the 'mother/housewife' role became established as the 'primary role for all women'.

So, once the initial phase of industrialization was over, married women were systematically removed from the labour market. Barrett and McIntosh (1980) put this down to fears about the potential disruption to family life caused by working wives. The Acts in large part embodied the state's desire to bolster the family as the normal social unit through the construction of a 'familial ideology' according to which women (and children) should be confined to the domestic sphere, and their employment outside of it increasingly came to reflect this belief. In terms of the limiting effects on women's employment opportunities of the expectations associated with their dual roles as mothers and employees, strong links between domestic responsibilities and employment were evident before and during industrialization, as they still are today (see Chapter 1, pp. 3–4).

Barrett and McIntosh also ascribe the success of the factory legislation to the material and patriarchal interests of male workers. In support of this argument it may be noted that many trade unions excluded women from membership and collaborated with employers in discriminating against them.

At the same time there was a decline in the employment of child labour and a curbing of its worst excesses. According to official figures, 50,000 children were employed full time in 1851, whereas this number had fallen to 22,000 by 1871 (Department of Employment 1971). For the first time child labour came to be seen as inhumane where previously there had been little concern about children's welfare as 'home workers'.

According to Grint (1991, p. 79) these developments illustrate the resilience of the moral economy, which refers to the way in which the economic system continues to be influenced by moral or social considerations and not just the cold rationality of the market economy: 'market forces alone would have stripped work from expensive men to cheap children and women but the moral economy that supported the patriarchal family was a critical resource in the demise of employment for married women and children'.

Convergence theory

Some have argued that there is a 'logic of industrialism', according to which industrial societies tend to become increasingly similar over time. This theory, sometimes known as 'convergence theory', is most closely associated with the work of Clark Kerr *et al.* (1960). The theory predicted that, as both capitalist and communist economic systems were increasingly characterized by industrial production, the similarities between them would increase. This prediction was overtaken by the fall of Soviet communism, but the theory is still applied to comparisons between different capitalist societies.

Recent articles in the sociological journals have considered the case of Britain and Sweden (Scase 1989; Fulcher and Gould 1993). The debate is about the extent to which politics and ideology shape the nature of industrial societies and whether there are deeper changes to the mode of production that are making countries more and more alike. Fulcher and Gould hold that there is a convergence, but it is due not to the imperatives of industrialism but to the dynamics of capitalism as it becomes increasingly global in its scope. In Chapter 9 we will examine the issue of globalization in detail.

 Try to obtain a copy of the Sociology Review *article by Fulcher and Gould (1993) and answer the following questions:*

1) *Explain the concept of convergence in your own words.*
2) *Suggest one implication of the demise of Soviet Communism for the theory of convergence.*

3) *In what sense, if any, has convergence theory remained significant in sociology?*

4) *Explain the distinction between the 'imperatives of industrialism' and the 'dynamics of capitalism' as explanations of convergence, and assess their relative importance according to Fulcher and Gould.*

Technology, control and the experience of work

The word 'technology' is difficult to define in the context of work. It can refer simply to the use of different types of machinery or it can encompass holistic organizational aspects of work. Winner (1985) distinguishes between inanimate machinery ('apparatus') the technical activities of humans ('technique') and the social arrangements whereby these two are coordinated ('organization'). In practice, however, it is virtually impossible to separate the social and the technical spheres.

Technology is thought by some to possess a logic or dynamic of its own, a concept referred to as 'technological determinism'. According to this view technology advances spontaneously and inevitably; appropriate technological developments emerge, and the organizations that adopt the most progressive technology will survive. The nature of work and work relationships are shaped by the march of technology, which is beyond the control of any one individual or group. This school reflects the structural approaches that dominated sociology in the 1950s and early 1960s (notably Blauner 1964 and Chinoy 1955) which did not regard workers as autonomous beings but saw them merely as players of roles determined by the technology of the workplace.

A contrasting approach, known as 'social determinism', sees technological change as the result of social or cultural factors. So technology (apparatus) cannot explain anything because it is itself socially constructed and its effects depend on the use to which it is put. Supporters of this approach include Goldthorpe *et al.* (1968), Silverman (1970) and Gallie (1978).

> *All three of these studies are summarized in Haralambos and Holborn (1995). Look them up, and identify the main conclusion of each study. Assess the extent to which each can be said to 'fit' within the tradition of social determinism.*

The social determinists' critique of technological determinism hinges upon a fundamental debate within sociology between structure and agency which can be expressed in the question: Do people choose their own circumstances or are they chosen for them? Social determinism is firmly rooted in action theory which claims that social reality is constructed through the subjective and interpretive meanings of individuals. In other words, technology does not exist in a vacuum – it has no objective existence outside the meanings given to it by individuals. In terms of its impact on work, Goldthorpe *et al.* and Gallie give technology very little importance as an independent variable. For these writers technology does not determine organizational features or behaviour; rather they point to factors external to the work situation (such as the general political climate, for example) that influence the formation of workers' attitudes and orientations, and these in turn explain what happens inside the workplace.

More recently, attempts to bring technology back into the picture as either an independent or a dependent variable have resulted in a variety of approaches which accept that both technology and socio-cultural forces have a part to play. The essence of these approaches is a concern to explain the social processes whereby a particular form of technology comes to be used, in whose interests it operates and its consequences for the work experience.

This approach, known as 'socio-technical systems theory', considers the nature of the relationship between the technical system of production and the social system of work to be reciprocal. It assumes that work is essentially a social activity, and any model that attempts to maximize productive efficiency by taking into account only the technological aspects of work, to the detriment of human relationships, will be inadequate. To put it simply, unhappy workers tend not to work efficiently. Equally, a workplace based on a human model of maximum social efficiency without regard to the technology of production would also fall short of maximum efficiency. The optimum socio-technical system is therefore one that achieves a compromise between technical efficiency and social efficiency.

Scientific management

Having unveiled his ideas to American engineers as early as 1895, in 1911 Frederick Taylor published the celebrated text, *The Principles of Scientific Management*. The aim of this book was to outline a scenario for industry that would increase productivity, and therefore profits and wages, with the result that workers and management would experience a 'mental revolution' and learn to cooperate for their mutual benefit.

There were three main principles:

1) The 'dissociation of the labour process from the skills of the workers', which in practice means making the labour process independent of craft, tradition and workers' knowledge by reducing it to rules, laws and formulae based on knowledge exclusively controlled by management.

2) In order to ensure management control and to cheapen the cost of labour power, conception and execution were separated. Design and planning were removed from the factory floor to a specialized department, once again beyond the control of the workers themselves.

3) The results of the scientific study of work were to be communicated to workers only in the form of simplified instructions for simplified jobs which it would be their duty to follow unthinkingly and without comprehension of the underlying technical reasoning.

Taylor believed that the adoption of the techniques of scientific management would encourage both management and workers to take their eyes off the division of the surplus and divert their attention towards increasing the size of the surplus. Taylor's ideas can be traced back to the work of the classical economists, notably Adam Smith. They were the first to approach the organization of labour within capitalist relations of production from a theoretical point of view.

The essence of scientific management or 'Taylorism' was that managers should study jobs scientifically in order to discover the optimum combination of tools, human operations, groupings of workers and rest periods. This came to be popularly known as 'time study' because stop watches were used to measure work in the minutest detail. Frank Gilbreth, one of Taylor's followers, added to time study the concept of motion study, that is, the classification of the basic movements of the human body. In time and motion study the elementary movements were visualized as the building blocks of every work activity; they were called, in a variant of Gilbreth's name spelt backwards, 'therbligs'. Each therblig was given a time for its completion in ten-thousandths of a minute. The philosophy extended to break times, as is evident in this account from the automotive industry:

> In the section where they press out the car bodies in one car company, workers in 1973 were subject to an agreement on the make up of their rest allowance. The elements are as follows:
>
> | | |
> |---|---|
> | Trips to the lavatory | 1.62 minutes. It is computer precise; not 1.6 or 1.7 but 1.62! |
> | For fatigue | 1.3 minutes |
> | Sitting down after standing too long | 65 seconds |
> | For monotony | 32 seconds |
>
> Cooley (1987), p. 33

Taylor assumed that the primary motive for work was money, and in order to maximize effort on the part of the worker and to overcome resistance, incentive schemes were devised including the piecework system – payment according to the amount of work done. According to Taylorism, workers were being paid to work and not to think. Indeed, the ideal specification of the worker according to Taylor was 'that he should be so stupid and so phlegmatic that he more nearly resembles in his mental make-up the ox, than any other type' (Taylor 1947, p. 59).

The best-known example of the application of such methods was the Ford Motor Company; in fact, the term 'Fordism' has become almost synonymous with Taylorism (see Chapter 3, p. 50ff). Though only a few industries introduced this system wholesale, the philosophy of scientific management permeated industry and 'justified' the right of management to use a variety of techniques to increase their control of the work process in the name of increased productivity.

Not surprisingly, Taylor's ideas have been the subject of intense criticism, both on a practical level from workers who have been subject to them and academically on the grounds that his underlying assumptions were flawed.

First, the assumption that people are primarily motivated to work for money is undermined by the historically high incidence of absenteeism, labour turnover and industrial disputes that have tended to characterize industry run along these lines.

Second, Taylorism treated workers as if they worked in isolation rather than in a complex social group. The notion that levels of productivity can also be influenced by social considerations was highlighted by the famous Hawthorne experiments, conducted at the Western Electric Company in Chicago from 1927 to 1932 (see Haralambos and Holborn 1995, pp. 295–7), which indicated that workers respond to being treated as humans rather than as bits of machinery. It was also discovered that output was significantly influenced by peer group pressure rather than money alone. This finding gave rise to the 'human relations' school of management, which advocated schemes to increase productivity that took workers' interests into account, such as job enrichment, worker participation and 'caring personnel management' (see Chapter 4, pp. 83–6).

Taylor's belief that his methods would increase industrial harmony has been severely criticized. For Harry Braverman (1974) scientific management allows managers to monopolize all existing knowledge and separate the labour process from the skills of the workers. For the worker, work is deskilled in terms of knowledge, responsibility and discretion. The chief attraction for employers of such a system is the increase in managerial control brought about by this separation of mental from manual work, and management from workers. Other advantages to management include the depression of wages and the dispensability of workers.

Why might the fragmentation of work have these effects?

Both scientific management and human relations approaches have been criticized for their managerial bias. They were not the sciences of work so much as the sciences of management, the primary aim of which is profit maximization. Both approaches have also been accused of failing to consider the wider social and economic context in which work takes place.

How far do scientific management and human relations share the aim of controlling the workforce? (For further information on the human relations approach, see Haralambos and Holborn 1995, pp. 294–9; or O'Donnell 1992, p. 273.)

Technology and alienation

According to Blauner, 'the most important single factor that gives an industry its distinctive character is its technology' (1964, p. 6). He attempted to operationalize Marx's concept of alienation by studying the effect technology can have in giving rise to, or protecting the worker from, alienation. Although no industry has completely homogeneous technology, most have their characteristic forms of production. For Blauner technology, 'more than any other factor, determines the job tasks performed by blue collar employees and has an important effect on a number of aspects of alienation' (p. 8).

Blauner thought the concept of alienation as used originally by Marx was too ideologically biased and 'unscientific'. He was attempting to recast it in what he saw as an objective, value-free way so that he could assess the extent to which it featured in different industries according to their level of technological development. Blauner's operationalization of the concept was nevertheless closely based on Marx's original conception, as can be seen from Table 2.1.

Table 2.1 A comparison of Marx's and Blauner's concepts of alienation

Marx	Blauner	
Man is alienated from:	Alienation refers to a sense of:	Implied non-alienative states:
The product of labour	Powerlessness	(control)
The performance of work itself	Meaningless	(purpose)
His 'true' self	Self-estrangement	(self-involvement)
His fellow man	Isolation	(social integration)

One of the main points of difference between these views is that, whereas for Marx alienation is an objective feature of capitalist society that affects everyone whether they realize it or not, according to Blauner alienation can only be said to occur when it is experienced in a subjective sense.

Blauner identified four distinct levels of production technology in existence at the time he was writing in the early 1960s. These were:

1) craft,

2) machine tending,

3) assembly line, and

4) continuous process (early automation).

Each of these was typically characteristic of particular industries, as summarized in Table 2.2.

Table 2.2 Blauner's correlation of production technologies and industries

Production technology	Industry	Characteristics
Craft production	Printing	Much work still done by hand Unique products Low in mechanization High in skill
Machine tending	Textiles	High in mechanization Fairly standardized product Worker controls the machinery Reduced skill
Assembly-line	Automobiles	Highly rationalized Highly standardized Machinery controls the worker Low in skill
Continuous flow	Chemicals	Highly rationalized Highly standardized Worker monitors production and responds to emergencies Responsibility high Knowledge high

As a result of his findings, Blauner suggested an evolutionary perspective on alienation, which can be depicted as an inverted U-curve (see Figure 2.2). He stated:

> In the early period dominated by craft industry, alienation is at its lowest level and the worker's freedom at a maximum. Freedom declines and the curve of alienation (particularly in its powerlessness dimension) rises sharply in the period of machine industry. The alienation curve continues upward to its highest point in the assembly line industries of the twentieth century. In automotive production . . . a depersonalized worker, estranged from himself and larger collectives, goes through the motions of work in the regimented milieu of the conveyer belt. [Blauner 1964, p. 182]

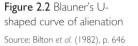

Figure 2.2 Blauner's U-shaped curve of alienation

Source: Bilton *et al.* (1982), p. 646

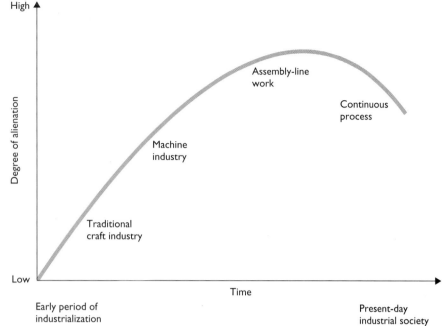

His findings from research in the chemicals industry suggested a downturn in the level of alienation with the introduction of continuous flow processes, and an increase in freedom or autonomy. In comparison with assembly-line work:

- workers had more of a sense of control over the work process as a whole;

- they experienced a greater sense of responsibility;

- they had considerable variety in their tasks and a certain amount of excitement and uncertainty related to the fact that things could go wrong (the 'fireman syndrome');

- they felt involved, tended to identify with the aims of the company and worked as an integrated team with little supervision.

Thus Blauner was extremely optimistic about the potential of such work for reducing levels of alienation in the future, and claimed that because work in continuous process industries involves control, meaning and integration it tends to be 'self-actualizing' rather than self-estranging. The term 'self-actualization' was used by Maslow (1943) to describe the highest order of human need in his 'needs hierarchy'. In other words it is the ultimate need that people aspire to satisfy, once other more basic needs, such as hunger, security, companionship and status, have been met.

 Assuming that self-actualization is the opposite of alienation, explain in your own words what the term means.

Because he saw everything else as being determined by the technology used, Blauner believed that reductions in the level of alienation would require changes in production technology. He saw the solution in terms of automation and thought it would lead to the emergence of workers with a new social personality – cooperative, non-unionized and loyal to the company – which would tend to reduce class consciousness and class conflict. This optimism places Blauner's work among a wide range of academic studies which have predicted that work in the late twentieth century was likely to experience this kind of upgrading.

Blauner's work has been criticized on the following grounds:

- It shows methodological weakness in terms of its reliance on the validity of results from questionnaires, and it is questionable whether the chemical industry is representative of industry as a whole.

- There are ambiguities about the task of monitoring continuous process production. There are negative aspects of such work which Blauner may have ignored.

- He assumed that technology at work was neutral in nature and design, rather than seeing it as a means to secure control over the workforce.

- From a Marxist point of view he ignored the basic cause of alienation – the objective position of the worker in the relations of production in capitalist society. Marxists such as Marcuse would argue that automation simply creates 'happy robots'.

- As a technological determinist, Blauner limited his considerations to what was going on inside the plant and could not account for the influence of external factors on workers' orientations to work.

- Blauner claimed to be value free, but he accepted the values of American capitalism.

1) *Which different types of production technology did Blauner investigate?*
2) *Illustrating your answer with examples, explain why Blauner attached so much significance to technology in determining the nature of work.*
3) *To what extent would you describe him as a technological determinist?*
4) *Why did Blauner think that automation would be the solution to the problem of alienation?*
5) *How valid do you consider Blauner's findings to be?*
6) *Blauner claimed that Marx's use of the concept of alienation was too ideologically biased. Why do you think he said this? How far do you think his own definition of alienation avoids such accusations?*
7) *When you have read the rest of this chapter and the following one on 'post-Fordism', critically evaluate Blauner's theory about the future of alienation in the light of developments that have taken place since his time.*

Labour process theory

Labour process theory (LPT) has developed since the mid-1970s under the influence of Marx's writings, updated by Braverman's *Labour and Monopoly Capital* (1974). As Paul Thompson (1989) suggests, the emphasis in this movement has been on who owns, controls and designs work, matters clearly related to the issue of technology discussed in the previous section.

LPT considers the effects of the capitalist mode of production (especially the relations of production) on the nature of work. The starting point is the unique property of labour as a commodity. Employers purchase only potential labour, which then has to be turned into profitable labour. In wage negotiations the primary aim of labour is to maximize rewards and protect or improve conditions of work, while the primary aim of management in a competitive market is to reduce the costs of production, of which labour remains a substantial part. In order to achieve profitable production the employer has to drive down the cost of labour by dividing it or by replacing skilled workers with unskilled. Capital also has to exercise control over labour through managerial structures and functions. Thus in this view the labour process is a site of conflict over who controls work and wage levels. This conflict determines how technology is utilized by management to subordinate labour.

There are a number of possible ways in which both the cheapening and the control of labour might be effected. For instance, labour costs might be reduced through sub-contracting or switching production to the Third World. Similarly, increased control over the workforce might be achieved through an intensification of surveillance and bureaucratic rules or alternatively by engendering in the workforce a sense of loyalty and cooperation through corporate culture.

LPT thus tries to understand the general structure of relations between capital and labour in the workplace. The debate among adherents of this broad approach tends to revolve around the extent to which capitalist social relations either constrain and set limits upon the use of workers' skills and creative powers, or rather facilitate the democratization of work organization. This has produced different schools of thought, arranged broadly around the question of whether or not increasing managerial control over the work process ultimately results in deskilling or enskilling (upgrading) of the workforce.

Braverman: deskilling and the degradation of labour

Harry Braverman was firmly of the opinion that the major feature of monopoly capitalism in the twentieth century would be a continuation of a process that had begun in the previous century – the deepening degradation of work. What Marx referred to as the real subordination of labour would only be completed in the twentieth century.

The use of increasingly sophisticated science and technology to deskill work and the strengthening of managerial control would inevitably result in a long-term tendency to degrade occupations. The widespread adoption of the 'principles of Taylorism' (see p. 27) was the prime mover of this process, since these principles transferred personal initiative and discretion from the workers to the machines they operated and to management's sphere of responsibility.

According to Braverman, the division of labour and the hierarchical organization of work do not simply enhance productivity and efficiency; the detailed subdivision of tasks is also a means of controlling the workforce. It is also makes possible the hiring of less skilled and thus cheaper labour. General skills are reduced to job-specific ones, and the skills and knowledge of craft workers are broken down, allowing companies frequently to dispense with skilled labour. From the workers' point of view, possession of skilled status provided them with some power to resist managerial domination at work, as well as enhancing their market situation in terms of pay and conditions. Braverman felt that the allied tendencies towards deskilling and increased managerial control would persist through changes in technology and work organization.

Automation

Braverman claimed that the dominant view of automation – that it is qualitatively different from mechanization, as Blauner held – was profoundly mistaken; in fact, like mechanization, in the long run automation reduces the skill requirements of the workforce:

> . . . the chemical worker has been singled out time and again as the outstanding beneficiary of 'automation', and the praises of this job are sung in countless variations. The work of the chemical operator is generally clean, and it has to do with 'reading instruments' and 'keeping charts'. These characteristics already endear him to middle class observers, who readily confuse them with skill, technical knowledge, etc. Yet few have stopped to think whether it is harder to read a dial than tell the time. [Braverman 1974, p. 224]

He goes on to argue that even in industries where operators have been eliminated from the physical process of production, such as chemicals, the supervision of machinery in more congenial surroundings has often been confused with actual increases in the use of skills and knowledge.

Braverman cites the work of James Bright (1966). Bright devised a classification of seventeen levels of mechanization and traced their relationship to sources of power and control. He then charted the way in which each level of mechanization affected the experience of work (see Figure 2.3).

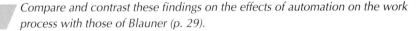

Compare and contrast these findings on the effects of automation on the work process with those of Blauner (p. 29).

Figure 2.3 Why advances in automation can have contrary effects on skill requirements

Source: Adapted from Bright, J., quoted in Braverman (1974), p. 221

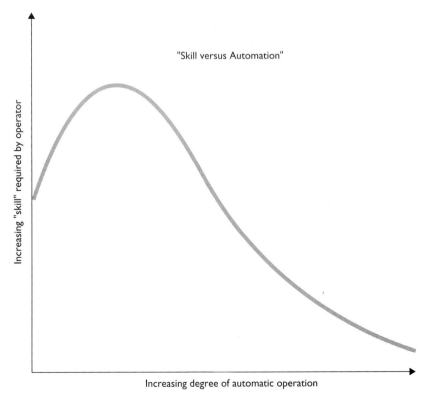

Defining skill

Defining the concept of skill is by no means simple. Try to write your own definition.

Braverman saw skill as the equivalent of 'craft mastery' which, crucially for him, involves an ability to conceive and imagine as well as 'do'. He criticized the conventional view of skill as a technical and objectively measurable thing relating to the possession of knowledge and experience in terms of 'a specific dexterity'. Such a definition 'becomes degraded along with the degradation of labor and the yardstick by which it is measured shrinks to such a point that today the worker is said to possess "skill" if his or her job requires a few days' or weeks' training' (Braverman 1974, pp. 443, 444).

He argued that skill is socially constructed and therefore influenced by ideological notions. He cited an official reclassification of jobs in the USA which tended to give the impression that there was more skill in contemporary jobs than there really was. This sort of false and arbitrary reclassification misleadingly added weight to the 'upgrading thesis' that Braverman was attacking.

As Slattery states, 'skill can refer to real attributes of knowledge and/or manual dexterity, or to labels used by management and workers to up- or down-grade a particular job. Skills may be technical or personal and often a job is labelled "skilled" even though the work involved is largely unskilled. Jobs may be deskilled but workers may not – they may be reskilled or redeployed' (Slattery 1991, p. 35).

Some have developed Braverman's 'social constructionist' view of skill along the lines that skill differentials have been construed by management as a way of artificially dividing a potentially unified workforce. Others, particularly feminists, have considered the ways in which skill labels have emerged as a product of worker resistance both to managerial attempts to deskill, and to competition from cheaper, often less organized groups of workers.

Ainley (1993, pp. 21–2) draws some useful distinctions:

- 'Enskilling' extends and develops existing skills.

- 'Multi-skilling' retains existing skills while combining them with new skills in other areas (sometimes referred to as functional flexibility or systems competence).

- 'Reskilling' means learning new skills in place of old ones at an equivalent level of complexity.

- 'Deskilling' means the loss of skills that would formerly have been acquired through study in a discipline or apprenticeship to a trade or profession.

What implications might these distinctions have for Braverman's deskilling thesis?

In the last two decades many areas of work, whether in factories or offices, have come to be mediated by computers, and the debate concerning the extent to which such work will be degraded or upgraded has continued. For the Marxists, any attempt by employers to introduce new technology and redesign jobs is an attempt to increase managerial control. This view was supported by the findings of Shaiken (1979), showing that machine tool operators had been deskilled by the removal of their decision-making power to office-based programmers.

Figure 2.4 Behind the screens

Source: Phil Evans (1986)

Despite the greater stress, new technology is much more –

– fulfilling.

Braverman also rejected the idea that a general upgrading of work had occurred as a result of changes in the occupational structure since 1945. He argued that even jobs which were once seen as of being high status have been deskilled in a process of proletarianization and homogenization in which many 'white-collar' jobs had become marked by the 'proletarian condition'. Certainly it has been suggested that many jobs in the expanding service sector have been deskilled (see p. 44 for more detail on this).

Professional workers, according to Braverman, have also been proletarianized – they have become merely the trained servants of capitalism, in many cases undertaking alienated labour in large corporations. The massed ranks of draughtsmen, accountants and technicians are the new proletariat, and the terms 'worker' and 'working class' refer to everyone who has to work for a living, whether they are professional, middle class, routine white-collar or manual workers.

> *What criticisms could be made of Braverman's classification of the professions as proletarian?*
>
> *The debates on proletarianization nd deskilling are interwoven, why might this be the case?*
>
> *What differences, if any, are there between proletarianization and deskilling? Explain your answer.*
>
> *How far do you believe each of these processes is occurring in capitalist society? You could refer to Haralambos and Holborn (1995)* Sociology Themes and Perspectives *for evidence to support your argument.*

Criticisms of Braverman

Braverman's work has been extended, modified and criticized. Some fellow Marxists criticized him for failing to address the issue of class consciousness by confining himself to an analysis of the working class as a 'class in itself' rather than a 'class for itself', portraying the working class as powerless and docile.

Explain this criticism in your own words.

Several Marxist-inspired case studies to support Braverman were conducted in the USA during the 1970s (see Zimbalist 1979). Perhaps not surprisingly, they found evidence that work had been degraded in a wide range of manual and non-manual occupations. However, critics of these findings, and the deskilling thesis in general, argue that they tend to present a romanticized image of craft production in the past, overstating the skill and autonomy of such work and thereby making comparisons with contemporary work unrealistic. Pahl (1984), for instance, believed Braverman was deluding himself about a past 'golden age' of work.

Braverman himself has been criticized on the grounds that he overestimated the pervasiveness of Taylorism and the ability of management to relentlessly pursue a strategy of deskilling and controlling the workforce, and that he underestimated the ability of workers to resist. Edwards (1979) proposed that the type of control found in an industry is the outcome of the interplay (the contested terrain) between management control and worker resistance; he identified several stages of control.

In similar vein, Friedmann (1977) argued that managerial control strategies range from 'direct control' over every aspect of the production process to 'responsible autonomy' whereby workers have considerable discretion in their work. The latter privilege is likely to be confined to skilled and functionally important (core) workers, while the rest (the disorganized periphery) are more likely to be subject to 'direct control'.

Another criticism of Braverman has been that, by concentrating on scientific management, Braverman ignored other management strategies, such as 'human relations', and the different industrial relations scenarios that prevail in different industries. In more recent years attention has turned away from explanations of management control in terms of conflict at shop-floor level to wider issues such as the importance of the product market and the state of the economy in general.

Some have seen Braverman's labour process analysis as an example of Marxist 'conspiracy theory'. Winch (1983) and Knights and Collinson (1983) argue that employers are not simply motivated by a desire to control the workforce. The deployment of new technology is the result of competitive market pressures as much as power relations in the workplace. According to Winch, although some deskilling may occur, there is no single tendency towards deskilling or reskilling; rather there is room for choice and manoeuvre over which type of technology to adopt and how work is organized.

This idea was supported by an investigation into the introduction of word processing (Buchanan and Boddy 1983), which found that technology itself does not determine anything. Changes in the overall pattern of jobs and skills were only weakly and indirectly influenced by technology, but more strongly by managerial policies.

Braverman's work has also been criticized on the grounds that it is historically inaccurate in terms of the timing, extent and pace of deskilling. According to Batstone (1988), even the most obvious aspect of Taylorism – work study – is practised in only half the workplaces in a range of recent surveys of Britain.

Braverman could not have predicted some of the developments that have occurred since his death in 1975. For example, the introduction of so called 'smart machines' may empower workers because, as Zuboff (1988) pointed out, 'information technology supercedes the traditional logic of automation' because information technology 'is characterised by a fundamental duality that has not yet been fully appreciated'. Information technology, according to Zuboff 'informates as well as automates'. Quoted in Ainley (1993), p.22.

Ainley (1993) suggests that Braverman's description of 'the degradation of work' came too soon to appreciate the capacity of computers not only to automate and deskill industrial and office work, with resultant labour shedding, but also to generate information potentially accessible by all employees and not just their managers. In this way some reskilling and even enskilling occurs among the core of remaining employees and their managers.

Recent empirical work suggests a more complex pattern of responses to automation than Braverman envisaged:

> Daniel concluded a national survey of the introduction of new technology in Britain: 'Our results provided support for those who have argued that the spread of advanced technology would enrich the jobs of workers affected, certainly in comparison with the quality of work under the characteristic systems of production or working for manual workers during the first half of the century. We found little comfort for those on the other side of the debate who have taken the view that the development of automation represents a further stage in the dehumanisation of work. The generally favourable picture we found of the impact of the new technology upon the content of jobs applied to both manual and office workers. [Daniel 1987]

> A large study conducted on behalf of the Economic and Social Research Council concluded that technological advances in the workplace had not in fact caused much downgrading of skills. Over half the employees reported that they had gained skills in the previous five years. Less than one in ten felt their job had been deskilled. This pattern, furthermore, was evident in both the manufacturing and service sectors of the economy. There was, however, some difference in the experiences of the higher skilled and the lower skilled workers on this issue. The evidence seemed to point to a widening of the skills gap in which those who already had more skills experienced an increase in the skills demanded by their work. Those who were relatively unskilled were more likely to find their work less skilful over time. Part-time female workers were worst hit. [Denscombe 1991, pp. 24–5]

> *How far do you agree with Braverman that jobs involving the monitoring of automated processes are little more demanding than reading a watch?*
> *(See page 33)*

Thus it appears that to talk of an inevitable process of deskilling and degradation of work in the twentieth century does not do justice to the complexity of the situation. As Ainley puts it, 'Enskilling, multi-skilling, reskilling and deskilling can all happen simultaneously to individuals within one employment and to the workforce as a whole as technology changes' (1993, p. 22). This makes it difficult to comprehend the overall effect of the rapid introduction of technology, particularly information technology.

Braverman has also come under fire from another quarter. Feminists have applauded him for giving a portrait of the exploited position of women in the labour process, which he expressed largely in terms of their constituting a reserve army of labour. However, they have been less impressed by his apparently traditional view of work, which has been described as highly 'productionist' and as overemphasizing the three Ms: male, manual, manufacturing work.

The feminist critique centres on the fact that Braverman failed to take a sufficiently broad view of work, embracing the sexual division of labour and the large amount of unpaid work typically done by women in the informal economy. Feminists also charge that he assumed deskilling was purely caused by management rather than the actions of male trade unionists and their sexist ideological assumptions about work.

Feminists argue that definitions of skill have also been influenced by ideology (see Cockburn 1991). Beechey (1983) points out that many of the jobs traditionally done by women are defined as unskilled when in fact they require a considerable amount of complex knowledge and ability.

Services, employment and post-industrial society

In terms of the conventional taxonomy of three sectors of the industrial structure – primary (agriculture and mining), manufacturing and services – there have been

Figure 2.5 Employment by sector, 1946–86

Note: ¹Includes electricity, gas and water

Source: Data from Ministry of Labour and Department of Employment; reproduced in Warde (1989), p. 11

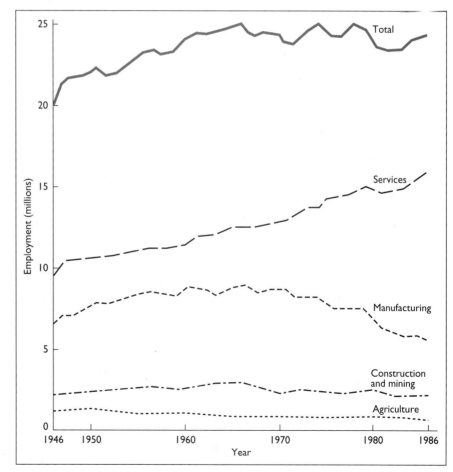

39

profound changes since 1851 when more than half the British workforce worked on the land, compared with about 2 per cent today. The relative changes in the numbers employed in each sector since the Second World War are clearly visible in Figure 2.5. (Note that construction and mining have been separated out.)

The term 'de-industrialization' refers to a situation in which there is a significant decline in the proportion of people employed in the manufacturing sector. Such a decline has occurred rapidly in Britain during the last 30 years, especially since 1980, and this has only been partially matched by the growth in employment in service industries.

Discussing the way the British economy has apparently moved (without state intervention) from being an industrial to a 'post-industrial' society, Bazen and Thirlwall (1989, p. 1) comment, 'there is an amusing acronymic classification of the countries of the world into HICs (hardly industrialized), PICs (partly industrialized), NICs (newly industrialized), MICs (mature industrialized) and DICs (decadent industrialized). The United Kingdom is a prime DIC!'

Explain in your own words what is meant by the term 'decadent industrial society'.

Britain is not the only DIC. As Nigel Harris (1983) pointed out, by 1982 more than twice as many people sold McDonalds' hamburgers in the United States as made steel. This raises the question of whether an economy can sustain itself by specializing in service-type activities. Can people survive in the long run by selling hamburgers to each other?

Sony's Chairman, Akio Morita, has warned that, far from being the sign of a maturing economy, de-industrialization is a destructive trend. 'In the long run an economy which has lost its manufacturing base has lost its vital centre. A service-based economy has no engine to drive it . . . Service industries cannot flourish in isolation, they depend on manufacturing to support them' (quoted in Stefanou 1992, p. 1). By the mid–1990s it was becoming clear that service industries did not hold the key to Britain's future prosperity.

While economists debate whether de-industrialization is a cause or effect of Britain's poor economic performance, others discuss the meaningfulness of the term when the term 'services' can refer to a number of different things. Abercrombie and Warde (1994) provide a useful typology of services (see Table 2.3).

In this scheme intermediate services are those that involve circulating money, commodities or information, for example banking. When provided to firms they are

Table 2.3 Different types of service industry

	Producer service	Consumer service
Intermediate service	Warehousing Management Consultancy	Retailing
Final service	Auditing of accounts	Package holidays Medical treatment

Source: Abercrombie and Warde (1994), p. 91

called producer services, and when provided to individuals they are called (intermediate) consumer services. Final services are those where a function is being directly provided that is used immediately in a particular time and place, though there may not be a tangible product, for example a sociology lecture. Many service industries have expanded; those which have gained in employment terms include the financial services in the intermediate sector, and the human services (health, education and social services) in the final service sector. Meanwhile other personal final consumer services, notably public transport, have contracted.

The growth of the service sector has given rise to several theories about its supposed effects for the future of work and the social structure. One of the earliest and most famous was Bell's (1973) 'post-industrial society' thesis which he developed to account for the long economic boom of the 1950s and 1960s. This thesis became part of the post-war orthodoxy of social scientists, whose main themes were:

- separation of ownership and control;

- the consequent rise of a managerial technocracy;

- fragmentation of social classes into clusters of overlapping interest groups; and

- the end of ideology and polarized class politics.

The term 'post-industrial' implied that work was becoming more pleasant for the majority as employment shifted from industrial production to information processing. This 'de-industrialization' process was marked by the relative decline of manufacturing and an increase in service sector jobs, creating a new 'knowledge society elite' workforce. The rise of a service economy and the central importance of the possession of knowledge were thought likely to produce a shift in the dominant values, norms and culture of this 'post-industrial' society. The traditional work ethic would be replaced by a greater emphasis on individual freedom and pleasure seeking; market forces would be subdued by an increased stress on social welfare and economic planning; and class-based conflict over the distribution of wealth would decline.

Other 'futurologists' shared these views and extended them. Stonier (quoted in Rowe 1986) predicted that, by the year 2000, 40 per cent would work in what he calls 'the knowledge industry' leading to the idea of a 'post-service stage'. Toffler (1980) describes a similar phenomenon in terms of three 'waves' – agricultural, industrial and post-industrial. The first lasted thousands of years, the second about

Figure 2.6 Towards a post-service society

Source: Rowe, C. (1986) *People and Chips: human implicationf of Information Technology*, London: Paradigm

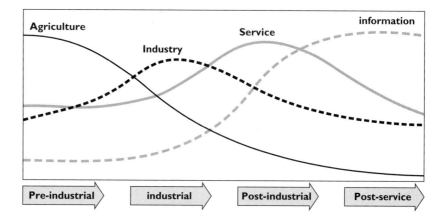

300, and the latest, which began in about 1955, will reach maturity in a few decades. What all these views have in common is their tendency towards technological determinism (see p. 25), whereby a dominant technology is taken as the over-riding influence on a given historical epoch.

Quantitative criticisms of the post-industrial society thesis

Kumar (1978) points out that employment in manufacturing never accounted for a majority of the workforce, peaking at 48 per cent in Britain in 1955. Furthermore, the concept of de-industrialization was initially premised on the relative decline in numbers employed in manufacturing compared with services, rather than an absolute decline, and this is partly a function of the increased productivity of labour, meaning that fewer workers are required for the same level of output. Thus de-industrialization does not necessarily entail lower output, though it does appear to entail fewer jobs in the long run.

Callinicos (1989) argues that de-industrialization has socially regressive results. Taking the example of what he calls the 'paradigmatic post-industrial society' – California – the

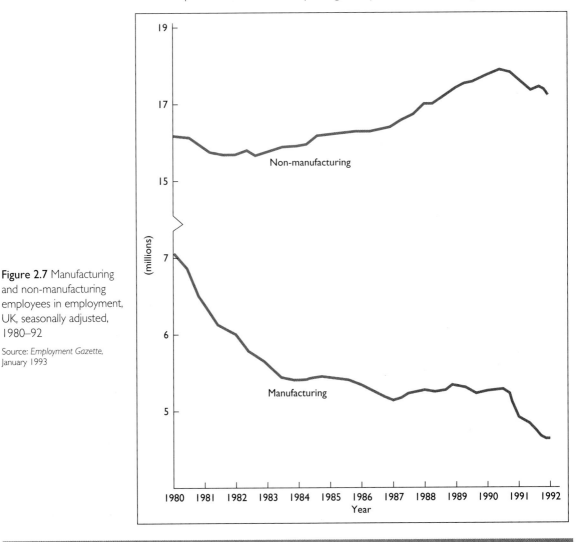

Figure 2.7 Manufacturing and non-manufacturing employees in employment, UK, seasonally adjusted, 1980–92

Source: *Employment Gazette,* January 1993

1979–82 recession which wiped out most of the state's main industry was followed by an expansion of labour-intensive, low-wage manufacturing, and while an increase in services also occurred, wages there were some 40–50 per cent lower. He claims that post-industrialists and post-modernists have been too eager to announce the 'obsolescence of the production paradigm' and have exaggerated the contraction of manufacturing employment in the advanced economies. The need for manufactured products does not disappear : humans have the same mundane needs as ever, and on a global scale there are more industrial workers than at any time in history.

The rise of service sector jobs in Britain has not been inexorable (see Figure 2.7); there have been periods of decline, partly as a result of economic recession, and partly as a result of changing patterns of consumption. Callinicos argues that there is no necessary tendency for services to supplant manufacturing. For example, the growing popularity of 'white goods' (fridges, etc.) has entailed the replacement of services by goods, as has the purchase of private motor cars and consumer durables which provide home-based leisure. In fact, 'there is a continual incentive to manufacture goods which can substitute for previously purchased services' (Prowse 1987).

Which services have been replaced in these examples? Suggest another example of a manufactured product which replaces a final consumer service.

Gershuny (1978) discovered a contraction in demand for some final consumer services as people bought the manufactured goods with which to 'service' themselves. He argued that an embryonic 'self-service' grey economy was developing in which an increasing number of services are being produced outside the formal economy, with no money passing hands. After considering the various ways in which services can be obtained, Gershuny concluded that the prospects for increasing the amount of paid employment in the service sector were not promising.

While demand for the services bought in the formal marketplace may remain relatively stable, consumption of state-provided services has declined as a result of public sector spending cuts under the Conservative government, with a resulting fall in state employment in the service sector. Some of the demand may be displaced into the formal (private) sector where people are able to pay. Some work is done on a communal or reciprocal basis, though its impact on paid employment is quite small.

The biggest threat to growth in employment in the formal market for services probably comes from the domestic mode of (self) provisioning. This suggestion was supported by Pahl (1984) and Pahl and Wallace (1985). These studies of adaptations to recession and unemployment on the Isle of Sheppey noted that, rather than the informal (black) economy expanding, the largest amount of work was being done in the domestic mode, such as DIY. Interestingly, this was only really affordable to households with at least one member in full-time paid employment ('work-rich' households); the unemployed did not use their extra time to improve living standards by working either in the black economy or in the domestic mode. Pahl concludes that the unemployed cannot get by through substituting time for money.

Explain Pahl's conclusion about the unemployed. Suggest two reasons why they cannot substitute time for money.

There is a decline in demand for marketed services from both the employed and the unemployed, because the former can afford to 'self-provision', thereby saving money on marketed services, while the latter cannot afford either option. Pahl saw this as the basis for further social divisions in times of recession. (See also the section on 'the peripheral workforce', p. 56)

It seems therefore that Bell's prediction of unlimited growth in the service sector is questionable, to say the least.

Qualitative criticisms of the post-industrial society thesis

It is difficult to draw any general conclusions about the alleged upgraded quality of service sector jobs due to the sheer variety of such jobs. Callinicos (1989) argues from a Marxist perspective that most service sector jobs lack the qualities anticipated by Bell. He makes the point that service industries do not employ only white-collar workers; many occupations in the services are not particularly 'clean' or attractive and are, to all intents and purposes, manual in character.

Suggest some examples of the kinds of jobs Callinicos may have had in mind.

Furthermore, the term 'white collar' itself includes at least three distinct class positions:

1) 'managerial capitalists';

2) the 'new middle class'(higher professional, managerial and administrative staff); and

3) routine white-collar workers whose insecurity, relatively low earnings and lack of autonomy place them in the same position as manual workers.

Callinicos argues that 'employment in the service industries proper hardly matches the profile of the "knowledge society" elite portrayed by Bell' (1989, p. 124). To support his argument he cites the following examples. In the USA in 1986 average weekly earnings in manufacturing were $396, but only $275 in services. Between 1972 and 1984 the biggest growth in employment in the service sector was in restaurants and the retail trade. Average hourly earnings in that subsector were 38 per cent below those in manufacturing.

While Callinicos concedes that manual industrial workers no longer form the majority of wage labourers in advanced societies, this does not imply the beginning of the end of the 'work-based society'. Wage labour has if anything become a more pervasive feature of social experience in the past half century. The fact that this involves interacting with people rather than producing goods does not change the social relations involved, or the proletarian character of most service jobs. In this view the term 'post-industrial' is a misnomer for monopoly capitalism or late capitalist society. (The section on 'post-Fordism' in Chapter 3 is also relevant to this discussion.)

Clearly many of the points discussed here are relevant to the 'proletarianization' debate normally dealt with in the stratification topic at A-level. Read up on this debate and assess the extent to which evidence supports or rejects the post-industrial society thesis. Haralambos and Holborn (1995), pp. 65–9, and O'Donnell (1992), pp. 139–44 would prove useful for this exercise.

The future occupational structure

New Scientist magazine recently made predictions about the future shape of the job market, as shown in Figure 2.8.

Study Figure 2.8, and answer the following questions:

1) Are there any specific examples over which you disagree with the prediction?
2) How important is technology in the rise and fall of certain occupations?
3) What would be the significance of such a shift in the occupational structure as far as the post-industrial society thesis is concerned? Would it finally confirm it? Would it mean we have gone beyond it? Or neither of these? Give reasons for your answer.

Figure 2.8 Growing, shrinking and changing trades over the next twenty years

Source: *New Scientist,* 16 April 1994, pp. 30–1

Shrinking or disappearing trades:

Air couriers (replaced by high-speed data networks); Answering machines (computers); Insurance claims assessors (neural networks); Bailiffs (electronic credit freezes); Checkout staff (image recognition software); Cash register suppliers (computers); Coal and solid fuel merchants (electricity); Company registration agents (networks); Dictation and secretarial services (voice recognition software); Layout artists (computer templates); Duplicating equipment (computers); Factory cleaning (intelligent robots); Film processors (digital, chemical-free film); Hotel booking agents (software); Industrial relations arbitrators (employment deregulation); Notaries and commissioners of oaths (video recordings); Draughting equipment makers (computer-aided design); Typewriter manufacturers (computers); Window cleaners (intelligent robots); Airlines (rising fuel prices); Middle managers (networks)

Growth areas:

Advertising (fuelled by opportunities in new media); Alarms and security equipment (rising crime due to unemployment); Corporate entertainment (to keep staff and consumers happy); Sports equipment (more leisure time); Hi-Fi and computer dealers (convergence of technologies); Cellular radio dealers (more networks); Cable manufacturers (more networks); Environmental systems (tighter laws); Recycling (tighter laws, higher material costs); Computer programmers (need for better interfaces); Designers (producing and choosing computer templates); Telemarketing (chance for wider access to public); Career consultants (increased redundancies); Trauma consultants (rise in random criminal acts); Personal matchmakers (less time for workers to socialize); Escort services (importance of appearing sociable in public); Cruise companies (for leisurely business trips)

Change from physical to electronic:

Market research

Novelty goods

Lawyers

Doctors

Surveyors

Cinema

Detective agencies

Estate agents

Journalists

Writers

New trades:

Internet plumbers (PC won't talk to your fridge? Call one out they'll solve it); Workgroup synthesizers (bringing together ideas from staff on different projects in remote locations); Systems hosts (the DJs and talk-show hosts of the Internet, who will be famous for the discussions they provoke each day. The true megastars of the future)

Essay Questions

1) Assess the sociological significance of the increase in relatively low-paid, part-time employment in the service sector. (InterBoard Syllabus, Specimen Question Paper, 1994)

2) Assess the view that technological progress will eliminate alienation at work. (ULEAC, June 1992)

Structured Question

A post-industrial society?

Item A

Overall the new jobs are likely to arise in skill-intensive, knowledge-based occupations, in services and manufacturing. An increase in higher-level qualifications and skills will be needed to match such occupational change. Not only are highly skilled occupations increasing, but the occupations themselves are now requiring increased skills.

A recent analysis by the Centre for Research in Employment and Technology in Europe (CREATE) considers that the critical skills gap facing employers in the 1990s is associated with the emergence of a new category of 'knowledge worker' (Group 1) who will have a higher level

Figure 2.9 Jobs affected by changes in numbers and skill levels

Source: Rajan (1993), p. 28

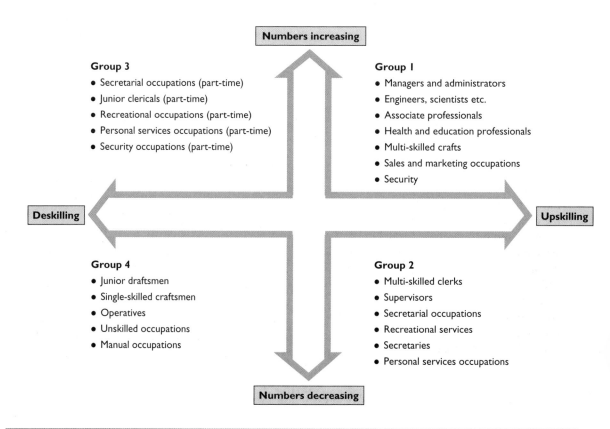

of education and training qualifications; intellectual skills geared to problem solving and decision making; and the ability to shoulder various responsibilities in the work place.

At the other extreme are occupations which are going to go through both numbers and skill contraction (Group 4). These occupations, concentrated in manufacturing, will be the victims of continuing automation, resulting in deskilling and labour shake-out.

Other occupations will also feel the effects of technology. It will enhance the skills content of the work done in some occupations (Group 2) by reducing their numbers. Conversely technology will increase the number of employees in Group 3 occupations by making more jobs amenable to part-timers, through task simplification and reduced responsibilities.

Source: Adapted from Rajan (1993), pp. 28–9

Item B

. . . much employment now requires more than the 'general mechanical intelligence' that the Crowther report on 15–18 education (HMSO, 1959) assumed was necessary for all citizens. Many occupations require at least keyboard familiarity with computers, and modern European languages are increasingly in demand.

For optimists, these increasing demands being made upon the new generations of the workforce are reason to believe that at last the old divisions between white and blue collar, office and shop floor, those who decide and those who do can be overcome as the country moves towards a high-skill economy requiring the extension to all of life-long education, training and retraining combined in a mass system of universal higher education. For pessimists, the collapse of industry into a low-skill service economy merely replaces the old divisions of labour and class with a new core–periphery pattern of employment in which power and the information to make decisions rest with a narrowing elite of managers.

Source: Ainley (1993), p. 24

Item C

If, as many historians from Marx onwards have suggested, capitalism took three or more centuries to emerge from feudalism, why expect its decline and demise to take so much less? Industrial capitalism was established, on a reasonably general scale, only by the end of the nineteenth century. In the course of this century it has extended its reach and intensified its hold. The very novelty of its full operation, and the dynamism intrinsic to its mode, have misled some into seeing the emergence of a 'post-industrial' society – barely half a century after industrial society itself had in any real sense come of age. This would be rapid change indeed and, one might add, unprecedented. Social orders change somewhat more slowly than intellectual fashions. Post-industrial theorists have sought to foreshorten capitalism's past and foreclose its future every bit as roughly and arbitrarily as revolutionary socialists.

Source: Scase (1989), p. 41

1) What characteristic is shared by those occupations which are both increasing in number and experiencing deskilling (Group 3,) according to the information in Item A? (**1 mark**)

2) In terms of the 'core–periphery pattern of employment' referred to in Item B, which group of occupations in Item A typically constitutes the core and which the periphery? (**2 marks**)

3) Using material from Item A and elsewhere, assess the relative importance of technology as a factor in either the deskilling or upskilling of the workforce. (**9 marks**)

4) Suggest how the information in Item A could be interpreted as support for the views of both the optimists and the pessimists outlined in Item B. (**4 marks**)

5) How far does sociological evidence support the view contained in Item C that post-industrial theorists have been 'misled . . . into seeing the emergence of a post-industrial society'? (**9 marks**)

Coursework suggestions

1) On the theme of occupational change it would be possible to investigate how patterns of employment in a local area have changed over a certain period of time. Which occupations have disappeared or declined and which have been created or grown?

   The decline or growth of various industries is likely to differ from area to area according to a variety of factors (historical tradition, local infrastructure, government policy, technological change, transnational corporation policy). The relative impact of these factors on the local community/occupational structure could become the focus of the investigation. Local census reports may provide detail, and local histories can be a good source of information about the rise and fall of local industries. Local authorities, such as the city council, can provide much up-to-date information about trends in employment, unemployment,

incomes and population changes. This could also be studied in relation to gender or ethnic stratification in the job market.

How does the occupational structure compare with national change? Does it seem to support the claims about the emergence of a post-industrial society?

2) For other alternatives, you might wish to explore the relationship between technology and levels of alienation, as did Blauner, or investigate the relative importance of factors that determine attitudes to work.

One of the biggest problems will be gaining access to groups of workers. Remember that because coursework is fraught with potential pitfalls and hazards, especially when dealing with official organizations, it is important to make sure that your aim and methods have been approved by your tutor before you carry out any primary research. If you have a job yourself you will have

Bibliography

Abercrombie, N., Warde, A., Soothill, K., Urry, J. and Walby, S. (1994) *Contemporary British Society*, 2nd edn, Cambridge: Polity

Ainley, P. (1993) *Class and Skill: Changing Divisions of Knowledge and Labour,* London: Cassell

Barrett, M. and McIntosh, M. (1980) 'The "family wage": some problems for socialists and feminists', *Capital and Class,* No. 11

Batstone, E. (1988) *The Reform of Workplace Industrial Relations: Theory, Myth and Evidence,* Oxford: Clarendon

Bazen, S. and Thirlwall, T. (1989) *Deindustrialization,* Oxford: Heinemann

Beechey, V. (1983) 'The sexual division of labour and the labour process: a critical assessment of Braverman', in Wood, S. (ed.) *The Degradation of Work: Skill Deskilling and the Labour Process,* London: Hutchinson

Bell, D. (1973) *The Coming of Post-Industrial Society,* New York: Basic Books

Blauner, R. (1964) *Alienation and Freedom,* Chicago, IL: Chicago University Press

Braverman, H. (1974) *Labour and Monopoly Capital:*

The Degradation of Work in the Twentieth Century, New York: Monthly Review Press

Buchanan, D.A. and Boddy, D. (1983) *Organizations in the Computer Age: Technological Imperatives and Strategic Choice,* Aldershot: Gower

Callinicos, A. (1989) *Against Postmodernism,* Cambridge: Polity

Chinoy, E. (1955) *Automobile Workers and the American Dream,* New York: Doubleday

Cockburn, C. (1991) *Brothers: Male Dominance and Technological Change,* 2nd edn, London: Pluto Press

Cooley, M. (1987) *Architect or Bee? The Human Price of Technology,* London: Hogarth Press

Daniel, W. W. (1987) *Workplace Industrial Relations and Technical Change,* Dorset: PSI

Denscombe, M. (1991) *Sociology Update,* Leicester: Olympus Books

Department of Employment (1971) *British Labour Statistics,* London: HMSO

Edwards, R. (1979) *Contested Terrain,* London: Heinemann

Friedmann, A. (1977) *Industry and Labour,* London: Macmillan

Fulcher, J. and Gould, A. (1993) 'Convergence or divergence?', *Sociology Review,* April, pp. 8–12

Gallie, D. (1978) *In Search of the New Working Class,* Cambridge: Cambridge University Press

Gershuny, J. (1978) *After Industrial Society? The Emerging Self Service Economy,* Basingstoke: Macmillan

Goldthorpe, J.H., Lockwood, D., Bechhofer, F. and Platt, J. (1968) *The Affluent Worker in the Class Structure,* London: Cambridge University Press

Grint, K. (1991) *The Sociology of Work: An Introduction,* Cambridge: Polity

Haralambos, M. and Holborn, M. (1995) *Sociology: Themes and Perspectives,* 4th edn, London: Collins Educational

Harris, N. (1983) *Of Bread and Guns: The World Economy in Crisis,* Harmondsworth: Penguin

Kerr, C., Dunlop, J.T., Haribson, F. and Myers, C.A. (1960) *Industrialism and Industrial Man,* Cambridge, MA: Harvard University Press

Knights, D. and Collinson, D. (1983) *Shop Floor Culture and the Problem of Management Control,* Manchester: UMIST

Kumar, K. (1978) *Prophecy and Progress: The Sociology of Industrial and Post-Industrial Society,* Harmondsworth: Penguin

Maslow, A. (1943) 'A theory of human motivation', *Psychological Review,* Vol. 50, pp. 370–96

Oakley, A. (1974) *Housewife,* London: Allen Lane

O'Donnell, M. (1992) *A New Introduction to Sociology,* 3rd edn, Walton-on-Thames: Nelson

Pahl, R.E. (1984) *Divisions of Labour,* Oxford: Blackwell

Pahl, R.E. and Wallace, C. (1985) 'Household work and strategies in the recession', in Redclift, N. and Mingione, E. (eds) *Beyond Employment,* Oxford: Blackwell

Prowse, M. (1987) 'Why services may be no substitute for manufacturing', *Financial Times,* 22 May

Rajan, A. (1993) '1990s Where the new jobs will be', in *Labour Market and Skill Trends 1994–5,* Nottingham: Skills and Enterprise Network

Rowe, C. (1986) *People and Chips,* London: Paradigm

Scase, R. (1989) 'Theories of convergence and the comparative study of society', *Social Studies Review,* March, pp. 153–5

—— (ed.) (1989) *Industrial Societies: Crisis and Division in Western Capitalism and State Socialism,* London: Unwin Hyman

Shaiken, H. (1979) 'Numerical control of work: workers and automation in the computer age', *Radical America,* Vol. 1, No. 6

Silverman, D. (1970) *The Theory of Organisations,* London: Heinemann

Slattery, M. (1991) *Key Ideas in Sociology,* Basingstoke: Macmillan

Stefanou, R. (1992) *Understanding Industry Now,* 3rd edn, London: Heinemann

Taylor, F. (1947) *Scientific Management,* New York: Harper & Row

Thompson, P. (1989) *The Nature of Work,* 2nd edn, Basingstoke: Macmillan Educational

Toffler, A. (1980) *The Third Wave,* London: Collins

Winch, G. (ed.) (1983) *Information Technology in Manufacturing Processes: Case Studies in Technological Change,* Rossendale

Winner, L. (1985) 'Do artefacts have politics?', in Mackenzie, D. and Wajccman, J. (eds) *The Social Shaping of Technology,* Milton Keynes: Open University

Zimbalist, A. (1979) *Case Studies on the Labor Process,* London: Monthly Review Press

3 The new flexibility: from Fordism to post-Fordism?

'The nineteenth century is not yet over.'

Richard Sennett

Fordism

Fordism is the term given to the particular form of industrial production that is said to have characterized work and society in 'mature industrialized countries' from the 1920s to the mid to late 1970s. The origins of this term lie in the fact that the Ford Motor Company became synonymous for many people with assembly-line mass production techniques. Although assembly-line production itself was not new, having its roots in the slaughterhouses of the Chicago meat industry of the 1890s, it was Henry Ford who first employed the principle of semi-automatic moving line assembly with the famous single-colour, single-model, mass-produced Model T at the Highland Park, Detroit, plant in 1913.

Ford himself enthused in his autobiography (1923) that the benefits of such a highly specialized division of labour were such that, out of the 7,882 operations involved in making the Model T, 949 required 'strong, able bodied and practically physically perfect men', 3,338 needed men of 'merely ordinary physical strength', most of the rest could be performed by 'women or older children', while '670 could be filled by legless men, 2,637 by one legged men, two by armless men, 715 by one armed men and 10 by blind men'. Specialization can go so far that many jobs require, not a whole person, but only a part!

Ford defended assembly-line work against its critics. He was well aware of the problem of monotony, but cited the most monotonous task in the whole factory, in which a man picked up a gear with a steel hook, shook it in a vat of oil and turned it into a basket. The motion never varied; it required no muscular energy or intelligence. Yet the man who had been doing the job for eight solid years had saved $40,000 and resisted attempts to move him to a 'better' job.

This method of production meant that a Model T previously made in twelve and a half hours could be built and tested in one and a half hours. By 1923 annual output reached 2 million (capturing more than half the US market), and over 15 million were made in all by 1929.

According to Robin Murray (1989), Fordist production was based on four principles from which all else followed:

- *Standardization.* Each task and each part could be standardized. Unlike craft production – where each part had to be specifically designed and fitted – for a run of mass-produced cars the same headlight could be fitted to the same model in the same way.

- *Mechanization.* If tasks were the same, some could be mechanized; thus mass production plants developed special-purpose machinery for each model, much of which could not be switched from product to product.

- *Scientific management.* The tasks that remained were subject to scientific management or Taylorism: each task was broken down into its component parts and then redesigned by work-study specialists on time-and-motion principles. The specialists then instructed manual workers on how the job should be done.

- *Flowline production.* Flowline replaced nodal assembly, so that instead of workers moving to and from the product (the node), the product flowed past the worker.

Standardization is a fundamental feature of industrial society. It extends far beyond the factory, affecting every aspect of life. Alvin Toffler's book The Third Wave *(1980) describes how it was not just machinery and products (hardware) that became standardized during what he calls the 'second wave' of human civilization (roughly equivalent to Fordism), but procedures and administrative routines (software) also.*

Write down as many aspects of your own life as you can that you would describe as 'standardized'. (Examples might be that you own a CD collection, or sometimes eat at a McDonalds restaurant.) Now look at the arguments on in Chapter 8 which suggest that working life and patterns of consumption have changed in such a way as to allow for flexibility, variation, individuality and choice. How far does your experience provide evidence for or against such suggestions?

The word 'Fordism' was first used by the Italian Marxist Antonio Gramsci in his article 'Americanism and Fordism', written in prison in approximately 1931–32 (see Gramsci 1971). At that time Italy itself had little or no assembly line production. For Gramsci American Fordism was heralding a new era of civilization within advanced capitalism because it was more than the development of just another form of production, it was accompanied by a whole new economic culture extending to many other areas of social life and transcending national and political boundaries.

Because Fordism is characterized by large-scale production, standardized products, huge initial investment start-up costs and long production runs, it requires (and creates) the following economic conditions:

- a mass of semi-skilled workers primarily motivated by high wages and with a strong sense of collective solidarity expressed in labour movement politics;

- fragmented routine tasks and rigid demarcation between jobs;

- hierarchical organization of work, with close supervision of the workforce in a low-trust system;

- predictable mass consumption;

- mass advertising for stable demand;

- competition based on cost rather than quality;

- some degree of protection over home markets;

- some degree of protection for the workforce from the vagaries of the market (unemployment, low wages), in the form of institutionalized collective bargaining procedures and extensive state welfare; and

- an economy with some degree of central planning.

In economic terms the model suggested by all this is a Keynesian one. John Maynard Keynes, writing in the 1930s, rejected the idea that there was a natural tendency in a competitive economy towards full employment. An economy could get stuck due to recession or lack of demand for products and services. Thus Keynes believed it was necessary for the state to intervene to manage demand levels – 'fine-tuning' the economy to maintain a buoyant labour market. The aim was essentially to establish a virtuous circle of consumption (demand) and production. In the case of Britain this was achieved, in part, through the nationalized industries which operated with the benefit of state subsidies, and state welfarism.

State intervention in the economy and the policy of 'full employment' have long since been abandoned in Britain by the Conservative government. An unwelcome effect of Keynesian policy was high inflation; coupled with increasing global competition and falling rates of profit in capitalist enterprises, this fuelled the development of 'market liberal theory', which was espoused by the New Right.

The theory of market liberalism was based on the notion of 'free market economics' propagated by Milton Friedman and Friedrich Hayek, among others. In practice it meant keeping the money supply under tight control (monetarism) and consequently resulted in cuts in public spending. It has created a deregulated economy in which market forces are unleashed and state intervention is kept to a minimum. Inflation has been curbed but at the cost of unprecedented levels of long-term unemployment. In 1992, when he was still Chancellor of the Exchequer, Norman Lamont summed up the policy when he said high unemployment 'was a price worth paying'.

The limits of Fordism

While Ford was singing the praises of the assembly line it quickly became seen by many as a symbol of human oppression and misery – the most alienating, dehumanizing form of work imaginable. The 1936 Charlie Chaplin film, *Modern Times,* provides a graphic example of the ambivalence with which Fordist methods and values were greeted by many people. Try to see this film if you get the opportunity.

The division of labour and alienating work soon led to productivity problems due to absenteeism and high labour turnover. Training new workers was costing Ford more than $2 million per year. One solution that was attempted, and only partially succeeded, was to buy off labour unrest with a $5 a day offer which included an incentive for employees to modify their behaviour outside the factory as well as within.

The following extracts from *Rivethead* by Ben Hamper illustrate some of the factors that might produce an intractable workforce. Hamper worked at General Motors Truck Division for many years (as well as doing some freelance journalism), before writing his memoir of life and work in what he called the 'fat choke hold of Papa GM'.

> My pal Roy ... was having major difficulty coping with the drudgery of factory labor. Unable to arrange a double-up system with Dan-O, he wallowed in the slow-motion injustice of the time clock. His job, like mine,

Figure 3.1 A still from *Modern Times*

wasn't difficult, it was just plain monotonous. . . . We had been able to conquer the other annoyances. We adjusted to the heat and grew accustomed to the noise. After a while, we even got used to the claustrophobia of the wheel wells. . . . The one thing that was impossible to escape was the monotony of our new jobs. Every minute, every hour, every truck and every movement was a plodding replica of the one that had gone before. The monotony gnawed away at Roy. His behavior began to verge on the desperate. The only way he saw to deal with the monotony was to numb himself to it. [Hamper 1992, p. 41]

1) How might workers numb themselves to this kind of work?
2) What tactics might be used to 'fight back the clock'?
3) Do you think the kinds of experiences described here are exclusive to manual work in auto plants? How would you support your view?
4) From the evidence of this extract, how far can Hamper's account be seen as more journalistic than sociological? What are the differences?

Taylor and Walton (1971) provide numerous examples of the ways in which workers attempt to 'take on the machine' and assert some control over the work process.

These range from damaging equipment to breaking rules and cutting corners.

There are numerous accounts of what it is like to work on an assembly line. Huw Beynon's Working for Ford *(1973) is probably the best known such study by a sociologist. Others include Ruth Cavendish's* Women on the Line *(1982) and R. Linhart's* The Assembly Line *(1981). Satoshi Kamata's* Japan in the Passing Lane *(1984) describes the human cost of Japanese 'economic success'. Try to obtain one of these books, or Hamper's* Rivethead *(1992), and carry out the following tasks:*

1) Describe the methodology used and assess its sociological validity.
2) Evaluate its usefulness to a sociological understanding of the experience of work.
3) On the basis of the evidence presented, discuss the relative importance of technological and cultural factors as determinants of the experience of work.

Aside from the labour problems and diseconomies of scale faced by Fordist companies at the microeconomic level, it also soon became apparent that at the macroeconomic level demand for products was not infinite or stable. The great weakness of the Fordist method of production is its inability to respond quickly to changes in demand or to stimulate variable demand. The Ford Motor Company itself fell victim to this problem in the 1920s when General Motors began to produce a range of cars 'for every purpose and every purse' and 'flexible mass production' was born. According to Hounshell (1984), mass production, as Ford had made it and defined it, was for all intents and purposes dead by 1926.

Sales of cars, as of everything else, collapsed in the Great Depression of the early 1930s following the Wall Street crash of 1929, and mass production of consumer goods only revived in the boom following the Second World War. Fordism survived largely as a result of state intervention in the form of subsidies to industry and policies to promote 'full employment'.

In the later stages of the Fordist era firms in mature industrialized countries faced another problem, in that it is relatively easy to copy such production techniques and transport them to places where a pool of even cheaper labour exists. First Japan, and later Taiwan, were both very successful in this respect. In this sense Fordism created global competition; the response to this, some would argue, was the development of a deregulated, 'global' form of capitalism that demanded a radically new way of organizing production.

It has been claimed (for instance by Clegg 1992) that the modernist (Fordist) model had run out of steam by the 1970s, and organizational responses to this changing state of affairs became evident in the 1980s, particularly in Japan. The terms 'postmodern' or 'post-Fordist' organization were used to describe the nature of these Japanese organizations.

Flexibility

Few can doubt that in many respects the world of work has undergone a considerable transformation in recent times. It is generally agreed that, as Sabel (1982) claims, the 'high point' of Fordism has passed. One word more than any other became synonymous with survival in the lexicon of business organizations in the

Figure 3.2 The flexible
workforce

Source: *Guardian,* 14 March 1994

hostile economic climate of the 1980s and 1990s: 'flexibility' – the quality that pure
Fordism lacked. A less charitable interpretation of flexibility is to be found in the
lexicon of the Left, as Harman (1994, p. 7) attests: 'The slogan for ruling classes
everywhere has become "flexibility" – making the rest of us bend our lives to fit in
with the ups and downs of capitalist accumulation.'

Atkinson (1985) has drawn a distinction between two dimensions of the flexible
deployment of labour. *Numerical flexibility* refers to a company's ability to adjust
labour supply to product demand through the use of external labour markets and
the development of a two-tier internal labour market with its small 'core' of critical
(full-time, permanent) workers and a much larger 'periphery' of less critical (part-time
and/or temporary) casualized or subcontracted workers. *Functional flexibility* is the
company's ability to use the same workforce for a wide variety of tasks.

Figure 3.3 The flexible firm

Source: Atkinson (1985), p. 19

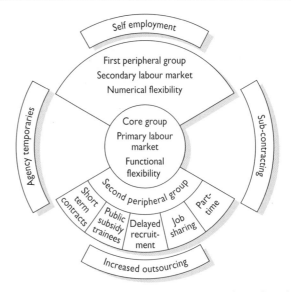

These principles are clearly evident in the following description of work in the 'fast food' industry which shows that service sector workers are by no means immune from flexible working practices:

> McDonalds' secret recipe for success comes not from the Big Mac sauce but from a new production process, using a combination of the Fordist conveyer belt with a Japanese emphasis on flexibility. Each store is a factory where workers' skills have been kept to a bare minimum. No chefs, no apprentices wanted on this burger-line: everyone has been levelled down to the uniform 'crew member' rushing between stations to perform tasks learned in a day. From Oxford Street to Manila, McDonalds' workers follow identical steps to produce identical burgers.
>
> Labour costs should never exceed 15 per cent of an outlet's sales. 'It is very tight,' said one manager. 'If sales are down, labour costs must come down. You have to cut the staff and make those remaining work harder.' Workers hired for busy sessions are later shown the door.
>
> Such 'flexible working practices' are as contagious on the high street as on the industrial estate. By employing part-timers, stores can cover unsocial hours without paying overtime and adjust workers' hours on a weekly, or even daily, basis as sales and staff numbers fluctuate. As one manager put it, 'We don't have full and part-timers here. Everyone at McDonalds works flexible hours.' The new tribe of so-called 'peripheral' workers is becoming increasingly central to the economy. Today, one in four British workers is part-time and 90 per cent of them are women. [Adapted from Lamb and Percy 1987]

Which aspects of this description of work at McDonalds exemplify functional flexibility and which represent numerical flexibility?

Alan Warde (1989, p. 12) identifies four aspects of industrial production in which tendencies towards increased flexibility can be seen (see Table 3.1).

Let us examine each of Warde's aspects of production in turn:

Table 3.1 Aspects of Fordist and non-Fordist production

	Fordist	Non-Fordist
1 Technology	• fixed, dedicated machines	micro-electronically controlled multi-purpose machines
	• vertically integrated operation	sub-contracting
	• mass production	batch production
2 Products	• for a mass consumer market	diverse, specialized products
	• relatively cheap	high quality
3 Labour process	• fragmented	many tasks for versatile workers
	• few tasks	some autonomy
	• little discretion	group control
	• hierarchical authority	
	• and technical control	
4 Contracts	• collectively negotiated rate	payment by individual performance
	• for the job	dual market secure core, highly
	• relatively secure	insecure periphery

Source: Warde (1985), p. 12

1) *Technology.* Technological determinists (see p. 25) would have it that technology is the primary factor driving the reorganization of production. Whereas assembly-line machinery was 'dedicated' to a fixed product, the development of CAD (computer-aided design) and CAM (computer-aided manufacture) allows machine tools to be reprogrammed, thereby facilitating more efficient small-batch production. This has implications for the social organization of the factory floor and the labour requirements of the firm.

2) *Products.* According to Piore and Sabel (1984), increasingly variable demand is the motive force behind the move to flexibility. Faced with quickly changing consumer tastes and specialized or 'niche' markets, the flexible firm can now engage in customized or 'tailor-made', very short run products using the latest technology and craft labour.

3) *Labour process* (Atkinson's 'functional flexibility'). One way in which the flexible firm strives to eliminate waste is by reducing the amount of time that each worker spends doing nothing, the aim being to eliminate unnecessary workers. Fewer, more versatile workers are employed to carry out a greater number of tasks, which requires the removal of demarcation barriers between different crafts.

4) *Contracts* (Atkinson's 'numerical flexibility'). The flexible firm also seeks to eliminate unnecessary workers by reducing the number of workers doing nothing at any point in time. So only those workers who can be fully occupied for 40 hours per week will be employed on a permanent and full-time contract. The extra capacity is made up when required using casual or subcontracted workers depending on the degree of expertise involved. At its extreme this results in the infamous practice of 'zero-hour' contracting whereby workers have no guaranteed hours of work and are often 'on-call' waiting for work. A well-known high street fast food outlet has recently been forced, through bad publicity, to suspend an unofficial policy operating in some branches that required counter staff to 'clock-off' when trade was slack.

Several different terms have been used to describe the production process in this 'new phase' of industrial capitalism, including 'neo-Fordism', 'flexible specialization' and 'post-Fordism'.

1) *Carry out a survey of job advertisements in your local newspaper (or a local job centre), categorizing them according to whether or not they mention the word 'flexible' (there are usually quite a few that do!).*
2) *Using Atkinson's distinction between functional and numerical flexibility, suggest which type(s) of flexibility might be implied by each of the advertisements that contain the word 'flexible'. Devise a way of presenting your results in a quantitative form.*
3) *How is it possible to tell in each case, if at all, what type of flexibility is involved?*
4) *To what extent does the nature of 'flexibility' in each case appear to be related to the qualifications and experience required and the pay and conditions offered?*
5) *How useful did you find Atkinson's distinction in this exercise?*

There are two main pathways which the increasing flexibility of the labour market might take. If, as the post-Fordist paradigm suggests, flexibility really is being driven by the need to respond quickly to changing markets, then it will require the workforce to become much more closely oriented to and knowledgeable about the production process. In this view it might be assumed that there will be an extension of democratized decision-making processes in the workplace. However, it is possible to discern an alternative pathway – the neo-Fordist paradigm, according to which management's primary goal is the intensification of work and its own control over the workforce.

Neo-Fordism

The term 'neo-Fordism', coined by the French Regulation Theory school – notably Michel Aglietta (1979) and Alain Lipietz (1987) – is used by some writers to refer to a half-way position between Fordism and post-Fordism. The suggestion is that in response to 'the crisis of accumulation' (falling rates of profit and increasing global competition) facing capitalist organizations, many companies have taken advantage of new technology to move away from the rigidities of pure Fordist production and create greater product variety but without relaxing the tightness of managerial control (Coriat 1981).

In other words, new technology may well allow companies to be more flexible in their response to the market than previously, but this is mainly achieved at the expense of the workforce, who have themselves been rendered both functionally and numerically more flexible. Hierarchical organization and centralized control are still present in many so-called flexible firms. For example, Smith *et al.* (1989), who studied changing work practices at Cadbury, did not find much evidence of workers becoming more autonomous in terms of their discretion over the work process.

So neo-Fordism describes flexible developments which remain within mass production. It involves the 'just-in-time' process (or *'kanban',* to use the original Japanese word) – a system of manufacture and distribution whereby, at each stage of the process, there is little risk of overproduction or overstocking. (See the extract from *Japan in the Passing Lane* on pp. 67–8 for a description of this.) It makes use of information technology as a tool used by core workers and as an organizer of production procedures for peripheral workers. It tends to result in a workforce with limited forms of multiskilling rather than attempting to create skilled craft workers with knowledge to contribute to the system of production. In neo-Fordism flexibility for the workforce is often a question of compliance, in other words 'liking it or lumping it'.

Crabtree (1992) provides an illustration of what he sees as neo-Fordist practices in the retail industry. This is based on straightforward observation at points of sale and interviews with staff in the Argos company.

> Consumers select their purchases from catalogues displaying over two thousand goods ... Each item in the catalogue has a stock number and customers purchase goods by completing stock request forms ... Because Argos competes mainly on price, customers spend considerable amounts of time queueing both at the till to pay and at the counter to receive their goods.
>
> The goods come from the 'back of the shop' and the stock request forms completed by the customer are recorded on the computer for automatic re-ordering and resupplying. The 'just-in-time' method of re-ordering stock enables Argos to hold sufficient stock in store to fulfil current demand without overstocking.
>
> Staff, who are generally part-time women and students aged 16–19 years, are employed to operate the till, and ... 'at the back of the shop' to get the goods from the shelves and then give them to counter staff for passing on to the customer. Full-time workers form the core at Argos and are normally store managers, area managers, buyers and decision makers. Full-time workers are a minority as the majority are part-time workers performing pre-programmed tasks around the demands of 'just-in-time' and automatic re-ordering stock control systems. There is little training for the part-time till, counter or 'back of shop' worker and this is only 'job related', not accredited, and generally not transferable to another job. Wages tend to be low, conditions of service minimal, and the worker is expected to be flexible about time and duties ... Decision making is not expected in the job because the computer programme deals with it all. With Argos, both as a consumer and worker, you fit in or go elsewhere.

1) In what sense do the working practices at Argos outlined above suggest that it is more aptly described as a neo-Fordist organization than a post-Fordist one?
2) How far do you think Argos is typical of the way retail work is organized?
3) Can you suggest any other similar examples?
4) How would you investigate the nature of work in the retail sector in your locality? (You may be able to apply your ideas on this to a piece of coursework; see p. 78 for some suggestions.)

Post-Fordism

The terms 'post-Fordism' and 'flexible specialization' (FS) entered the academic debate about increasing flexibility in the early 1980s with the work of Reich (1983) and Piore and Sabel (1984). In their view the ultimate flexible firm would be one where multiskilled, transferable workers and flexible production methods combine to meet flexible demand.

Describe in your own words what is meant by the term 'flexible specialization'.

Table 3.2 Fordism and flexible specialization (post-Fordism) compared

	Fordism	*Flexible specialization*
1 Production concept	Mass production; economies through fixed capital and labour productivity within the production process	FS/ flexible automation; economies through working capital productivity between production processes and in distribution
2 Technology	Machines purpose built and dedicated; R&D functionally separate and discontinuous	General purpose and adaptable machinery; importance of design
3 Products	Limited range of standardized products	Specialization, product variety; 'niche' markets
4 Inputs	Materials- and energy-intensive	Materials- and energy-saving; information-intensive
5 Work process and skills	Fragmented and standardized tasks; strict division between mental and manual labour; semi-skilled workers	Open-ended tasks/closer integration of manual and mental tasks/core of multi-skilled workers linked to subcontract and semi-skilled labour
6 Payment system	Rate for the job; formalized pay bargaining	Payment for person; rising income for skilled core; more informal wage settlement
7 Organization and management	Managerial hierarchies; centralization; multi-divisional corporation	Flatter hierarchies; centralized information and planning systems, decentralized production networks, franchising, sub-contracting
8 Markets and customers	Domination of manufacturers over retailers, producers over users; one-way relations/ mass advertising	Domination of retailing; two-way relations between customer and manufacturer; firm rather than product advertising
9 Suppliers	Arm's length; stocks held 'just in case'	Two-way relations/stocks arrive 'just-in-time'
10 Competitive strategy	Compete by full capacity utilization and cost-cutting; tends to over production, stockpiling, mark downs	Compete by innovation; respond to falling market through diversification, innovation, subcontracting or lay-offs

Source: Phillimore (1989), p. 81

According to Grint (1991) the difference between neo-Fordism and post-Fordism is that the former is still based on mass production for international mass markets, while the latter suggests product specialization for specialized, often localized markets. Post-Fordism is a relative concept and needs to be defined in relation to pure Fordism. The 'ideal typical' forms (or paradigms) of Fordism and post-Fordism are illustrated in Table 3.2.

> *Draw up a similar table for yourself which combines the information from Tables 3.1 (on page 57) and 3.2. (Make sure you do not duplicate points or headings.) Leave room at the bottom so that when you have read the section on 'Wider social, cultural and political implications' (pp. 72–5) you can add the further categories of 'Class', 'Politics' and 'Welfare state/education' as well as any other new points featured in Table 3.5 on p. 70.*

At the level of the organization post-Fordism is said to occur when versatile workers are engaged in a production system which depends on team working rather than isolated individuals, when there is a reduction in the division of labour and some flattening of the hierarchical authority structure, all of which might be summed up in the concept of semi-autonomous work groups. (Volvo introduced a prototypical and celebrated example of this as long ago as the 1970s at its Kalmar plant.) So post-Fordism implies getting rid of the assembly line, decentralization of management control, upgraded skills and versatility on the part of the workforce and the provision of teamwork structures. Piore and Sabel (1984) described these changes as a 'second industrial divide' in which craft production replaces mass production, as a result of which there is a decline in alienation and industrial unrest and a growth in the spirit of 'collective individualism' where people work together but benefit personally.

Piore and Sabel were certainly optimistic about the possible effects of 'post-Fordism'. They believed FS potentially contained positive features for both capital and labour, for capital because clusters of small innovative firms have been very successful in terms of increased growth, and for labour in the form of potential for job enrichment and greater autonomy.

Not surprisingly, the implications of these post-Fordist tendencies have not been universally acclaimed. They are viewed with pessimism by some and scepticism by others, both of which amount to criticisms of the concept of post-Fordism itself.

Post-Fordism: the pessimistic view

While the pessimists tend to agree that FS may well prove to be very successful for capital as a way of competing more effectively against low-wage mass producers, they believe it will spell a return to the worst excesses of industrial capitalism and will thus be bad news for the trade unions and the labour movement in general. FS in this view offers disproportionate benefits for capital, resulting in a decline in the relative bargaining power of labour. As long as competition between FS firms is based on cutting costs (and therefore wages) rather than on innovation there will be a negative effect on jobs in the form of increased redundancies and lay-offs, higher productivity demands, labour intensification, inferior contracts with reduced job security and an erosion of trade union rights.

The clothing industry has been the focus of some debate. Until recently it was thought to be the archetypal 'sunset' (declining) industry: firms in the advanced industrial countries, faced with competition from cheap mass-produced garments from low-wage Third World producers, increasingly come to resemble such producers, with their 'sweatshop labour' and low productivity. However, the success of companies such as Benetton, Next and Burton, achieved through pursuing a strategy of high-quality, innovative design and 'niche marketing', has been based on the FS model of work organization with its associated 'upgrading' of the workforce, revitalizing 'First World' producers and allowing them to regain lost market share.

The pessimistic view is that while an upgrading of work may have occurred for a minority of workers – the 'core' – the same cannot be said for the majority. In the case of Benetton, only 1,500 are employed directly but another 10,000 are employed indirectly, and these are largely subcontractors or homeworkers who allow the company to avoid direct responsibility for taxes and welfare payments. In addition Benetton makes use of seasonal and temporary workers such as pensioners, students, 'moonlighters' and married women. Some would argue that even 'core' jobs in the future may not be secure or full time because some large companies will shift wholesale towards the employment of part-time staff; this happened in 1993, when the Burton group replaced 1,000 full-time employees with 3,000 part-timers. In fact, of the extra jobs created in Britain in 1993, 90 per cent were part-timers, so while the so-called 'Burton effect' may contribute to a fall in unemployment, it means that those doing the jobs will receive relatively low incomes. This may account for the preponderance of women in part-time employment. (In 1993 only one in ten part-time workers was a man.)

What advantages would Burton have gained from shifting from full-time to part-time employment?

Find out the differences in employment rights accorded to full-time and part-time workers. A good place to start would be Sociology Update, *1991 and 1993, which contain features on part-time work. You could also write to the TUC, Congress House, Great Russell Street, London WC1B 3LS.*

Britain's flexible labour market

Unlike the pre-Thatcher era, when Britain's labour market was more regulated and highly unionized, employers in 1993 were more able to 'hire and fire' staff. More pressure was also put on unemployed people to actively seek work. In such a 'flexible' labour market, employers found it easier to adjust employee numbers in line with their requirements. Employers are quick to shed jobs when the business outlook is depressed – which may explain what has been described as 'oversacking' in the summer and autumn of 1992, when job shedding reached record levels. But employers are quick to create jobs once prospects recover (and find that unemployed people are prepared to take them). [Philpott 1994, p. 114]

1) What does it mean to say that the labour market has become more flexible in the 1990s?
2) Why has this happened?
3) Are there any advantages to a flexible labour market for those participating in it?
4) What are the disadvantages for employers, if any?

An international comparative survey conducted during the 1980s in seven advanced industrial societies investigated the organization of work and the extent of employee discretion (Boreham 1992). The aim was to provide some empirical evidence of the characteristics of the contemporary workplace and the extent to which these are in accord with post-Fordist rhetoric.

To operationalize the concept of control within the workplace the researchers employed three separate measures which they believed to encompass different practices of discretion at work:

• The extent to which individuals are constrained within the parameters of their own job (degree of control over the pace of work, for example). This measure was called '**autonomy**', and would be the foundation for the flexibility and deployment of skills required under post-Fordist production.

- Control over the methods of production, termed '**production decision making**' (degree of control over product or work process design, for example). There would need to be some evidence of involvement by lower-level employees if the hypothesized post-Fordist reorganization of work was to be confirmed.

- Economic control over the means of production, termed '**economic decision making**' (degree of participation in budgetary decisions within the workplace). Infiltration of policy decisions in this respect by lower-order workers would be evidence of the post-Fordist scenario of flexible production based on employees' knowledge of financial management.

Some of Boreham's findings are summarized in Table 3.3.

Table 3.3 Control in the contemporary workplace: international comparisons

Autonomy and occupational status (percentage of employees with high autonomy)

	Australia	Britain	Canada	Germany	Japan	Sweden	USA
Managers, administrators	75.6	49.6	74.2	49.0	83.8	82.4	81.4
Professionals	53.0	37.2	44.3	27.0	52.9	53.6	64.7
Clerks	32.0	21.8	28.4	18.4	38.8	28.7	33.5
Skilled workers	27.3	21.5	20.4	16.1	32.3	30.3	42.9
Semi- and unskilled workers	12.1	7.1	8.3	8.3	24.7	19.1	18.4

Production decision making and occupational status (percentage of employees with significant participation)

	Australia	Britain	Canada	Germany	Japan	Sweden	USA
Managers, administrators	75.6	29.2	46.7	32.7	60.5	59.4	43.0
Professionals	47.3	18.7	24.4	12.8	27.5	23.1	21.8
Clerks	14.5	3.4	7.3	2.8	10.5	11.3	5.5
Skilled workers	16.1	7.3	7.4	3.8	7.6	12.4	10.8
Semi- and unskilled workers	6.0	3.8	3.2	1.3	4.6	5.6	3.9

Economic decision making and occupational status (percentage of employees with significant participation)

	Australia	Britain	Canada	Germany	Japan	Sweden	USA
Managers, administrators	68.9	30.8	49.6	30.8	55.3	61.1	36.7
Professionals	34.7	14.4	19.0	10.6	19.2	16.9	18.4
Clerks	9.8	3.0	6.4	2.0	10.5	8.2	3.2
Skilled workers	7.2	3.8	4.2	3.2	4.5	9.6	5.4
Semi- and unskilled workers	1.5	1.3	2.3	0.5	3.5	2.0	2.5

Source: Boreham (1992), p. 103

1) *Suggest two examples to illustrate what autonomy in the workplace might mean in practice.*
2) *Describe the relationship between occupational level and degree of autonomy, according to the information in Table 3.3.*
3) *According to the table, which countries contain the highest and lowest percentages of semi-skilled and unskilled workers reporting a high level of autonomy?*

4) *Which of the two categories of decision making (economic or production) shows the smaller amount of 'significant participation' on the part of the three lowest-status categories of employees?*

5) *To what extent does the information in the table regarding the position of skilled workers provide evidence for or against the view that the contemporary workplace is 'post-Fordist'?*

Boreham concludes that the results attest to what Fox (1974) described as the low discretion and low trust accorded to white-collar, skilled and blue-collar employees in Britain, Australia, Canada and Germany. In all countries the extension of involvement in decision making is scarcely evident other than for a small percentage of professional emoloyees. He also adds: 'The data strongly suggest that it is location in the traditional power and status hierarchy of the enterprise that determines participation in workplace decision making. The predicted extension of new participation arrangements at the level of the skilled worker is not evident.'

This research also produced interesting findings in relation to factors such as gender, age, public/private sector and union membership. It suggests that gender is strongly associated with autonomy in every country. At all levels men were more likely to be able to control various aspects of their employment conditions. Age did not appear to be significant since work experience with age failed to provide much in the way of participation. Nor did the public/private enterprise distinction prove significant in determining autonomy. Union membership, it seems, cannot produce empowerment at the micro level, and was in fact negatively associated with autonomy in every country studied except Germany.

To sum up, the anticipated involvement of those with skill and experience was not evident, so it still appears that in the contemporary workplace 'it is hierarchy that matters, not the rational application of skill'. This suggests that production in advanced capitalist societies is currently largely organized along neo-Fordist lines. 'Flexible production techniques and organizational forms do not appear to have usurped the Fordist organization of the labour process, and there is little evidence . . . to suggest that participative organizational practices have made any significant incursion into traditional managerial prerogatives.'

Boreham is pessimistic about the effects on the labour market of the transition from Fordism to flexible working practices. The results of his study suggest that there is a steadily shrinking core of employees who are involved in strategic decision making, and a periphery made up of two parts. One part consists of a large number of clerical, secretarial and blue-collar workers who play little or no part in decision making and have limited access to career opportunities; the other part includes the growing numbers of mainly female, casual, part-time workers, outworkers and subcontractors with no job security and no discretion over their working arrangements. In this sense, in Britain at any rate, the evidence for the arrival of post-Fordist employment practices may primarily indicate a continuing process of deindustrialization, as secure full-time employment disappears from older manufacturing industries.

The outlook for women is especially pessimistic since the move towards flexible working practices has been achieved largely through the exploitation of female labour. Quoting Harvey (1989), Boreham comments: 'not only do the transformed market structures make it easier to exploit the labour power of women, as casual

Figure 3.4 Two
perspectives on part-time
work

Source: *Economist*, 22 May 1993

and part-time workers, and to substitute the labour of female workers for core male
workers, but also the revival of subcontracting, homeworking and family labour
systems permits a resurgence of patriarchal practices'.

Finally, Boreham argues that neo-Fordist organizational practices and the deployment
of new technologies have extended the opportunities for an intensification of control
and a devaluation of the labour power of many traditional forms of employment,
very much as Braverman had contended it would.

New forms of control and surveillance

Paul Thompson (1993) points out that although some new production systems
devolve responsibility to teams, this does not in itself result in individual autonomy.
Quoting a study of 'lean production' in North America by Berggren (1993), he refers
to 'rigorous factory regimes' which involve detailed conduct and discipline codes,
minute regulation of work and the elimination of personal attributes. The kind of
'autonomy' which prevails is self-policing by the group, such as peer surveillance as in
the case of Nissan UK's 'Neighbour Watch' system. Plant layout is used to facilitate
surveillance, and this is encouraged by competition between teams and plants, with
'incentive' schemes including information systems that can trace defective work back
to source, and prominently displayed productivity quotas.

> *In what sense might it be said that employers are currently implementing one of
> the lessons of the Human Relations school's 'bank wiring observation room
> experiment' conducted by Elton Mayo? (See Haralambos and Holborn 1995, pp.
> 295–6.) To what extent is their strategy pure Taylorism? Or is it perhaps a
> mixture of both? Give reasons for your answer.*

This paradox of enhanced worker autonomy coupled with increased managerial
supervision (responsibility without power) has been confirmed by studies of UK
engineering plants. Use of computerized 'work-to-lists' allows for operators' performance
to be quickly monitored. Such equipment is increasingly being applied in the areas of

clerical and service work, most obviously in electronic point-of-sale technology.

On a broader level, Thompson notes that there is now greater subordination of personality to corporate culture and norms – a trend apparent in selection, psychological testing and appraisal procedures which stress attitudes as well as performance. Referring to the work of Fuller and Smith (1991; quoted in Thompson 1993), he comments: 'the shift to behavioural controls can be observed in the service sector, where there are increasing attempts to police appearance and emotions to create added value in circumstances where products are fairly standardized'.

Explain the last paragraph in your own words.

Intensification of labour

Those with a favourable view of post-Fordist production methods claim that it involves working 'smarter not harder'. However, Thompson argues that there has actually been an intensification of labour.

He concludes that it is wrong to talk of a qualitative break in the nature of work, and that some post-Fordist rhetoric exaggerates the extent of empowerment of workers. While an upgrading of work may occur in a small number of cases, in Britain generally it seems more likely to result in deskilling because changes in production have occurred against the backdrop of the low-trust industrial and employment cultures espoused by British management. Countries with cooperative and egalitarian traditions are more likely to develop the social relations that resemble the optimistic claims made for post-Fordism. The historical, sectoral and social contexts play an important part in shaping the contemporary work process.

Figure 3.5 A post-Fordist scenario?

Source: David Bocking, Leeds Postcards

To sum up, the pessimists argue that flexible specialization is about a 'trade-off' between wages and jobs (unless most people accept lower pay there will be a growing number of unemployed), the necessity of 'flexible labour markets' (greater job insecurity) and 'flexible working hours' (less guaranteed leisure).

The following extract from *Japan in the Passing Lane* illustrates some of the features of the so-called 'art' of Japanese management in its early days, before it was adopted by its competitors as the model for flexible mass production:

> The keynote of Toyota rationalization is the elimination of all waste:
>
> * waste from overproduction;
> * waste in waiting;
> * waste in the shipping process;
> * waste in processing;
> * waste in inventories;
> * waste in motions; and
> * waste from producing defective products.
>
> The rationalization here is not so much to eliminate work as, as more directly, to eliminate workers. For example, if 33 per cent of 'wasted motion' is eliminated from three workers, one worker becomes unnecessary. The history of Toyota rationalization is a history of the reduction of workers, and that's the secret of how Toyota shows no increase in employees while achieving its startling increases in production. All free time during working hours has been taken away from assembly line workers. All their time, to the last second, is devoted to production. Subcontractors deliver parts directly to the conveyor belts. Assembly conveyors in each plant are subordinate to the main conveyors that ship out finished cars, and the conveyor belts in subcontracting firms are 'synchronized' to the conveyor belts in each Toyota plant. This '*kanban* method', which has been widely heralded in the mass media, is meant to compel subcontractors to deliver parts exactly on time, which is just another sign of the increasing 'synchronization' in the industry.
>
> If production was lower because of some minor malfunction of machines, the conveyor speed was increased to make up the delay. If production was delayed owing to a fellow worker's absence, overtime became necessary. Even without such incidents, production goals were always just beyond what seemed like the human capacity to produce, and no worker knew what time he might go home once he was in the shop. The workers were bound to the conveyors until they stopped, and the conveyors never stopped until the production goal for the day was achieved.
>
> Should someone in the team make a mistake, the wage would decrease correspondingly. Tied to the conveyor belts, everyone works desperately, hoping that he is not a burden to the others.
>
> While management journalism may applaud Toyota's high profit and the '*kanban* method' which they see as supporting it, the human costs of Toyota methods – suicides, injuries, job fatalities, and occupational disease – increase at a horrifying rate. The situation at Toyota is a sad but typical example of the victimization of workers in modern society. Workers suffer every day in front of the conveyer belts. The panel in Toyota Hall increases every six seconds.* Whenever I come to this city and talk to the workers, I

feel as though I have strayed into some fantasy land. But this is a nightmare that I have lived, and the anger will not go away.

*This signifies the number of Toyotas produced up to the present. One new vehicle every six seconds!

[Adapted from Kamata 1984, pp. 199–202 and 211]

How far does such evidence tend to invalidate the claim that Japanese organizations are the prototypes of a post-Fordist age?

The elimination of 'waste' described by Kamata was also happening in the British car industry. In 1983 there was a dispute at what was then the British Leyland Cowley plant that was dubbed 'the washing-up war'. It was about what management buys when it purchases 'labour power'. Does it buy the job the worker does, or does it buy the worker? The specific dispute was over whether or not workers should wash in the last three minutes of the shift (i.e. management's time) or after the shift has finished (i.e. their own time). While on the face of it such a dispute may appear to be over a trivial thing, it was symptomatic of the overall attempt by management to man up to 100 per cent – to get as close as possible to 60 minutes' work in every hour.

Japanese car producers now have plants in the UK, and by comparison with the 1970s and 1980s industrial relations in the car industry in the 1990s appear to be harmonious. The industry now operates on the basis of a slimmed-down workforce who accept the rigour of work in lean production systems and whose 'loyalty' is encouraged through 'self-policing teams', individual accountability and, not least, fear of unemployment. For the pessimists the primary feature of a post-Fordist scenario such as this appears to be a workforce with little alternative but to fit in with the requirements of corporate standards at a time when the balance of power clearly lies with management.

Changes on the line? The 1990s

The following are extracts from an article by Ian Elliot in *Mini 35 Official Souvenir Magazine*, 1994:

Mini building at Longbridge has always followed the same basic sequence. Brian Dipple should know – he started working on Mini bodyshells in 1960.

'In those days if someone was getting a bit behind the rest, the lads might start tapping hammers against the track to encourage them to catch up . . .

'In some ways we were more dependent on each other then than we are now. It was an "us and them" situation – you feared management, if you wanted to discuss a problem you'd have a battle to even get past the secretary. Now our manager's door is genuinely open and there's a spirit of working together instead of the old conflict.' . . .

John Roberts recalled his impressions of starting work in 1964. '. . . In the old days you just did your job; you didn't have much contact with other areas. Now we have greater exchange of ideas and information.'

Down in the East Works, where the famous A-series engine and gearbox for the Mini have always been made, you can find a compact and busy team assembling automatic gearboxes to meet the demand from Japan.

Ron Taylor . . . says: 'I began by assembling parts like sub-frames onto the track ready for the body drop, then spent time working under the "cakestand" [a Longbridge term for the raised platform allowing the assembly of underbody components]. We tended to stick to one operation then, but there's far more flexibility now.'

Geoff Powell and John Speed are from Conformance (a modern multi-disciplinary department that blends functions like quality control and industrial engineering). . . and Samantha Humphreys has just become the first woman auditor in the Longbridge quality audit department.

1) *Identify examples from these extracts that might be seen as features of post-Fordist work organization.*
2) *Which aspects the post-Fordist paradigm referred to in Table 3.1 on p. 57 are not mentioned in the extract?*

Post-Fordism: the sceptical view

As well as being pessimistic about the way in which increasing flexibility is being deployed in the workplace, people like Boreham are also clearly sceptical about post-Fordist claims of the extent to which work has been substantially democratized.

In support of this view, Jones (1988) studied the engineering industry and found little empirical evidence of a revolution in work roles. Other sceptics doubt that flexible specialization is of any significance at all. Pollert (1988) argues that proponents of the increasing flexibility of production have oversimplified the picture. To begin with, Fordist methods were never as widespread as the post-Fordists suggest, and despite the rapid diffusion of Ford's techniques to other industries Fordism never became a universal or typical form of capitalist production. Ginsberg (1982) estimated that assembly-line techniques only ever absorbed a maximum of 7 per cent of America's workforce during this century. FS was always present to some extent in industries that were resistant to Fordism, such as small-batch engineering. Moreover, mass production is much more flexible than critics give it credit for. Ford himself was familiar with the concept of flexible specialization, and the pursuit of 'segmented markets' goes back to the big US mail-order firms of the 1890s and was very well established in the heyday of Fordism in the 1950s and 1960s. Since then market segmentation and product choice in the 'mature' consumer goods industries have increased markedly under a mass production regime.

Conversely, it is also pointed out that, quantitatively, mass production is currently more important within manufacturing than FS, which is still confined to relatively few regions and industries. Mass production is ubiquitous, and the idea that small, dynamic firms pioneer the use of 'hi-tech' equipment is countered by the fact that usually only large companies can afford it. Some of the innovations are still in their infancy, and while the use of computers in retailing has revolutionized stock control there are few examples of link-ups with manufacturing.

The sceptics also point out that in any case manufacturing is declining in significance, occupying less than a quarter of the British workforce, so FS is not likely to be the 'wave' of the future. The real measure of the concept will be the extent to which it can flourish in the service industries (currently occupying about 70 per cent of all workers). There is some evidence of increased autonomy in a growing number of professional jobs, but the number of menial service jobs has also grown. Both functional and numerical flexibility can be achieved in services, as we saw in the case of MacDonalds on p. 56. Irving Leveson (quoted in Williams 1985) argues that we are seeing the rapid industrialization of the service sector. Gabriel's research (1990) noted how the catering industry traditionally relied on the human factor – the social and technical skills of its workforce – but now there is a shift towards the 'industrialization of service'. Low cost and standardized operations mean flexibility across a range of deskilled tasks, rule-driven processes and loss of creativity.

> *Make a list of products and services with which you are familiar that are mass produced. Keep the list for use in the next activity.*

Pollert also argues that flexibility within the work process does not inevitably reskill workers. Its effects vary according to the balance of power between management and workforce at the time. In some cases it can lead to an upgrading of the skills required, while in others it leads to deskilling. Goss's (1987) study of the instant print industry illustrates how technology paved the way for the displacement of craft skills with young, inexperienced and relatively untrained personnel who are unable to withstand employer pressure.

Wood (1989) has also questioned the view that an upgrading of skills occurs with the introduction of new technology. In the British steel industry many workers were already skilled, while for others it meant moving between semi-skilled jobs. Wood argues that the extent of FS has been exaggerated. Taking the example of cars, he points out that although many manufacturers offer a comprehensive range of optional specifications, this is far removed from individual custom-built products.

> *Investigate the number of possible specification choices available to the purchaser of a new car at a number of local main dealers. Is it possible for those choices to be built into the manufacture of a particular vehicle? How far does this information support or reject the idea of post-Fordism?*
>
> *Make a list of products that are either hand made, custom built or made in very limited numbers. Compare this with the list of products you made in the last activity. How many of the items in each list have you ever purchased? What conclusions do you draw from this about the relative importance of mass production?*

Further scepticism about the post-Fordist paradigm is based on the fact that the increase in the number of part-time workers associated with it does not seem clear cut or inevitable. Pollert points to the falling number of such workers as a proportion of manufacturing workers between 1979 and 1986. The Labour Force survey of 1986 (Department of Employment 1986) calculated that one third of the workforce belonged to the category of part-time workers, temporary workers or the self-employed; so two thirds did not belong to this 'flexible workforce'. If there has been an increase in part-time work in recent years, this is seen as the expedient result of recessionary pressures rather than a conscious step towards the long-term implementation of post-Fordist ideals.

Similarly the notion of the 'core' group of privileged workers who are able to protect themselves from attack has been criticized. It is a mistake to believe that any jobs can be secure in the face of economic recession. At the UIE shipyard on Clydeside, where management had tried to implement a division based on the core/periphery notion, a recent dispute occurred when the management tried to sack half of the workforce in the 'core' category (Incomes Data Services survey, quoted in Callinicos and Harman 1987). It appears that, because of the economic recession, the supposed privileges of the core group disappeared.

Finally, in a major survey of employers sponsored by the Employment Department, it was found that the main reasons for employing part-time employees were:

• to cope with fluctuating levels of demand for the product or service;

• to fill jobs which require only short time spans of work; and

• to meet preferences for part-time work among the available workforce.

More than half the employers questioned thought that the turnover of labour and the absentee rate for their part-timers were about the same as for their full-timers. Around a quarter thought they had a better employment record in these respects. Most of the employers, nearly nine out of ten, offered the same rates of pay for full-timers and part-timers doing similar work. Most employers did not regard their part-time workers as 'peripheral' workers, but saw them as a crucial element of the workforce (*Employment Gazette,* 1992, quoted in Denscombe 1993, p. 34).

However, on a more negative note, given that the majority of part-time workers are women, it should be pointed out that there are still instances where women doing 'broadly similar' work to men, often alongside men, actually still earn less.

Try to discover some examples of this.

Supporters of flexibility would point to the fact that many women appear to take part-time jobs because they do not want full-time jobs (see Table 3.4).

Table 3.4 Reasons for taking a part-time job: by sex and marital status, Spring 1993 (percentages and thousands)

| | | Females | | |
	Males	Married	Non-married	All females
Student/still at school	29.4	0.6	33.4	6.9
Ill or disabled	3.3	1.0	1.3	1.1
Could not find a full-time job	29.0	8.4	18.3	10.3
Did not want a full-time job	36.2	88.0	45.4	79.9
Part-time workers (=100%) (thousands)	886	4,078	967	5,045

Part-time is based on respondent's self-assessment.
Includes those who did not state the reason for taking a part-time job.

Source: Department of Employment (1994)

How would you explain this situation?

Summary

Overall the picture is complicated by the fact that the optimisitic, pessimistic and sceptical perspectives are not mutually exclusive. Pessimists would agree with many of the points raised by the sceptics, but they are more concerned with the threat to organized labour. Many of the optimists are guarded and are aware of the uncertainty of the outcome of these changes, and they are also acknowledging the sceptics' arguments about the continued importance of mass production.

Both the optimists and the pessimists have valid points. Some workers have experienced an upgrading of skills, but many have simply been marginalized, and the situation varies by region, by country and by industry. In the case of Britain, economic restructuring so far only appears to have resulted in a 'perfunctory sort of post-Fordism' (Lovering 1990).

Wider social, cultural and political implications

If the post-Fordist paradigm is the scenario of the future, its repercussions will reach far beyond the workplace itself. As the foregoing analysis suggests, it will affect the basis of industrial relations and class solidarity, but it is also thought to have implications for politics, education and training, and culture. In all of these areas the traditional class basis of action is said to be breaking down, supplanted by an increasing emphasis on individualism, as witnessed in the growth of new social movements and patterns of consumption based around individual choice. Table 3.5 indicates the various ways in which the concept of post-Fordism has been extended.

Table 3.5   The politics of post-Fordism

Area of society	Fordism	Post-Fordism
Industry	Low technological innovation	Accelerated innovation
	Fixed product lines, long runs	High variety of product, shorter runs
	Mass marketing	Market diversification and niche-ing
	Steep hierarchy, vertical chains of command	Flat hierarchy, more lateral communications
	Mechanistic organization	Organismic organization
	Vertical and horizontal integration; central planning	Autonomous profit centres; network systems; internal markers within firm; out-sourcing
	Bureaucracy	Professionalism, entrepreneurialism
	Mass unions, generalized wage bargaining	Localized bargaining; core and periphery; workforce divided; no cooperation
Class	Unified class formations; dualistic political systems	Pluralized class formations; multi-party systems
	Institutionalized class compromises	Fragmented political markets
Welfare state/ education	Standardized forms of welfare, prescribed 'courses' in education	Consumer choice in welfare, credit transfer, modularity, self-guided instruction, 'independent' study
Politics	Class parties, nationwide	Social movements; multi-parties; regional diversification
Private consumption style	Standardized consumption (cars, houses, dress) and styles	More varied consumption and personalized styles

Rustin (1989), adapted and extended by O'Donnell (1992), p. 240

The idea that capitalist industrial society is entering a new phase is not new. Throughout the post-war period there have been predictions about the impending changes in social solidarity and class relations in capitalist society brought about by technological change and the reorganization of work. These have been expressed in terms of Daniel Bell's post-industrial society thesis (see p. 41), Ralf Dahrendorf's post-capitalism thesis, Alvin Toffler's 'third wave' of civilization (see pp. 41–2), Gorz's 'farewell to the working class' and more recently the 'New Times' thesis of Hall and Jacques (1989) which is most overtly based on post-Fordist assumptions. All of these share, to a greater or lesser extent, the belief that we are witnessing the end of ideology and polarized class conflict.

Chapter 2 discussed Bell's famous post-industrial society thesis, which predicted that the traditional work ethic would be replaced by a greater emphasis on individual freedom and pleasure seeking, that market forces would be subdued by increased stress on social welfare and economic planning and that class-based conflict over the distribution of wealth would decline. Of all these things, social welfare and economic planning appear to have actually receded as capitalism has entered what Lash and Urry (1987) have called a 'disorganized phase'. However, supporters of post-Fordism would argue that Bell's predictions about the decline of class alignment are still relevant.

Lash and Urry suggest that post-Fordism has signalled the end of 'organized capitalism' and the start of 'disorganized capitalism'. With more reliance on market forces, less government intervention, increased flexibility of labour, the adoption of microelectronic technology and the decline of the manufacturing sector, employment becomes less secure and more fragmented. The result is the emergence of a 'postmodernist' culture based on fragmentation and pluralism in which class is 'decentred' as the source of identity, being replaced by individualist consumption. Work is no longer a way of identifying oneself, more a means of acquiring desirable goals, a tendency that leads to a decline in traditional class politics and the end of the possibility of working-class revolution, (see Chapter 8 p177 and Chapter 9 pp203–5 for further information).

Figure 3.6 New chains?

Source: Gomm (1991), Vol. A, p. 101

Marxists critical of these postmodernist ideas argue that post-Fordism does not represent a significant break in the development of capitalism and capitalist class relations. For the old Left, nothing fundamental has changed to alter the exploitative character of capitalism. There is little opportunity for the masses of the Third World to exercise choice, though one does not have to go to Calcutta to find people who are in no position to choose lifestyles and define identities on the market. Callinicos (1989) asserts that the basic position of many working-class people under capitalism has worsened. As Ainley (1993) puts it, 'the recrudescence of quite primitive and grossly exploitative employment in sweatshops under paternal management, of child labour and new types of domestic service, is a marked feature of the metropolitan economies'.

Callinicos adds that the revival of nineteenth-century sweated trades in the world's richest cities is to some extent a function of the rise of the 'newly industrialized countries' of the Third World, leading to a growth of the working class on a global scale. This global competition in a unified world economy will mean that some work will command much the same pay regardless of where it is performed, and the threat to wages is such that some commentators see in the USA the beginnings of a Third World economy. Davis (1988) gives a flavour of this when he says that 'LA industry has been turned back from Fordism to bloody Taylorism of an almost east Asian standard.' Callinicos accuses the postmodernists of parochialism in their failure to acknowledge this global picture of poverty and insecurity.

> *Reuter:* Thirty per cent of the world's labour force – more than 820 million people – are either unemployed or working for less than a subsistence wage, the International Labour Organization said yesterday. [Guardian, 3 February 1994]

Chronic insecurity affects nearly all levels of the labour hierarchy, but the new labour market conditions of the 1980s and 1990s have re-emphasized the vulnerability of disadvantaged groups. In 'New Times' Britain some 8–9 million people live below the poverty line, and such people can exercise precious little choice and express little of their identity with the money they have left after paying the cost of basic subsistence.

Far from enabling individuals to overcome the coercive features of capitalist society, the world of consumption can only serve to reinforce the limitations on individual freedom that result from capitalist domination. The paradox is that most products and services are still produced by large-scale organizations; there is greater choice, but within the restrictions of a standardized range of products. There are also the associated evils of consumer fetishism and the creation of false needs.

It could be argued that the apparent fragmentation and decomposition of social class is a temporary phenomenon reflecting the balance of power between employers and unions; the employers currently have the upper hand and therefore the ability to extract cheaper and more flexible labour from a weaker and less unionized workforce. The solution advocated by the radical Left is, of course, to overthrow through collective struggle the social relations of production that define the capitalist system. However, they may be hard pressed to explain the paradox noted by Brown and Scase (1991) that at the end of the 1980s 'the restructuring of class relations has increased material inequalities but reduced the subjective level of awareness of them'. The problem for the Left is that radical appeals to the electorate appear to be falling on deaf ears. How far this reflects the fact that the proletariat has dissolved into a competing crowd of individuals or how much it is due to apathy, or a sense of powerlessness, remains debatable.

Fiona Devine's (1992) study of 'affluent workers' in Luton sheds some light on this. She found that there was resentment at what was perceived as the inequitable distribution of resources in society at present, in particular the notion of inherited wealth. Her respondents aspired to a more equal society, in which people were rewarded more fairly. This vision of an ideal society was not confined to the capitalist system.

Devine concludes that the everyday economic realities of people's lives act as a powerful constraint on their doing anything other than accepting things as they are. But this constraint in itself implies a lack of acceptance of the existing system. She suggests that lack of collective action on the part of the working class can largely be put down to the failure of the trade unions and the Labour Party to mobilize working-class support for change.

Essay Questions

Assess the extent to which sociological evidence supports the view that 'peripheral workers' are becoming increasingly central to the economy of advanced industrial societies. (25 marks)

Structured question

Item A

'Functional flexibility' describes the ways in which workers are moved around from job to job within the factory as required. An alternative is 'numerical flexibility'. Here firms . . . either . . . employ workers on a temporary, part-time or casual basis, thereby avoiding paying wages for wasted time. Or they sub-contract out certain activities for which there is insufficient demand . . .

Some authors consider the growth of flexible organization and working practices so significant as to constitute the basis for a major new phase in the development of capitalist societies . . .

However, there are two kinds of objection that might be raised about this view . . . First there is an empirical problem of how many people are being affected by these changes. Second . . . it is not entirely clear that these changes are part of a new, coherent or unified system of manufacturing production, still less that they are the harbinger of a new age. In Britain the conditions of employment have altered in the last 10 years, with some functional flexibility and many more insecure jobs . . .

It is ironic that the growth of less secure forms of employment should be seen as indicative of a new employment scenario, for casual and temporary work was very much the norm in Victorian times . . . What is more, outside the manufacturing sector there have always been plenty of jobs that are seasonal or temporary – for instance in the tourist and catering trades. In this context it is equally ironic that so much attention is being paid to changes in manufacturing industry, since it now employs a relatively small proportion of the labour force.

Source: Warde (1989)

Item B

More than one million employees in Britain are temporary workers. This means that six per cent of all employees are employed on a temporary basis. Although the number of temporary workers has risen since 1984, there has been no comparable increase in the share of employment of temporary work.

Fifty-seven per cent of temporary workers are female. Three fifths of these are employed part-time as are nearly a third of male temporary workers. Consequently, for both sexes, a much higher proportion of temporary, than permanent, employees work part-time.

Almost half of all temporary employees are employed on fixed short-term contracts and one in five are casual workers.

Temporary workers by type of work

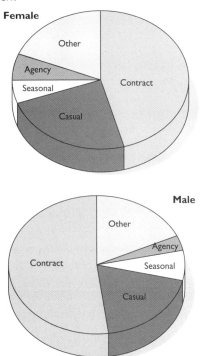

Source: Equal Opportunities Commission (1993)

Item C

Undoubtedly the labour market is more flexible. Non-standard types of work such as part-time and contract jobs and self-employment have boomed in the past decade. One British worker in four is now a part-timer. Add in temporary

staff and the self-employed and two workers in five are outside permanent, full-time employment. Firms such as Burton Group in tailoring, British Home Stores and British Airways are rushing to convert full-time workers into part-timers. As many as two-thirds of Sears, the Saxone-to-Selfridges group, are now part-timers. These firms say part-time work enables them to boost staff at busy periods, improving customer service.

In the long run more flexibility in the labour market should mean more jobs . . . if firms are now hiring two part-timers rather than one full-timer it . . . may explain why unemployment has started to fall earlier than expected.

Other implications of the part-time boom are less palatable. A grim *Panorama* programme . . . highlighted the problems of Britain's increasingly insecure workforce: milkmen working longer hours for the same money, CD stackers sacked just before the two years after which their jobs would be legally protected, betting-shop workers thrown out if they refuse to work evenings. Flexibility for employers means new chances to save money and to fire unwanted workers.

Part-timers may be on lower rates than full-time workers. Most do not qualify for redundancy pay, pensions, sick pay or national insurance benefits until they have been with a firm for two years. Employers escape paying national insurance contributions for workers on less than £56 a week.

An economist would say this is market forces working: cheaper labour means more jobs. Trade unionists cry 'exploitation' and want part-timers protected.

More protection would mean fewer jobs. Many women, especially those with children, like part-time work. A recent Department of Employment survey found that only 13 per cent of part-timers did such jobs because they could not find full-time work. Paradoxically, to 'protect' them might mean that they ended up with no jobs at all.

Source: *Economist,* 22 May 1993

Item D

The post-Fordist argument suggests that there has been – or at least can be – a qualitative transformation of the economy. The Fordist economy with its mass production and deadening work for the majority can be usurped by the development of a high skill, high trust economy and society. In this vision of the future we are offered the possibility of job satisfaction for all. So what's new? We have heard similar arguments throughout the post-war period, camouflaged within notions of the post-industrial society, post-capitalism and in some of the more fanciful versions of embourgeoisement.

They suggest that the labour process characteristic of post-Fordism requires teamwork, creativity, control and commitment. Each of these carries a democratizing thrust. If firms are to compete effectively they will have to develop work relations such as these, which will themselves undermine hierarchy and existing patterns of authority. Work will be a decidedly social and collective enterprise. It is here that the progressive and radical nature of post-Fordism is said to lie.

However, there are serious problems. Such an analysis marginalizes the uneven development of the economy. Are we merely talking about a small primary labour market surrounded by a larger secondary and hidden economy? Capitalist social relations are evacuated from the discussion, being at the same time silenced and normalized they are rendered more palatable and we are offered, not the possibility of transformation but a new stage in capitalist development predicated on a direct relation

between individual creativity, collective work and a successful economy.

This vision ignores the presence of a variety of economic functions within a post-Fordist economy. The patterning of social relations along class, race and gender lines is also marginalized. The systemic nature of antagonism revolving around these is apparently transformed by post-Fordist practices. By stealth as it were, capitalist social relations will be undermined by the logic of an economic imperative which creates the conditions for a fairer and juster society.

Source: Avis (1992)

1) According to the information in Item B, in which two types of work are female temporary workers more likely to be found than their male counterparts? (**2 marks**)

2) Explain in your own words the difference between 'functional' and 'numerical' flexibility (Item A). (**2 marks**)

3) Explain which type of 'flexibility in the labour market' is indicated by the information in Item C, illustrating your answer with two examples contained in the item. (**4 marks**)

4) Using information from the items and elsewhere, assess the extent to which empirical evidence supports the claim that the labour process characteristic of post-Fordism 'undermines hierarchy and existing patterns of authority' (Item D). (**8 marks**)

5) Using information from the items and elsewhere, evaluate the argument that the systemic nature of antagonism revolving around class, race and gender is 'transformed by post-Fordist practices' (Item D). (**9 marks**)

Coursework suggestions

As a key feature of the 'flexible labour force', part-time paid employment is an important area to investigate. You might approach the topic from a 'macro' angle, using secondary sources to provide a picture of the structural significance of part-time employment by industry or by sector for

the national, and indeed, global economy. You could provide a demographic and social profile of the part-time workforce. Social Trends, Labour Research, Department of Employment and Equal Opportunities Commission publications would all provide details on this. It might then be possible to link your findings to feminist theory in order to give possible explanations for your findings. Abbott and Wallace (1990) would be very useful here. One possible line of enquiry is to investigate any links between women's part-time employment status and the informal 'grey' or black economies, although the latter could be a sensitive area!

You could combine the secondary data mentioned so far with a local survey of employers and perhaps interviews with a number of part-time employees about their reasons for working part time. Bear in mind that employers are unlikely to say that they treat some of their workers as peripheral! Has there been an increase in part-time employment in your area? Or has there always been a tradition of part-time work there?

If you yourself are a part-time employee you are in an excellent position to carry out covert participant observation of the experience of flexible employees in the workplace, perhaps with particular reference to gender relations. You might consider pay, conditions, employment rights, job satisfaction and informal power structures. You might look for instances where part-time workers suffer discrimination. Some observations may be statistical, others more qualitative. (As always, this method can have a number of potential hazards, and you should always discuss your plans with your tutor beforehand.)

Bibliography

Abbott, P. and Wallace, C. (1990) *An Introduction to Sociology: Feminist Perspectives*, London: Routledge

Aglietta, M. (1979) *A Theory of Capitalist Regulation*, London: Verso

Ainley, P. (1993) *Class and Skill: Changing Divisions of Knowledge and Labour*, London: Cassell

Atkinson, J. (1985) 'The changing corporation', in Clutterbuck, D. (ed.) *New Patterns of Work*, Aldershot: Gower

Avis, J. (1992) 'Post-Fordist idylls: whither education?', *General Educator*, No. 18

Berggren, C. (1993) 'Lean production: the end of history', *Work, Employment and Society*, Vol. 7, No. 2

Beynon, H. (1973) *Working for Ford*, Harmondsworth: Allen Lane

Boreham, P. (1992) 'The myth of post-Fordist management', *Management Decision*, Vol. 30, No. 6

Brown, P. and Scase, R. (eds) (1991) *Poor Work, Disadvantage and the Division of Labour*, Milton Keynes: Open University Press

Callinicos, A. (1989) *Against Post-modernism*, Cambridge: Polity

—— and Harman, C. (eds) (1987) *The Changing Working Class*, London: Bookmarks

Cavendish, R. (1982) *Women on the Line*, London: Routledge

Clegg, S. (1992) 'Modern and postmodern organisations', *Sociology Review*, Vol. 1, No. 4, pp. 24–8

Coriat, B. (1981) 'Restructuring the assembly line: a new economy of time and control', *Capital and Class*, Vol. 11

Crabtree, D. (1992) 'Fordism, post-Fordism and neo-Fordism', *General Educator*, No. 16

Davis, M. (1988) 'LA: civil liberties between the hammer and the rock', *New Left Review*, No. 170

Denscombe, M. (1993) *Sociology Update*, Leicester: Olympus Books

Department of Employment (1986) *Labour Force Survey*, London: HMSO

Devine, F. (1992) *Affluent Workers Revisited: Privatism and the Working Class*, Edinburgh: Edinburgh University Press

Equal Opportunities Commission (1993) '1992 Labour Force Survey', in *Women and Men in Britain 1993*, London: EOC

Ford, H. (1923) *My Life and Work*, New York: Doubleday

Fox, A. (1974) *Beyond Contract: Work, Power and Trust Relations*, London: Faber & Faber

Gabriel, Y. (1990) *Working Lives in Catering*, London: Routledge

Ginsberg, E. (1982) 'The mechanization of work', *Scientific American*, September

Gomm, R. (1991) *Sociology A Level*, Cambridge: NEC

Goss, D. (1987) 'Instant print: technology and capitalist control', *Capital and Class*, No. 31

Gramsci, A. (1971) *Selections from Prison Notebooks*, London: Lawrence & Wishart

Grint, K. (1991) *The Sociology of Work*, Cambridge: Polity

Hall, S. and Jacques, M. (1989) *New Times: The Changing Face of Politics in the 1990s,* London: Lawrence & Wishart

Hamper, B. (1992) *Rivethead: Tales from the Assembly Line,* London: Fourth Estate

Haralambos, M. and Holborn, M. (1995) *Sociology: Themes and Perspectives,* 4th edn, London: Collins Educational

Harman, C. (1994) *Socialist Review,* No. 177

Harvey, D. (1989) *The Condition of Postmodernity,* Oxford: Blackwell

Hounshell, D. (1984) *From the American System to Mass Production 1880–1932,* Baltimore, MD: Johns Hopkins University Press

Jones, B. (1988) 'Work and flexible automation in Britain: a review of developments and possibilities', *Work, Employment and Society,* Vol. 2, No. 4, pp. 451–86

Kamata, S. (1984) *Japan in the Passing Lane,* London: Unwin

Lamb, H. and Percy, S. (1987) 'Big Mac is watching you', *New Society,* 9 October

Lash, S. and Urry, J. (1987) *The End of Organized Capitalism,* Cambridge: Polity

Lipietz, A. (1987) *Mirages and Miracles: The Crisis of Global Fordism,* London: Verso

Linhart, R. (1981) *The Assembly Line,* London: John Calder

Lovering, J. (1990) 'A perfunctory sort of post-Fordism', *Work, Employment and Society,* Special Issue, May, pp. 9–28

O'Donnell, M. (1992) *A New Introduction to Sociology,* 3rd edn, Walton-on-Thames: Nelson

Phillimore, A.J. (1989) 'Flexible specialisation, work organisation and skills: approaching the second industrial divide', *New Technology, Work and Employment,* Vol. 4, No. 1

Philpott, J. (1994) 'The labour market', in *Focus on Britain 1994,* Deddington: Phillip Allan

Piore, M.J. and Sabel, C.F. (1984) *The Second Industrial Divide: Possibilities for Prosperity,* New York: Basic Books

Pollert, A. (1988) 'The flexible firm: fact or fiction?', *Work, Employment and Society,* Vol. 2, No. 3, pp. 281–316

Reich, R.B. (1983) *The Next American Frontier,* New York: Times Books

Rustin, M. (1989) 'The politics of post-Fordism', *New Left Review,* No. 175

Sabel, C.F. (1982) *Work and Politics: The Division of Labour in Industry,* Cambridge: Cambridge University Press

Smith, C., Child, J. and Rowlinson, M. (1989) *Innovation in Work Organisation: Cadbury Ltd 1900–1985,* Cambridge: Cambridge University Press

Taylor, L. and Walton, P. (1971) 'Industrial sabotage: motives and meanings', in Cohen, S. (ed.) *Images of Deviance,* Harmondsworth: Penguin

Thompson, P. (1993) 'The labour process: changing theory, changing practice', *Sociology Review,* Vol. 3, No. 2

Toffler, A. (1980) *The Third Wave,* London: Collins

Warde, A. (1989) 'The future of work', *Social Studies Review,* September

Williams, M. (ed.) (1985) 'The future of work', *New Society,* 25 October

Winner, L. (1985) 'Do artefacts have politics?' in MacKenzie, D. and Wajcman, J. (eds.) *The Social Shaping of Technology,* Milton Keynes: Open University Press

Wood, S. (1989) 'The transformation of work?', in Wood, S. (ed.) *The Transformation of Work?,* London: Unwin Hyman

4 *Recent patterns of industrial conflict*

A 'strike' is a social phenomenon of enormous complexity which, in its totality, is never susceptible to complete description, let alone complete explanation.

Alvin Gouldner

Official figures on strikes in the UK

Official statistics on industrial conflict are collected by local offices of the Department of Employment. Table 4.1 summarizes the official figures for strikes in the UK for the period 1974–93.

Table 4.1 Stoppages in progress, 1974–93				
Year	Working days lost (000s)	Working days lost per 1,000 employees	Workers involved (000s)	Stoppages
1974	14,750	647	1,626	2,946
1975	6,012	265	809	2,332
1976	3,284	146	668	2,034
1977	10,142	448	1,166	2,737
1978	9,405	413	1,041	2,498
1979	29,474	1,273	4,608	2,125
1980	11,964	521	834	1,348
1981	4,266	195	1,513	1,344
1982	5,313	248	2,103	1,538
1983	3,754	178	574	1,364
1984	27,135	1,278	1,464	1,221
1985	6,402	299	791	903
1986	1,920	90	720	1,074
1987	3,546	164	887	1,016
1988	3,702	166	790	781
1989	4,128	182	727	701
1990	1,903	83	298	630
1991	761	34	176	369
1992	528	24	148	253
1993	649	30	385	211

Source: *Employment Gazette*, June 1994, p. 200

*Which of the four measures shown in this table do you think gives the best
indication of the level of industrial conflict over the period?*

*Convert this table into a graph (you will need to think of how to deal with the
different scales). Write a short summary (about 1,000 words) of the changes over
the period, using both the table and the graph you have constructed.*

*Compare the figures for a) 1974 and 1979; b) 1981 and 1983. Write a short
paragraph comparing patterns of industrial conflict in each case.*

The two key statistics used to measure the incidence of industrial conflict are the
number of working days lost and the number of stoppages.

There are, as always, a number of issues concerning the way these statistics are
constructed that must be borne in mind. First, they exclude stoppages involving fewer
than ten workers or lasting less than a day unless the total number of 'working days
lost' is over 100 (working days lost are calculated by multiplying the number of
workers involved by the number of days the stoppage lasts). Richard Hyman (1977)
has pointed out that 'working days lost' is a loaded term since it implies a rather
negative effect of strikes, and he uses the term 'striker-days' instead.

Second, the figures exclude any disputes deemed political and not directly related to
terms and conditions of employment. As a result a stoppage in the coal industry in
1986 in protest at the visit of an MP was not included.

Third, the figures do not include industrial action short of the stoppage of work (a strike)
and therefore do not include forms of protest such as go-slows and work-to-rules.

Which of the following would be included in these statistics?

A) Eight workers going on strike for two weeks over a pay claim.
B) Eleven workers going on strike for one day over a pay claim.
*C) An unofficial strike at a construction site involving 100 workers and lasting
three days.*
*D) An unofficial strike at an FE College where seven lecturers go on strike for
four weeks.*
*E) Eight workers striking for the day over government policy towards the health
service.*
F) 500 workers instituting a work-to-rule in protest at proposed pay-cuts.

Despite these problems the figures are viewed as a fairly valid picture of the extent
of labour disputes in the UK. Looking at the recent trends indicated by the table, it
can be seen that the number of stoppages has fairly constantly declined over the
period shown. The 211 stoppages recorded in 1993 is the lowest figure for a year
since records began in 1891. However, this figure cannot give a full picture on its
own since it tells us nothing about the number of people involved in these disputes
or how long they lasted. It is for this reason that the other statistics are presented.

To take an example, the number of stoppages in 1926 was 323, a relatively low
figure compared to recent years. But the total of 'striker-days' in that year was
162,233 – which dwarfs recent figures. The reason is that there was a general strike
in 1926. It counted as only one stoppage, but clearly a general strike is more
important that a one-day strike involving 25 workers at a local factory.

Strikes in the twentieth century

Summarizing the trend this century (up until 1976) on the basis of comparable earlier figures, Hyman (1977) argues that the pattern of strikes in the UK was characterized by a rising number of stoppages. There were over 1,000 for every year between 1941 and 1976, with an average figure of over 2,000.

This rising trend in the number of stoppages was matched by a falling trend in the number of 'striker-days'. The average figure up to 1933 was 15 million, while for the rest of the period covered by Hyman's study it fell to an annual average of under 3 million. The size of the labour force had increased consistently throughout the study, which means that the figures are not strictly comparable over time. The rise in the number of strikes is less than one would expect if they had risen in line with the growing labour force, and the decline in striker-days is greater.

At the time Hyman was writing, Britain was viewed as a strike-prone country. His analysis of the statistics refutes this suggestion.

Figure 4.1 One point of view on trade unionists!

Source: adapted from Joseph (1986) p. 117

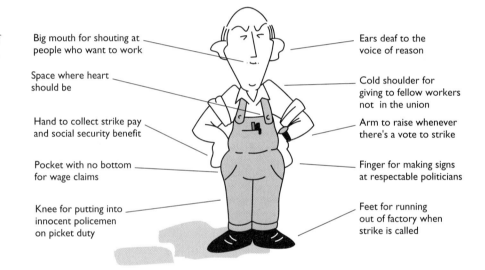

Big mouth for shouting at people who want to work

Space where heart should be

Hand to collect strike pay and social security benefit

Pocket with no bottom for wage claims

Knee for putting into innocent policemen on picket duty

Ears deaf to the voice of reason

Cold shoulder for giving to fellow workers not in the union

Arm to raise whenever there's a vote to strike

Finger for making signs at respectable politicians

Feet for running out of factory when strike is called

1) *What kind of picture of trade unionists do you think is portrayed in this cartoon? How accurate do you think it is?*
2) *Write alternative labels to those on the diagram to represent your view of trade unionists.*
3) *What labels would you put on a picture of an employer?*

The trade unions

The key organizational innovation by workers in the field of industrial relations was the development of trade unions. They arose because workers were aware that there were conflicts of interest in industry.

Such conflicts and their origins and effects were central issues for the classical sociologists. Emile Durkheim (1893) viewed the rise of the new form of organization based on specialization and the division of labour as potentially problematic. If relations between people were to be based purely on self-interest (as classical economists such as Adam Smith argued) and people merely looked out for themselves, the system of social norms that held society together would be eroded. Durkheim argued that the rise of industrial society and the greater development of the division of labour had undermined the old mechanical basis of solidarity in society. A new form of solidarity, which he termed organic solidarity, would be required.

This new form of solidarity would not arise simply out of self-interest; society needed a moral foundation. The danger inherent in the development of the division of labour was that this moral foundation would break down, leading to a condition of 'normlessness' which he called *anomie*.

One of the key indicators of *anomie* for Durkheim was industrial conflict. His solution was that society should be regulated by professional associations which would develop codes of conduct for the ethical running of business and society. His model for such associations was the medieval guild system, and elements of this system also shaped the early trade union movement. In fact Durkheim's vision can be seen as something of a model for the era of industrial relations in the UK between 1945 and 1979, often known as tripartism, which gave prominence to discussions between the government, employers' associations and trade unions.

Karl Marx offered an alternative view of the effects of the Industrial Revolution. He argued that the rise of capitalism led to a distortion of the true nature of work and labour. Work was central to Marx's view of human fulfilment, by which he meant the possibility of unleashing the potential for human creativity to produce a better society. However, work under capitalism is for Marx an example of 'alienation' since it provides no satisfaction for the workers but rather constitutes the basis for their exploitation.

Alienation is the process whereby the products made by workers appear to be outside their control since they cannot afford to purchase them. Alienation results from a system of production based on the 'commodification' of life, meaning that everything is reduced to monetary relations. Since this is the basis of the free market which lies at the heart of capitalism, it follows that alienation cannot be overcome by mere adjustments to the system of capitalism, but only by the overthrow of the system of production upon which capitalism rests.

> *Draw up a table contrasting the views of Durkheim and Marx on industrial relations. Remember to include reference to the key concepts of anomie and alienation.*

These two views of the effects of the rise of modern industrial capitalism fed into the consciousness of workers and the emerging trade union movement. However, the logic of the two views is quite different. Following Durkheim, *anomie* can be overcome within capitalist society by allowing for the inclusion of professional associations, which could include trade unions. In modern terms, according to this approach the role of trade unions is to achieve an input into economic planning and control over the process of production. The Marxist view, in contrast, is that alienation cannot be overcome within capitalist society, and that in conjunction with the political organizations of the working class – the socialist and communist parties – the trade unions should struggle to overthrow capitalism and institute a society based on the common ownership of the means of production.

These two contrasting views, which might be called the reformist and the revolutionary perspectives on industrial relations, have competed for influence within the trade union movement since its foundation.

History of the British trade union movement

The origins of trade unionism in the UK lie in the breakdown of the system of regulating wages operative since 1349. With the rise of capitalism, calls for the free market were effectively challenging this system. The free marketeers argued that wages should be fixed by individual contracts struck between worker and employer. Fairly soon it became evident that the aim of this was to reduce the cost of labour to employers, and to protect themselves from exploitation workers resorted to collective organization. Their first attempts were fiercely resisted by the employers, and workers' organizations were declared illegal by the Combination Acts of 1799 and 1800. These laws did not apply to the employers, although they also grouped themselves together, as Adam Smith pointed out in *The Wealth of Nations*:

> We rarely hear . . . of the combinations of masters, though frequently of those of workmen. But whoever imagines, upon this account, that masters rarely combine, is as ignorant of the world as of the subject. Masters are always and everywhere in a sort of tacit, but constant and uniform combination, not to raise the wages of labour above their actual rate . . . Masters, too, sometimes enter into particular combinations to sink the wages of labour even below this rate. [1974 edn, p. 59ff]

1) *Adam Smith wrote* The Wealth of Nations *in 1776. To what extent do you think his view is still valid?*
2) *The Trades Union Congress (TUC) is the national body representing trade*

Figure 4.2 Trade union banner

Source: Gorman (1973), p. 123

unionists. Find out if there are any equivalent national bodies representing managers and employers.

It was not long before groups of workers came into conflict with the law. In 1834 the Tolpuddle Martyrs, six agricultural workers from Dorset, were transported to Australia when their attempt to form a trade union was discovered. Trade union members were continually prosecuted: Coates and Topham (1980) report that there were 10,000 prosecutions a year between 1858 and 1875. In the face of such intense repression, by 1870 only 4 per cent of the population of the UK were members of unions.

This situation changed dramatically with the rise of the 'New Unionism' in the 1880s. What was new about this period was the formation of general unions for all workers as opposed to the previous organizations which had been largely restricted to craft workers (the skilled workers). The proportion of the workforce in trade unions had risen to 25 per cent by 1914.

What views on the role and methods of trade unions can be gleaned from this photo of a National Union of General Workers' banner?

Discuss the relative importance of the various methods outlined on the banner in the contemporary trade union movement.

The economic depression after the First World War created mass unemployment, resulting in a decline a trade union membership that was accelerated by the defeat of the General Strike in 1926. The 1927 Trade Disputes and Trade Union Act outlawed the closed shop (100 per cent union membership agreements), restricted picketing rights, constrained the right of civil servants to belong to trade unions and outlawed certain categories of strike. This law was not repealed until 1946; in fact the decline in the trade union movement was only really reversed after the Second World War, when Keynesian economic policies ensured that the economic depression after the First World War was not repeated.

Membership of the trade unions grew steadily, reaching a peak of 13,289,000 in 1979, when 58 per cent of the workforce were unionized. The unions' influence was strongly felt during this period, which was the heyday of tripartite structures such as the National Economic Development Council, a body overseeing long-term economic planning comprising representatives of the government, the Confederation of British Industry (the employers' organization) and the Trades Union Congress.

Trade unions, industrial democracy and worker directors

As we noted in Chapter 2 (p. 28), the 'human relations' school of management arose in reaction to the practice of Taylorism or scientific management, with its insistence on the strict division of labour and control over workers.

Use any standard sociology textbook to write reports (of about 500 words) each on the approach to work and industrial relations advocated by the schools of scientific management and human relations.

Discuss in class whether you feel anything from either of these approaches is apparent in contemporary industrial relations.

In the late 1920s a team of researchers led by Elton Mayo conducted the 'Hawthorne experiments', which were an attempt to investigate the links between working conditions and productivity. They concluded that workers act in groups according to social norms and are not motivated by pay levels alone (Mayo 1933). This finding undermined the centrality of pay levels as a key incentive to harder work in Scientific Management approaches. The application of these findings led management to concentrate more on workers' social needs at work in an attempt to improve productivity by making workers relatively happy rather than simply paying them more. After the Second World War the growth of organizational psychology led to a neo-Human Relations school which concentrated on changes to the work process itself rather than the work environment. The classic example of this was the use of work groups to replace Taylorist assembly-line procedures at Volvo. These ideas achieved a degree of popularity in the 1960s and 1970s, and partly under their influence there were demands for more formal involvement of workers in industrial decision making.

However, Daniel and McIntosh (1972) identified two separate arguments for greater worker involvement in decision making:

- Greater involvement in decision making would result in higher motivation to work and greater productivity. This idea is based directly on the Hawthorne experiments. It can be called the argument based on production values.

- Work is central to people's lives, both in terms of time spent there and as a source of social identity. According to this more radical argument, if democracy is to have any real meaning it must be extended to the economic sphere. This might be called the argument based on social values.

These two very different arguments should alert us to the possibility that there may be very different motivations for espousing the same course of action. Marxist sociologists such as Harry Braverman were critical of the human relations approach since, although it differed from scientific management, it shared the idea that there

Figure 4.3 Management and workers have different goals

Source: TUC education cartoon, quoted in Joseph (1986), p. 102

Management and workers have different goals

were no fundamental conflicts of interest between managers and workers and viewed greater productivity as benefiting all. The human relations approach did not take into account differences in power between managers and workers and the existence of perceived and real differences of interest between them.

'Management and workers have different goals.' Think of as many possible resolutions to this problem as you can and write them down. Confer with your classmates and produce a class list.

This blindness to conflicts of interest aroused workers' hostility to proposals for worker participation along the lines advocated by the human relations school. As Daniel and McIntosh (1972, p. 31) pointed out: 'Where management and its spokesmen are advocating, and seeking to use job enrichment as a tool to weaken unions and worker influence and bargaining strength, it is hardly surprising if they become suspicious of, and hostile to innovations.'

One of the demands of the 1970s arising from the more radical versions of the human relations approach was for workers to be involved in decision making through the appointment of worker directors. In fact as early as the 1950s legislation was introduced in West Germany requiring a form of worker directorship. However, research by Dahrendorf (1959) indicated that these changes did not lead to any great advance in worker influence. The only major experiment with worker directors in the UK was at the British Steel Corporation. However, the worker directors were appointed by management, not elected by the workforce, and surveys showed that a majority of employees were unaware of the existence of the scheme.

The following arguments were made in favour of worker-director schemes:

- They fostered greater harmony in the workplace.

- They encouraged better decision making, recognizing the plurality of interests in the workplace.

- They gave workers more of a sense of being part of the enterprise.

Figure 4.4 A trade union view of worker participation

Source: Evans, *Labour Research,* September 1989

Trade unionists and socialists, however, criticized such schemes for the following reasons:

- They gave the appearance of greater involvement while attempting to reduce the substance of involvement.

- They did nothing to change patterns of ownership and control, which remained in private hands.

- They were an attempt to weaken the independence of trade unions and undermine their influence.

Capitalists too levelled criticisms at worker-director schemes:

- They were said to be unnecessary because there was no conflict of interest, and managements responsive to shareholders would take decisions that were in everyone's interest.

- They undermined the notion of property rights.

Albeit for quite different reasons, both main groups in industry were thus suspicious of the idea of worker directors. It was influential for a period in the 1970s, but never really caught on in the UK, and in the 1980s there was a renewed emphasis on management's right to manage. As an example of the reaction against the human relations approach, Abraham Zalaznik, Professor of Leadership at the Harvard Business School, argued that 'observation tells me that too many managers put inter-personal matters . . . ahead of real work' as a result of the 'subordination of real work to psychopolitics' (quoted in the *Financial Times*, 6 February 1989). He went on to make the now familiar argument that companies should centrally concern themselves with pleasing their customers.

What do you think is meant by 'real work' in this context?

The influence of the trade unions began to wane in 1976 when the Labour government adopted monetarist policies which included a commitment to keep wage rises down. Conflict followed between the government and the TUC, culminating in the Winter of Discontent in 1978/9.

The decline of the trade unions?

The year 1979 witnessed the election of the first government led by Mrs Thatcher, whose attitude to trade unions can be described as hostile. New Right thinkers believe trade unions interfere in the free-market determination of wages, which should simply be a matter for negotiation between individual employers and employees. One of the central thinkers of the New Right, Friedrich Hayek, made the following comment on the trade unions:

> It is an illusion to imagine that the problems Britain now faces can be solved by negotiation with the present trade union leaders. They owe their power precisely to the scope for abusing the privileges which the law has granted them. . . . There can be no salvation for Britain until the special privileges granted to the trade unions three-quarters of a century ago are revoked. Average real wages of British workers would undoubtedly be higher, and their chances of finding employment better . . . It is a com-

plete inversion of the truth to represent the unions as improving the prospect of employment at higher wages. They have become in Britain the chief cause of unemployment and the falling standard of living of the working class ... There is no hope of Britain maintaining her position in international trade – and for her people that means no hope of maintaining their already reduced standard of living – unless the unions are deprived of their coercive powers. [Hayek 1984, pp. 57–64]

Imagine you are employed by the TUC and are asked to write a report refuting the view outlined here. Discuss what points Hayek is making, research their validity and write a report providing a defence of the role of trade unions. Your report should be about 1,000 words long.

If you are working in a class, divide into two groups. One group should represent Hayek and the New Right, and the other group the TUC. In these groups prepare for, organize and conduct a debate around Hayek's proposition: 'It is a complete inversion of the truth to represent the unions as improving the prospects of employment at higher wages.'

The Conservative governments elected since 1979 have enacted several pieces of legislation relating to trades unions which arguably reflect the New Right's negative view of them. The effect of these laws has been to seriously hamper the ability of trade unions to protect their members' interests and to tilt the balance of power in the industrial sphere markedly towards capital and away from labour.

Table 4.2 Legal attack

Since 1979 the Conservative government has passed eight Acts of Parliament aimed at reducing the power of trade unions:

1980 Employment Act
• Picketing restricted to own place of work
• 80 per cent ballot to establish closed shop
• State funds available for union ballots
• Secondary action restricted

1982 Employment Act
• Industrial action must relate to 'a trade dispute'
• Secondary action further restricted to 'own employer'
• Unions no longer immune from civil action – employers can take out injunctions and sue for damages
• 80 per cent ballot for all closed shops, every five years
• Right not to be dismissed for not being a member of a closed shop
• Removal of union-only labour clauses in commercial contracts

1984 Trade Union Act
• General secretaries, presidents and all executive committee members to be elected by secret ballot every five years
• Ballots on political fund every ten years
• Secret ballots before industrial action

1988 Employment Act
• Members have right to inspect union books
• Right not to be disciplined by union
• Right to ignore union ballot decisions

(continued over page)

- Right to stop check-off
- Unions cannot pay members' fines
- Commissioner for the Rights of Trade Union Members ('Crotum') established

1989 Employment Act
- Restrictions on paid time off for union reps

1990 Employment Act
- Unions liable for unofficial action unless written repudiation sent to all members
- Unofficial strikers can be selectively dismissed
- All secondary action other than picketing unlawful
- Unlawful to refuse to employ non-union member on the basis of closed shop
- Powers of Crotum extended

1992 Trade Union and Labour Relations (Consolidation) Act
- Brings together collective employment rights legislation (individual rights covered by Employment Protection [Consolidation] Act 1978)

1993 Trade Union Reform and Employment Rights Act
- 'Citizen's right' for members of the public to obtain injunctions against unions if they are likely to be deprived of goods and services by unofficial strike action
- New Commissioner for Protection against Unlawful Industrial Action to finance legal action against unions by members of the public
- Unions must give employers seven days' written notice of industrial action
- All strike ballots to be postal
- Independent scrutiny of strike ballots
- Postal ballots on union mergers
- Right to join union of choice (undermines 'Bridlington' agreement)
- Members must give written authorization for 'check-off' every three years
- New powers for Crotum to check union finances
- 'Wilson amendment': lawful for employers to offer incentives for staff to go onto non-union personal contracts

Other employment provisions
- Protection for employees raising health and safety concerns at work, or leaving hazardous workplace
- Maternity leave increased to 14 weeks, regardless of length of service
- Dismissal on the grounds of pregnancy automatically unfair
- Right to written statement of employment particulars
- Abolition of wages councils
- Amendment of Transfer of Undertakings (Protection of Employment) Regulations which implement the EC Acquired Rights Directive. In line with EC pressure, the requirement that the undertaking transferred be 'in the nature of a commercial venture' has been removed. Also, employees can refuse to transfer to a new employer without incurring dismissal
- Employers must consult with unions on redundancies

Source: *New Statesman and Society* (1994), p. 6

New Stateman and Society *claims that the eight Acts listed in Table 4.2 were 'aimed at reducing the powers of trade unions'. Use the information supplied to consider how far this is an accurate description of the content of these pieces of legislation. How might a Government minister respond to this claim?*

Use reports from old newspapers (or a CD-ROM) to investigate debate around the 1993 Act. Draw up a list of the reasons given by the government for its introduction and the benefits it claimed would arise. Draw up a list of criticisms made of the legislation.

Industrial conflict in the 1980s and 1990s

The free-market economics pursued by successive Conservative governments since 1979 have upset the economic stability enjoyed by the UK between the 1950s and the 1970s, creating greater insecurity in the job market. Added to the increased debt many households are carrying as a result of the credit boom of the late 1980s, the re-emergence of mass unemployment may offer an explanation for the caution many workers now show about taking industrial action (see Figure 4.4).

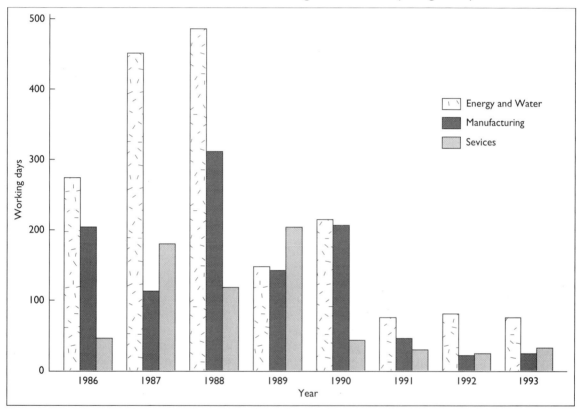

Figure 4.5 Working days lost per 1,000 employees, by broad industrial sectors, 1986–93

Source: *Employment Gazette,* June 1994, p. 201

- *Write a short report (75 words) on each of the three industrial sectors identified here, outlining trends in industrial conflict over the period shown.*
- *To what extent are there differences between the three?*
- *Apart from changes to the law, what other factors might explain the trends identified here?*
- *Is there any evidence to suggest that changes to the law were not particularly effective in reducing industrial conflict?*

Another factor had been the succession of defeats in industrial disputes suffered by the unions in recent years. This section will examine two major conflicts of the 1980s that helped to shape today's industrial relations landscape.

The National Graphical Association (NGA) and the Stockport Messenger

This was the first major dispute to test the 1980 and 1982 Employment Acts, and it also tested the attitude of the TUC to these pieces of legislation after the 1983 General Election. Its outcome paved the way for the changes introduced into Fleet Street shortly afterwards.

The *Stockport Messenger* was one of several free newspapers published and printed by the Messenger Newspaper Group Ltd, a holding company with nine subsidiary companies run by Eddy Shah. The dispute concerned the setting up of non-union workshops in Warrington and Bury to produce the *Messenger*. This brought the company into conflict with the National Graphical Association (NGA), the printers' union, since the rules of that union forbade members from handling work from non-union workshops. The NGA's strength had always been based on the closed shop – an arrangement by which everyone who works in a workplace is required to be a member of the union. This was a traditional trade union practice to ensure that all workers contributed to achieving their common goals.

By May 1983 the NGA had become aware that a printing operation had been set up in Warrington (at Winwick Quay in the Warrington Enterprise Zone) which breached the union's closed shop rules. The NGA suspected that the non-union plants would be used to replace the unionized plants. This fear was heightened when in June an advertisement appeared for word processor operators and studio staff to work in the Stockport area. The NGA national headquarters became involved in negotiations to try to settle the dispute, but a solution did not materialize and on 4 July NGA members at the Stockport offices (Fineward Ltd) came out on strike.

Production of the papers continued. The printers were picketing the offices of Fineward Ltd, but it became clear to them that work was being transferred elsewhere. The NGA therefore began to organize picketing at other offices in the Messenger group, particularly an industrial unit in Warrington where Messenger Printing Ltd, another of the subsidiary companies, was based.

The company invoked the Employment Acts, which outlawed 'secondary picketing', and court action followed. Although the company in Warrington was part of the same group as the company with which the NGA was in dispute, it was legally separate and therefore the union's action was deemed to be secondary picketing. This exposed the fact that the laws allowed employers to move work around but unions could not respond in like fashion. The very basis on which trade unions' effectiveness is built – support and solidarity – was directly threatened. The union refused to abandon its action, and eventually the court ordered the sequestration of the union's assets.

The NGA appealed to the TUC for help since a special conference of the TUC in 1982 had decided on outright opposition to the Employment Acts even if this meant engaging in illegal action. However, the General Council of the TUC refused the NGA's request, arguing that it must protect the TUC itself and therefore act only within the law. This meant it could not provide money to help with the dispute. Left-wing members of the General Council were said to be furious with this decision.

The same day a mass picket of the Warrington plant attracted about 5,000 people – showing how important many union members felt the dispute to be. The police closed the motorway exits nearest to the plant in an attempt to prevent the pickets from assembling, and then for the first time in an industrial dispute riot police were used. The frightening atmosphere created by this intervention is conveyed by the following account from one of the pickets, explaining what happened when the riot police charged at about 4 a.m.:

> I was running through the fields and I fell down in a ditch and nearly broke a leg. I very badly twisted my ankle as I went down, a sort of gap just opened up – no ground there any more. And then the Range Rovers, after they'd reversed at high speed, drove forward again, turned around and mounted this wet ground, this big field that we were on and again drove at high speed towards the pickets who were running away. [Quoted in Dickinson 1984, p. 143]

Figure 4.6 Having cleared pickets from the courtyard of the Warrington plant, police allow an armoured Land-Rover to deliver artwork

Source: Dickinson (1984), p. 127

The NGA was left trying to win a dispute with its funds confiscated and facing further fines for breaching injunctions issued earlier. The total fines imposed on the NGA of £800,000 and the feeling that it had not received adequate backing from the TUC eventually forced the union to wind down the dispute and in effect to admit defeat.

The tactics employed by Eddie Shah and the Messenger group were later used by Rupert Murdoch's News International group to move their printing operations to Wapping after sacking their existing print workers, and other national newspapers soon followed suit. Again at Wapping the riot police were very much in evidence against the mass pickets that gathered outside the new plant. What was new was that officers of a TUC union, the EETPU, helped recruit workers for the Wapping plant and thus assisted an employer in dispute with another union. This outbreak of 'business unionism' led to the suspension of the EETPU from the TUC.

The miners' strike of 1984–5

If there is one dispute that shaped the landscape of the 1980s and 1990s then it is the miners' strike of 1984–5. The cause of the dispute was a programme of pit closures and the fear that more and more pits would be shut.

Between 1981 and 1984, 41,000 miners' jobs had been lost; however, three strike ballots had also been lost and the National Union of Miners had not mounted significant resistance. This led some commentators to conclude that the miners – the archetypal traditional workers – were now affected by consumer affluence. This opinion took its inspiration, of course, from the general argument that the working class was in decline.

Yet in March 1984, when it was announced that Cortonwood mine was to be closed, the NUM branch there voted for strike action. The strike spread to the Yorkshire area, and then other areas of the union joined the action under Rule 41 of the union's constitution, which allowed for strikes at area level without a national ballot if supported by the National Executive of the union. Within a short period the vast majority of the pits in the country were shut down.

The NUM received only lukewarm support from the TUC and other unions. This created great bitterness among the miners: in a famous incident, a noose was lowered at a strike meeting in South Wales where the TUC General Secretary was talking about picket-line violence.

In contrast, the miners did receive mass support from rank-and-file trade unionists and the public at large. Dozens of miners' support groups were set up across the country. The Labour MP Tony Benn reported that £150,000 was raised in Chesterfield to support the miners, and Fleet Street trade unionists collected an estimated £2 million. Moreover, the organization Women Against Pit Closures was established by strikers' wives, and proved to be highly effective in sustaining the strike; it also challenged some of the traditional attitudes towards the place of women in mining communities.

Figure 4.7 A member of Maltby Women's Support Group

Source: Workers Revolutionary Party, *Newsline* (1985), p. 127

> *Investigate the role of Women Against Pit Closures. To what extent did the activities of this organization represent a change in the gender relationships in mining communities?*

An important background element to the strike was the role of the miners in bringing down the previous Conservative government in 1974. After that humiliation, Conservative MP Nicholas Ridley had developed plans to deal with the threat of a future miners' strike, involving the building up of coal stocks from 42 tonnes in 1981 to a massive 58 million tonnes in 1983.

The dispute marked an escalation in the involvement of the police in industrial disputes, with over 8,000 officers being sent to Nottinghamshire early on in the dispute. Nottinghamshire was the only significant area where the majority of miners continued to work. Another new feature was the construction of a network of roadblocks to limit the ability of people to picket.

James Anderton, Chief Constable of Greater Manchester, made the following comment on police behaviour:

> It does appear to the public that the police have imposed a kind of curfew on the community as a whole, not just on the miners, and also that they have restricted free movement. These features are things we normally only associate with countries behind the Iron Curtain. [Quoted in *Daily Mail*, 31 March 1984]

In an attempt to increase the impact of the strike, miners picketed several British Steel works, culminating in mass pickets in May and June 1984 at Orgreave, a coking plant near Rotherham in South Yorkshire. There were major confrontations between police and miners, with about 5,000 involved on both sides. The violence of Orgreave, relayed via TV cameras, sent shock waves through the whole trade union movement. The *Guardian* reported that on one day 'the battle lasted for 10 hours of horrifying clashes. At the end 93 had been arrested and 79 injured' (19 June 1984).

A tactic used to split the miners was the founding of the Union of Democratic Mineworkers, with the assistance of David Hart (at the time of writing an adviser to Michael Portillo, the Employment Secretary). This organization was composed of working miners, mostly from Nottinghamshire. Working miners were also instrumental in bringing and encouraging court action leading to the sequestration of NUM assets.

Isolated and deprived of its funds, the NUM kept up its struggle until March 1985, but eventually the miners returned to work knowing their struggle against pit closures had been lost. The rate of pit closures rapidly increased.

The failure of the TUC to support the NUM in line with the 1981 Wembley conference decision (the same one invoked by the NGA) was cited as a key reason for the defeat by the NUM President, Arthur Scargill: 'The trade union movement in Britain, with a few notable exceptions, have left this union isolated. They have not carried out TUC conference decisions, to their eternal shame' (Callincos and Simons 1985, p. 219).

> *Many books have been written about the 1984–5 miners' strike. Among the best are Benyon (1985), Callinicos and Simons (1985), Fine and Millar (1985), and Warwick and Littlejohn (1992). Read one of them (you might try a local Higher Education library) and write a summary of its contents, focusing on the social, economic and political effects of the strike and its outcome.*

One of the classic studies of working-class communities from the 1950s is
Coal is Our Life *by Dennis, Henriques and Slaughter (1956). You might see how*
views on mining communities in the 1980s compare with this account. You will
find reference to it in any textbook, or you may be able to locate the book itself.

The legacy of the 1980s

In the wake of the defeats suffered by the printers, the miners and other groups of
workers, the idea that class politics were no longer tenable and that strikes were now
obsolete became much more commonplace. This has had an enormous impact on
the trade union and labour movement. Within both the TUC and the Labour Party a
'new realism' has gained the ascendancy. Most leaders of the labour movement now
distance themselves from industrial conflict and certainly from any attempt to argue
that the laws can be broken because they are bad laws, designed to help employers
to defeat the unions and worsen workers' living standards. There is now pressure for
a new kind of union movement that will try to obtain the best deal for its members
without taking any form of industrial action. This has been called 'business unionism',
after a similar philosophy in the US labour movement.

However, a study of the link between policing in the miners' dispute and class
consciousness uncovers the great shift the strike caused in the consciousness of miners
and their supporters. The notion that the state was neutral disappeared, and in its place
an analysis of the strike in terms of 'us' and 'them' took root. Penny Green (1990)
found this view echoed in 90 per cent of her interviews, and 55 per cent argued that
the policing of the strike had opened their eyes to basic divisions in society.

The new industrial relations

Information on the changing nature of industrial relations has been collected in a
series of large-scale social surveys known as the Workplace Industrial Relations
Survey. The third of these was conducted in 1990. It covered 2,000 workplaces and
collected the responses of 2,550 senior managers and 1,466 worker representatives.
A follow-up analysis covering the industrial and commercial sector with a sample of
1,500 covered in detail the notion of the 'new industrial relations'.

The findings of the 1990 survey (reported in Millward et al. 1992; Millward 1994) can
be compared with the previous survey in 1984 (Millward and Stevens 1986) to
estimate the changes that have taken place. One of the main findings is a reduction in
the number of workplaces containing union members. This figure fell from 50 per
cent in 1984 to 39 per cent in 1990. The proportion of workers covered by
collective bargaining agreements fell from 58 per cent in 1984 to 43 per cent in
1990. There were several reasons for the latter trend. In the public sector, bargaining
rights were removed from teachers. In the private sector newer workplaces were
less likely to admit collective bargaining rights in the workplace. This is not simply
because they were new but because of their characteristics:

> Only 29 per cent of workplaces established since 1984 had recognized
> unions, compared with 40 per cent for all workplaces in 1990 . . . There
> seems little doubt that the characteristics of original new workplaces con-
> tributed to their lower rate of recognition. They were generally smaller,
> much more likely to be in the service sector (especially retailing and hotels

Table 4.3 Size, sector, ownership and workforce composition of new workplaces, 1990

	All trading sector	Original new workplaces estab. 1984 onwards	Original new workplaces estab. 1987 onwards
			Column percentages
Size of workplace			
25–49	52	54	39
50–99	26	30	32
100–199	13	11	15
200–499	7	4	15
500–999	1	1	–
1000+	1	*	–
			Means
Average size	96	77	106
			Percentages
Sector			
Manufacturing	29	13	10
Services	71	87	90
High-technology industry	6	9	2
Ownership			
Private sector	97	99	95
State owned	3	1	5
Branch or larger firm	68	82	83
Head office of larger firm	4	1	5
Independent establishment	28	17	12
Foreign-owned UK	9	13	7
Multinational	31	23	29
			Means
Workforce composition			
Percentage manual	54	59	49
Percentage of manual skilled	30	21	12
Percentage female	38	50	55
Percentage part-time	14	28	32
Base: establishments in industry and commerce			
Unweighted	*1510*	*74*	*41*
Weighted	*1452*	*91*	*41*

* means less than 0.5 per cent; – means zero

Source: Millward (1994), p. 20

and catering where union representation is particularly unusual), had fewer skilled workers (who have higher union membership) and had much higher proportions of part-time employees. [Millward 1994, pp. 21–2]

In so far as new workplaces having these characteristics were set up, the overall percentage of workplaces with union representation fell. Union strength was also greater in manufacturing industry, which was disproportionately hit by the recessions in the 1980s.

The surveys show an important trend towards the complete derecognition of unions: 'The decline in union representation between 1984 and 1990 was not generally a weakening of the role of unions from one of full negotiation and representation to a partial role . . . Rather, it involved a wholesale reduction of the trade unions' (Millward 1994, p. 33).

Only 29 per cent of workplaces established since 1984 had recognized unions. There are also considerable differences in the characteristics of these new workplaces, as shown in Table 4.3 (on page 97).

1) Write ideal-type description of the categories of workplace identified in Table 4.3 in terms of the characteristics outlined.
2) If the trends identified here continue, what implications does this have for trade unionism?
3) Do you think present trends will continue?

One of the interesting points to note is that there is a clear trend to an increase in the percentage of the workforce who are part-time, and in the percentage who are female. These findings have implications for the future of the trade union movement since it has been relatively weak in organizing part-time workers. Since one of the findings of the 1990 survey was that trade unions do improve both the pay and the working conditions of workers, one possible consequence will be an increase in the pay differentials between males and females. This points to the fact that equal opportunities in employment tend to be more notional than real unless there is a trade union movement able to enforce this type of policy.

Figure 4.8 The benefits of union membership

Source: Evans (1986), p. 2

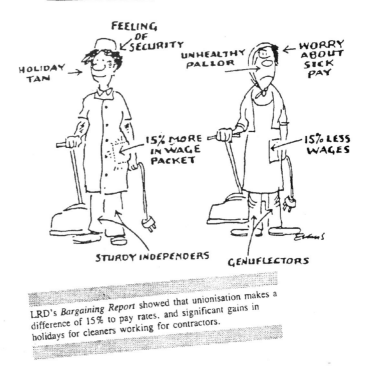

The decline of union density seems likely to increase wage inequality as a whole:

> without the constraint of union negotiations, pay levels were set unilaterally by management. ... commercial and financial considerations dominated management thinking on the size of pay settlements to a much greater extent than in the unionized sector. Pay was more a matter of individual performance, with formal job evaluation being rare. Again, reflecting the lack of union influence, differentials between the highest and lowest earners in non-union workplaces tended to be relatively wide. Lower-paid employees were more common. [Millward *et al.* 1992, p. 363]

Single-union deals

One of the areas considered in detail in the follow-up report issued by the authors of the Workplace Industrial Relations Survey was the extent of the spread of single-union deals, sometimes linked with no-strike agreements, which were seen as a crucial element of the new industrial relations.

Although single-union deals had attracted a lot of press comment, workplaces with no union were much more common but had been given very little attention. Moves from multi-union agreements to single-union ones were relatively rare (Millward 1994):

- 49 per cent of workplaces had no union members;

- 27 per cent had members of a single union;

- 23 per cent had members of two or more unions.

Single unions tended to be more likely in smaller workplaces, with a particularly sharp change at 500 or more employees. Above this size only 20 per cent of workplaces had single-union arrangements. They were also more common in the private sector than the public, more common in workplaces with a large percentage of part-time workers, more common in the services sector, and more common in newer workplaces.

Given that single-union deals are generally thought to be a phenomenon of the 1980s, an interesting finding of this research was that they were most common among workplaces set up in the 1970s.

Single-union deals were most popularly associated with unions such as the EETPU and the AEU, which were pushing a 'business unionism' approach. However, the survey found that these unions were not the most heavily involved. Of the ten unions most involved in single-union deals (and these accounted for 80 per cent of such deals), the TGWU was responsible for nearly a quarter and the EETPU for only 6 per cent, with the AEU on 7 per cent.

Turning to the effects of single unionism, the survey found that full recognition of the unions was less likely in single-union workplaces. The survey suggests that very little of this move to single unions was the result of management initiatives, which throws into doubt the idea that they arise from the different management style of the 1980s and 1990s. The merger of unions and job disappearances were much more common causes, and these are trends that antedate the 1980s.

No-strike agreements were rare, and single-unions deals were not necessarily of this nature. About 10 per cent of such deals involved a strong union winning sole negotiating rights with an employer, though 18 per cent of cases did involve what might be called a weak union in a weak situation.

In conclusion, despite much press comment, single-unions deals are not a new phenomenon, and they are not necessarily a reflection of the weakness of unions in the face of the legal and economic onslaught of the New Right.

Reasserting the right to manage

A clear trend in the 1990s has been the attempt by managements to reassert unilateral control over what goes on in the workplace. The only democratic organizations in workplaces – the trade unions – are weaker than they were, and authoritarian styles of management are more evident. This has negative consequences for workers. The 1990 Workplace Industrial Relations Survey found that compulsory redundancies were much more likely in non-unionized workplaces, and dismissal of workers was nearly twice as frequent in these workplaces as in unionized ones.

The 'human relations' approach of involving employees and employee representatives in the running of enterprises seems to have been replaced by the 'human resources management' approach, which involve things such as company newsletters, staff briefings and consultative committees or company councils. These techniques may recommend themselves to managements as a way of reducing communication between management and unions by communicating instead with employees on an individual basis or with employee (but not necessarily trade union) representatives.

At the extreme end of the reassertion of the right to manage are the cases of union derecognition and the much more common non-recognition of unions in new workplaces that we have already noted.

However, the New Right approach which views trade unions very negatively has not gone unchallenged. A report from the LSE's Centre for Labour Economics found that productivity grew faster in unionized companies than non-unionized ones between 1980 and 1984 (Nickell, Wadhwani and Wall 1989).

John Monks, TUC General Secretary, has pointed to the problem of insecurity created by the free-market reforms of the 1980s and 1990s. He argues that job security is the thing most people cherish, even above high wages. Undermining job security has economic costs due to the stress and absenteeism it causes, and social costs in terms of the destabilizing effects of the widening pay gap it has introduced. Therefore the trade union movement remains as relevant as ever (Monks, quoted in *New Statesman and Society* 1994).

Will Hutton (1994) argues that the problems created by the free market have rekindled interest in cooperative approaches: 'The future of trade unions is not as a key governing interest in the state or as the vanguard of the working class. They are the vital social partners in managing a capitalist system so that the gains are spread equitably.'

The renewal of worker resistance

There is a broad consensus that the 1980s and 1990s witnessed a decline in trade union power, but whether this has meant the effective end of trade unionism is much more open to debate. Some sociologists have appeared to support such a notion, talking of the end of the working class, but others have stressed the durability of the trade unions in this difficult period.

Table 4.4   Membership of top ten unions in 1987 compared with membership in 1992

1987 top ten unions	Membership (000s)	1992 top ten unions	Membership (000s)	Men per cent	Women per cent
Transport and General Workers Union	1,349	Transport and General Workers Union	1,037	82	18
Amalgamated Engineering Union	815	Amalgamated Engineering & Electrical Union	884	93	7
General Municipal Boilermakers and Allied Trade Unions	803	GMB	799	62	38
National and Local Government Officers' Association	759	National and Local Government Officers' Association	764	45	55
National Union of Public Employees	651	Manufacturing, Science and Finance Union	552	73	27
Association of Scientific, Technical and Managerials Staff	400	National Union of Public Employees	527	30	70
Union of Shop Distributive and Allied Workers	387	Union of Shop Distributive and Allied Workers	316	40	60
Electrical, Electronic, Telecommunication and Plumbing Union	369	Royal College of Nursing of the UK	299	8	92
Royal College of Nursing of the UK	270	Graphical Paper and Media Union	270	82	18
Union of Construction Allied Trades and Technicians	256	National Union of Teachers	214	25	75

Source: *Employment Gazette*, June 1994, p. 193

1) *Which social groups are most likely to be in unions in the 1990s?*
2) *What trends are identified in this table?*
3) *Find out which of the categories identified here are rising in importance in the economy and which are declining. What implications might this have?*

Batstone (1984, 1988; Batstone *et al.* 1977) argues that there were important continuities between the 1970s and 1980s. Shop-stewards' organizations remained resilient in the face of the New Right onslaught, and were still able to effectively represent their members. 'Leader' stewards could still achieve a strong bargaining position with management, Batstone argues, because they developed a sophisticated organization able to concentrate their resources and power; moreover, because they had developed close informal links with management they could improve their members' conditions through bargaining, opening the door for concessions and compromise.

This argument fits in with the 'new realism' currently popular in the labour and trade union movement, which views 'old-fashioned' tactics such as strikes, picketing and militant workplace unionism as counterproductive, and places much more emphasis on bargaining with employers. Negotiation is now considered more important and productive than industrial action.

Darlington (1994) opposes this view. He concedes that Batstone's analysis has some advantages in stressing the continued strength and resilience of trade union organization, but maintains that his assessment of the relative effectiveness of militant trade unionism versus negotiation and bargaining is mistaken. On the basis of studies of trade union organization in three Merseyside plants, Darlington argues that external pressures are the key component pushing shop stewards to adopt bargaining tactics rather than industrial action. Chief among these is the bureaucratization of local trade unionism with the proliferation of full-time officials who are distant from their members. This is a dangerous development, weakening the ability of workers to take action to defend themselves at a time when the balance of class forces is shifting towards capital. Since the power of the trade unions is ultimately dependent on their ability to take industrial action, Darlington argues for a reassertion of the tradition of industrial militancy rather than its abandonment. At the centre of his analysis is the idea that there exists a dynamic relationship between shop-steward organization and external pressures, meaning that effective trade unionism needs to take account of the wider power structures in society, and to develop a strong link with rank-and-file members – a relationship threatened by an emphasis on bargaining.

The outcome of this debate will obviously be affected by events in the 1990s. Despite the difficulties and defeats of the 1980s, recent years have seen a number of instances of trade unionists taking determined action to defend their conditions. Although the statistics overall show strike levels to be very low, the striker-day figures for 1993 are higher than those for 1992. The ending of the recession and a fall in unemployment, a perception that the government is weak and a desire to claw back some of the fall in living standards caused by the employers' offensive and the tax increases imposed by the 1993 and 1994 Budgets (the largest tax increases for over 15 years) have all contributed to the more militant mood.

One key example of this trend was the signal workers' dispute in Summer 1994. The dispute arose because the management of Railtrack refused to concede a pay rise unless restructuring of working contracts, designed to introduce flexibility, was also discussed. RMT (the relevant union) argued that these were separate issues.

There followed a series of one-day strikes. Significantly, it soon became clear that despite its stance on the free market the government was involved in this dispute as it had vetoed a deal reached between the two sides in June which would have cost Railtrack £4.3 million. As the dispute dragged on, the cost in terms of lost revenue greatly exceeded this figure. The government obviously did not want the signal workers to set an example to other workers of how to brush aside its pay policy.

The problem for Railtrack and the government was that support for the strike remained solid and the public consistently supported the strikers in opinion polls. The eventual outcome of the strike was a deal worth £8.7 million, with the signal workers achieving pay rises of up to 8 per cent. This clearly breached the government's guidelines on pay and underlined its weakness. This victory also confirmed the continuing importance of the trade unions as defenders of working-class living standards.

Management is still exerting pressure in various sectors for increased flexibility, and trade unionists have been taking action in response. Since 1993 lecturers in further education colleges have faced attempts to introduce a new contract increasing working hours by 23 per cent and decreasing holidays. Not surprisingly, the vast majority of lecturers have refused to accept such a drastic worsening of their conditions, and they have also been concerned that it would lead to a drop in the quality of provision they could offer. There has been a wave of strikes, many involving workers who were striking for the first time. This dispute again illustrates the bias in current employment law. It was held that a national strike of lecturers would be illegal because there was no national employer. The fact that all the colleges involved were affiliated to one organization and that the new contracts being introduced into each of these independent colleges were virtually identical suggests collusion on the part of management, but any matching collusion on the part of trade unionists would be illegal. This appears to constitute an uneven playing field.

Table 4.5 Membership of teaching unions 1992-93, showing percentage increase

	1993	1992	% rise
National Union of Teachers	182,644	176,022	3.76
National Association of Schoolmasters/ Union of Women Teachers	138,381	127,365	8.65
Association of Teachers and Lecturers	136,645	126,659	7.88
Professional Association of Teachers	40,223	41,265	–2.52
National Association of Headteachers	31,846	31,571	0.87
Secondary Heads Association	8,158	8,027	1.63
Total	537,897	510,909	5.28

TES, 19 August 1994

1) *What does this table indicate about patterns of union membership among teachers?*
2) *What explanations might be offered for the trends shown here?*
3) *What implications does this have for the trade union movement?*

Another serious dispute arose in the NHS over the defence of national pay bargaining and the nurses' anger at a 1 per cent pay offer. Feelings ran so high that in May 1995 the traditionally moderate nurses' union, the Royal College of Nursing, voted to abandon its traditional 'no-strike' policy.

These examples illustrate the continuing pressures on workers in the 1990s, but also the limits upon the ability of the government and employers to dictate to workers and the continuing centrality of trade unions and industrial conflict in the arena of work.

Essay Questions

1) How successful have sociologists been in explaining the declining incidence of strikes in Britain over the last twenty years? (**25 marks**) (InterBoard Syllabus, Specimen Question paper, 1994)

2) a) Briefly distinguish between strikes and other forms of industrial conflict. (**4 marks**)
   b) Describe two factors within the workplace that may cause strikes. (**4 marks**).
   c) Outline the effect of legislation on industrial conflict since 1979 (**7 marks**)
   d) Evaluate sociological explanation of industrial conflict. (**10 marks**) (Interboard Sociology A Level, Paper 2, June 1995)

Structured Question

Item A

Stoppages, workers involved, and working days lost in 1993 and 1992

	1993	United Kingdom 1992
Working days lost through stoppages		
In progress in year	649,000	528,000
Beginning in year	566,000	471,000
Workers involved in stoppages		
In progress in year	384,800	147,600
Of which: directly involved	383,100	140,100
indirectly involved	1,600	7,500
Beginning in year	382,700	142,300
Of which: directly involved	381,000	139,700
indirectly involved	1,600	2,600
Stoppages		
In progress in year	211	253
Beginning in year	203	240

Source: *Employment Gazette*, June 1994 p. 200

Item B

Most modern workers will never experience going on strike. However, involvement in strike action, such as it exists, varies according to social characteristics. The higher up the work hierarchy, the less likely individuals are to go out on strike. Statistics suggest that women are much less likely to be involved in strike action than men. In the search for explanations for this phenomenon, sociologists have suggested a range of possible reasons. Traditional explanations have focused on the more 'conservative nature' of women and their lack of membership of trade unions.

Source: Lawson (1993), p. 116

Item C

See table opposite.

Item D

The third hostile feature of Thatcherism has been an economic programme which created levels of unemployment unknown since the depths of the inter-war depression, and in a few years brought the loss of a quarter of all manufacturing jobs in the country. Closures and redundancies struck hardest in precisely those areas of employment where union organization had traditionally been strongest. Those new jobs which have been created have been primarily in the private service sector, often in small firms, and commonly involving part-time or temporary employment, precisely the type of work where unionization has always been exceptionally difficult. In addition, the proportion of female workers has been rising steadily, and unions have traditionally been less effective (some would say, less interested) in organizing women than men.

The attitudes of employers have also been altering. The process of industrial-relations reform formed part of a movement towards increased sophistication in the handling of labour relations. North American notions of 'human resource management' have become popular; employers seek increasingly to harness the loyalty and commitment of employees as individuals rather than relying on union officials or shop stewards as their main channel of communication. For some firms, such policies are pursued with the deliberate aim of excluding trade-union organization; for others, they are a means of reducing union influence.

Source: Adapted from Hyman (1989), p. 148

Table 4.4 Membership of top ten unions in 1987 compared with membership in 1992

1987 top ten unions	Membership (000s)	1992 top ten unions	Membership (000s)	Men per cent	Women per cent
Transport and General Workers Union	1,349	Transport and General Workers Union	1,037	82	18
Amalgamated Engineering Union	815	Amalgamated Engineering & Electrical Union	884	93	7
General Municipal Boilermakers and Allied Trade Unions	803	GMB	799	62	38
National and Local Government Officers' Association	759	National and Local Government Officers' Association	764	45	55
National Union of Public Employees	651	Manufacturing, Science and Finance Union	552	73	27
Association of Scientific, Technical and Managerials Staff	400	National Union of Public Employees	527	30	70
Union of Shop Distributive and Allied Workers	387	Union of Shop Distributive and Allied Workers	316	40	60
Electrical, Electronic, Telecommunication and Plumbing Union	369	Royal College of Nursing of the UK	299	8	92
Royal College of Nursing of the UK	270	Graphical Paper and Media Union	270	82	18
Union of Construction Allied Trades and Technicians	256	National Union of Teachers	214	25	75

Source: *Employment Gazette*, June 1994, p. 193

Item E

The Thatcher years were a pulverizing period for the unions. Under the impact of high unemployment, the shift to less unionized service industries, the growth of part-time employment and six Acts of Parliament designed to change the balance of power in industrial relations, membership of TUC-affiliated unions has fallen from 12 million to 8.1 million since 1979.

One response to falling membership has been to merge. The number of TUC unions has fallen from 112 in 1979 to 74.

The trend for the 1990s seems to be towards five or six 'superunions' dominating a few dozen supporting players.

The unions may have been going through a difficult period but, despite the lowest level of strikes since 1935, they can still point to the significantly higher wages paid to organized workers compared with non-union members. A quarter of a million workers still join the TGWU every year, real pay levels have held up well, and significant successes in recent years include the AEU's shorter working week campaign.

Source: Adapted from Milne (1991)

1) Explain the meaning of the term 'working days lost' in Item A. (**1 mark**)

2) Identify two social characteristics, other than those mentioned in Item B, which sociologists have seen as affecting the likelihood of involvement in strike action, and explain the effect of each. (**4 marks**)

3) Identify the union with the largest percentage of women members in 1992 according to Item C. (1 mark)

4) Assess sociological explanations for the assertion in Item B that 'women are much less likely to be involved in strike action than men'. (**8 marks**)

5) Explain the meaning of the phrase 'human resource management' in Item D. (**1 mark**)

6) Using material from the items above and elsewhere, examine the evidence for and against the assertion in Item E that 'The unions may have been going through a difficult period but . . . they can still point to the significantly higher wages paid to organized workers compared with non-union members . . . and significant successes in recent years'. (**10 marks**)

Coursework suggestions

Interview local union officials, whom you should be able to locate through your local trades council or from the addresses of local trade union offices kept in the reference library, about the changing nature of trade unionism in your area.

Question them about the changing composition of trade union membership and about the relative importance of the various problems which trade unions have faced in the 1980s.

Consider to what extent their views differ according to the type of union they are in. Consider how the explanations offered compare with national surveys and analyses of the effect of the 1980s on trade unionism. Offer explanations for any significant differences between the national picture and your local area.

Bibliography

Batstone, E. (1984) *Working Order: Workplace Industrial Relations Over Two Decades,* Oxford: Blackwell

—— (1988) *The Reform of Workplace Industrial Relations,* Oxford: Clarendon Press

——, Boraston, I. and Frenkel, S. (1977) *Shop Stewards in Action,* Oxford: Blackwell

Beynon, H. (ed.) (1985) *Digging Deeper: Issues in the Miners' Strike,* London: Verso

Callinicos, A. and Simons, M. (1985) *The Great Strike,* London: Socialist Workers Party

Coates, K. and Topham, T. (1980) *Trade Unions in Britain,* Nottingham: Spokesman

Dahrendorf, R. (1959) *Class and Class Conflict in Industrial Society,* London: Routledge & Kegan Paul

Daniel, W.W. and McIntosh, N. (1972) *The Right to Manage?,* London: Macdonald

Darlington, R. (1994) *The Dynamics of Workplace Unionism,* London: Mansell

Dennis, N., Henriques, F. and Slaughter, C. (1956) *Coal is our Life,* London: Eyre & Spottiswood

Dickinson, M. (1984) *To Break a Union,* Manchester: Booklist

Durkheim, E. (1893) *The Division of Labour in Society,* Paris: Felix Alain; English edn, New York: Free Press (1947)

Evans, P. (1986) *The Labours and Researches of Evans,* London: Labour Research Department

Fine, B. and Millar, R. (eds) (1985) *Policing the Miners' Strike,* London: Lawrence & Wishart

Gorman, Jo (1973) *Banner Bright* Harmondsworth: Allen Lane

Gouldner, A. (1955) *Wildcat Strike,* London: Routledge

Green, P. (1990) *The Enemy Without,* Milton Keynes: Open University Press

Hayek, F.A. (1984) *1980s Unemployment and the Unions* London: Institute of Economic Affairs

Hutton, W. (1994) 'Brother, can you spare a deal?' *Guardian,* 8 July

Hyman, R. (1977) *Strikes,* 2nd edn, London: Fontana

—— (1989) 'What is happening to the unions?', *Social Studies Review,* March

Joseph, M. (1986) *Sociology for Everyone,* Cambridge: Polity

Lawson, T. (1993) *Sociology: A Skills-Based Approach,* London: Collins Educational

Mayo, E. (1933) *The Human Problems of an Industrial Civilization,* New York: Macmillan

Millward, N. (1994) *The New Industrial Relations?,* London: PSI

—— and Stevens, M. (1986) *British Workplace Industrial Relations, 1980–84,* Aldershot: Gower

—— et al. (1992) *Workplace Industrial Relations in Transition,* Aldershot: Dartmouth

Milne, S. (1991) 'Charting a course for the 1990s', *Guardian,* 2 September

Newsline (1985) *The Miners' Strike 1984–5 in Pictures,* London: New Park

New Statesman and Society (1994) *Guide to Trade Unions and Labour Movement 1994,* London: NSS

Nickell, S., Wadhwani, S. and Wall, M. (1989) *Unions and Productivity Growth in the 1970s and 1980s: Evidence from Company Accounts,* London: LSE

Smith, A. (1776) *An Inquiry into the Nature and Causes of the Wealth of Nations,* 1974 edn, Harmondsworth: Penguin

Warwick, D. and Littlejohn, G. (1992) *Coal, Capital and Culture: A Sociological Analysis of Mining Communities in West Yorkshire,* London: Routledge

5 Patterns of unemployment

Measuring unemployment

The official statistics on unemployment in the UK, published every month and often quoted in the news, are very much open to questions concerning their validity. They are compiled by adding together the figures for people eligible to claim various social security benefits. The official definition of unemployment that is used, known as the 'claimant count unemployed', reads as follows:

> People claiming benefit, i.e. Unemployment Benefit, Income Support or National Insurance credits at Unemployment Benefit Offices on the day of the monthly count, who say that on that day they are unemployed and that they satisfy the conditions for claiming benefit. (Students claiming benefit during a vacation and who intend to return to full-time education are excluded.) [*Employment Gazette,* June 1994]

The rate of unemployment is calculated by taking the number of unemployed, so defined, and expressing it as a percentage of the workforce.

However, this is not universally accepted as the most accurate way of establishing the extent of unemployment. And since it is amenable to manipulation for political purposes it has been the target of detailed and continuing criticisms.

Problems with the official definition

The first problem with the official definition and method of counting the unemployed is that it only exists as a by-product of administrative procedures, namely providing welfare benefits. This is an important point since changes in the administration of benefits that in reality have no impact on whether someone is unemployed or not will affect the official statistics. For example, in November 1980 the government introduced a provision barring school-leavers from signing on as unemployed until the September after they finish. This had the effect of reducing the unemployment figures for June, July and August by between 100,000 and 200,000.

Since 1979 there have been 29 changes to the official method of counting unemployment, and all but one (the first, in October 1979) have had the effect of reducing the 'headline' figure of unemployment. Table 5.1 on page 108 provides a summary of some of these changes and their effects on the unemployment count.

Calculate the effect of these changes on the published unemployment total (claimant count). What might the unemployment total be if these changes had not been made?

These changes will not be the last. According to a report from the Unemployment Unit (Convery 1994), the government has admitted that the introduction of the 'Jobseeker's Allowance' to replace some of the present benefits for the unemployed from October 1996 will have the effect of reducing the claimant unemployment count by as much as 90,000.

In addition to these changes in the administration of benefits, there have been changes in the definition of the 'workforce' which have affected the calculated rate of employment. The 'workforce' was formerly defined as the sum of employees in employment and the unemployed. But in July 1986 the definition was changed to become the sum of employees in employment, the unemployed, those in self-employment and HM armed forces. In July 1988 those on government training

Table 5.1 Some recent changes in published unemployment statistics

Date	Change	Estimated effect on monthly count
Oct 79	Change to fortnightly payment of benefits	+20,000
Oct 79	Compensating adjustment to seasonally adjusted total	−20,000
Feb 81	First estimate of special employment and training measures	−495,000 (by Jan 86)
Oct 81	Compensation to seasonally adjusted totals for emergency measures taken during DHSS industrial action	−20,000
July 81	Unemployed men over 60 given option not to register for work	−30,000 (by May 82)
Oct 82	Change in definition and compilation of monthly figures from clerical to computer count	−190,000
Apr 83	Men over 60 no longer required to sign on	−107,400 (by June 83)
June 83	All men over 60 allowed long-term supplementary benefit rate	−54,400 (by Aug 83)
Oct 84	Change in Community Programme (CP) eligibility	−29,000 (by Jan 86)
July 85	Computer reconciliation with Northern Ireland DHSS records	−5,000
March 86	Introduction of two-week delay in publication of monthly totals	−50,000
June 86	New method of calculating unemployment rate, using larger denominator	−1.4 percentage points
Oct 86	Abolition of the right to claim either half or three-quarter unemployment rates	−30,000 (by Oct 88)
Oct 86	Voluntary unemployment deduction from unemployment benefit increased from 6 to 13 weeks	−3,000
June 88	New, larger denominator used in calculating unemployment rate	−0.1 percentage point
Sept 88	Benefit removed from all 16 and 17 year olds, removing them from the register	−120,000
Oct 88	Social Security Act contribution amendment	−38,000
Apr 89	26,000 redundant ex-miners no longer required to sign on	−26,000
Oct 89	1989 Social Security Act requires that all claimants must be able to prove that they are actively seeking work, or have not refused work because of the low wages offered	−50,000
Dec 89	Changes to effect of earnings on Unemployment Benefit. Some casual or part-time workers denied benefit	−30,000

Source: Adapted from Taylor (1990), Appendix 1

schemes such as Youth Training (YT) and Employment Training (ET) were also included in the definition of the 'workforce'.

1) *Explain why the unemployment rate can be affected by changes to the definitions of (a) unemployment, (b) the workforce.*
2) *What problems does this create for sociologists who wish to look at long-term trends in unemployment rates?*

The effect of these changes has been to reduce the declared rate of unemployment arising from any given total of unemployed people. Since the 'old' calculation of the unemployment rate is still provided by the Department of Employment, the difference can easily be seen. In April 1994, for example, the official rate of unemployment in Clacton in Essex was reduced from 18.8 per cent to 14.9 per cent as a result of the altered definition of the 'workforce'.

Alternative measures

The most widely used alternative measure of unemployment, adopted by most other countries, is based on a definition of unemployment provided by the International Labour Office (ILO), which reads as follows:

> People without a paid job in the reference week who were available to start work in the next fortnight and had either looked for work in the last four weeks or were waiting to start a job they had already obtained. [Quoted in *Employment Gazette*, June 1994]

The Department of Employment has summarized the advantages and disadvantages of each measure (see Table 5.2). In reality, since the ILO definition is effectively used

Table 5.2 Advantages and disadvantages of survey-based ILO unemployment and administrative claimant unemployed

Advantages	Disadvantages
ILO unemployment	
• Internationally standardized	• Relatively costly to compile
• Usable for inter-country comparisons	• Normally less timely
• Considerable potential for analysis of other	• Suject to sampling and response error
• Labour-market characteristics or of particular sub-groups	• Not always suitable for small areas due to sampling limitations
• Articulated with data from the same source on employment and the economically inactive	
Claimant unemployment	
• Relatively inexpensive	• Not internationally recognized
• Available frequently (normally monthly)	• Coverage changes whenever admin system changes although recalculation of consistent series allows the meaningful comparisons over time
• Available quickly	
• 100 per cent count gives figure for small areas	• Coverage depends upon admin rules; may not be suitable for other purposes
	• Limited analysis of characteristics of unemployed people

Source: *Employment Gazette*, July 1994, p. 250

in the Labour Force Surveys, both of these alternative measures appear in official statistics in the UK though the claimant count is the one used to provide the 'headline' figure of unemployment.

A third definition of unemployment is used by the independent campaigning group, the Unemployment Unit. They call their measure the 'Broad Labour Force Survey measure'. It is based on the ILO definition used in the Labour Force Survey but differs in that it also includes as unemployed those who say they have not sought work in the relevant period because they believed no jobs were available. As can be seen from Figure 5.1, the number of men in this category rose by approximately 450 per cent between 1979 and 1988.

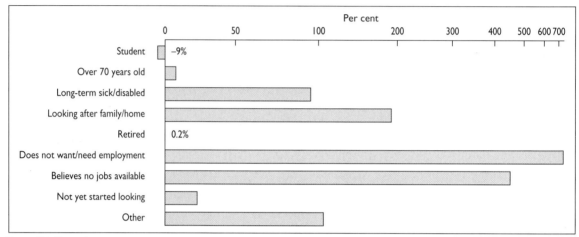

Figure 5.1 Percentage changes in the numbers of economically inactive men, 1979–88

Source: *Guardian*, 8 June 1990

People in this group are sometimes known as 'discouraged' because their assessment of their employment prospects discourages them from seeking work. This alternative measure has a particular impact on the gender imbalance of unemployment since the number of extra women included as unemployed in this broad definition is greater than the number of extra men. Fifty-two per cent of the 626,600 women in Winter 1993/4 who were not classified as unemployed on the standard Labour Force Survey were looking after families.

Table 5.3 provides a picture of unemployment in Winter 1993/4 according to the three definitions discussed above.

1) *Looking at the figures for Great Britain in Table 5.3, what is the difference in the numbers counted as unemployed by the three measures?*
2) *Different figures are supplied for men and women. Calculate the percentage of the total unemployed who are men and women on each measure.*
3) *What are the implications of this debate over unemployment definitions for the way we look at the following issues:*

the gender balance of unemployment;
regional differences in unemployment;
the overall importance of unemployment in Britain?

One further interesting point to emerge from the Unemployment Unit research is that the decline in unemployment in recent times has been greater than the rise in the number in employment. Between Winter 1992/3 and Winter 1993/4 the

Table 5.3   Unemployment totals and rates, Labour Force Survey, Winter 1993/4

	'Standard' LFS unemployed			'Broad' LFS unemployed			Claimants (averaged)		
	Total	Men	Women	Total	Men	Women	Total	Men	Women
South East	908,800	605,300	303,500	1,247,000	739,800	507,200	894,900	677,400	217,500
(Greater London)	461,700	316,000	145,700	642,300	391,200	251,100	455,600	339,900	115,700
East Anglia	95,800	60,900	34,900	129,400	72,000	57,400	81,900	61,600	20,300
South West	194,300	130,300	63,900	274,200	164,100	110,000	212,400	160,200	52,200
West Midlands	277,500	185,700	91,800	370,900	222,700	148,200	267,400	205,000	62,400
East Midlands	159,000	102,000	57,000	221,200	125,700	95,500	180,500	139,000	41,600
Yorks/Humberside	236,700	158,000	78,700	322,700	195,500	127,200	240,700	187,800	52,800
North West	318,300	219,200	99,100	422,400	261,200	161,200	313,500	245,500	68,000
North	165,400	122,100	43,300	228,600	142,800	85,700	169,800	136,200	33,500
Wales	132,000	90,600	41,400	202,300	118,700	83,600	131,500	103,700	27,800
Scotland	248,700	158,400	90,400	352,600	198,000	154,600	244,700	189,700	55,000
Great Britain	2,736,600	1,832,500	904,000	3,771,200	2,240,500	1,530,600	2,737,200	2,106,200	630,900
South East	10.2%	12.0%	7.8%	13.4%	14.3%	12.3%	10.0%	13.5%	5.6%
(Greater London)	13.7%	16.7%	9.8%	18.1%	19.9%	15.8%	13.5%	18.0%	7.8%
East Anglia	8.7%	9.7%	7.4%	11.4%	11.3%	11.6%	7.5%	9.8%	4.3%
South West	8.3%	10.0%	6.2%	11.3%	12.3%	10.2%	9.1%	12.3%	5.0%
West Midlands	10.7%	12.8%	8.1%	13.9%	14.9%	12.5%	10.4%	14.1%	5.5%
East Midlands	7.9%	9.0%	6.5%	10.7%	10.9%	10.4%	9.0%	12.3%	4.7%
Yorks/Humberside	9.8%	11.7%	7.4%	12.9%	14.1%	11.4%	10.0%	13.9%	5.0%
North West	10.6%	13.2%	7.5%	13.7%	15.3%	11.6%	10.5%	14.8%	5.1%
North	11.7%	15.4%	7.0%	15.5%	17.5%	12.9%	12.0%	17.1%	5.4%
Wales	10.3%	12.5%	7.4%	14.9%	15.7%	14.0%	10.2%	14.3%	5.0%
Scotland	10.1%	11.5%	8.3%	13.8%	14.0%	13.4%	9.9%	13.8%	5.1%
Great Britain	9.9%	11.9%	7.5%	13.2%	14.1%	12.0%	9.9%	13.6%	5.2%

The Winter 1993/4 LFS covers the quarterly period December 1993 to February 1994. The figures are not seasonally adjusted.

Source: Unemployment Unit and Youthaid, *Working Brief,* July 1994, Table 1, p. 14

claimant count fell by 188,800 but employment rose by only 157,000. Some people leaving the unemployment count are apparently becoming economically inactive (being classified as either sick or retired).

The two main official definitions of unemployment used are the claimant count and the figures derived from the Labour Force Survey.

Table 5.4 on page 112 has been constructed to show the differences between the two measures of unemployment. As presented here, it is incomplete. Copy the table out into your notes and then calculate and fill in all the missing figures (shown by a dash on the table) to give you a complete picture of where the main differences between these two measures of unemployment lie.

Answer the following questions about your completed table:

1) *Which measure gives the higher figure for total unemployment?*
2) *Which measure gives the higher figure for (i) men, (ii) women?*
3) *How do you account for the difference noted in question 2?*
4) *What was the percentage increase in unemployment over the year, according to each of the two measures?*

Table 5.4 ILO measure of unemployment compared with the monthly claimant count (Great Britain, millions)

	Spring 1993			Spring 1992			Spring 1992		
	All	Men	Women	All	Men	Women	All	Men	Women
Claimant count	2.86	—	0.66	2.61	2.01	—	—	—	—
Less									
Claimants not unemployed on ILO definition	1.00	—	0.27	0.85	—	0.24	+0.15	+0.12	+0.03
Of which									
1) Not seeking work	—	—	0.18	0.53	0.38	—	—	—	—
2) Employed	0.38	0.29	—	0.32	—	0.09	—	—	—
Plus									
People defined as unemployed on ILO Count but not claiming	0.95	0.43	—	0.89	—	0.50	+0.06	—	—
Total ILO unemployment	—	1.90	—	2.65	—	—	+0.16	+0.12	+0.04

Source: Adapted from *Employment Gazette*, October 1993, Table 1, p. 459

Consider whether the following would be classified as unemployed by each of the two measures:

1) An unemployed person who looks for work every day.
2) People who are employed part time but are still eligible for benefits.
3) Those unable to start work.
4) A married woman who does not work, although she would like to do so, but is not entitled to claim benefit as her partner is working or claiming benefit.
5) People aged 18 or under who do not take up an offer of a Youth Training place.
6) A student looking for part-time or vacation work.
7) Those who have not looked for work in the past four weeks.
8) A person who is working but claiming unemployment benefit.

Using information in Tables 5.2 (on page 109) and 5.4 consider which measure of unemployment is the most accurate.

Defining work and unemployment – an alternative sociological framework

As well as debating the validity of the official statistics on unemployment, sociologists have also questioned the accepted meanings of terms such as 'work' and 'unemployment'. Rosemary Deem (1988) has pointed out some of the anomalies in the official definitions. For example, those who are unemployed are defined as part of the economically active population (on the basis that they are seeking paid employment), which 'is an interesting categorization, since the one obvious characteristic of the unemployed is their lack of economic activity' (p. 61); in contrast, those with domestic labour responsibilities, overwhelmingly women, are classified as economically inactive. This is because the official statistics are based on a definition of work that is centred on the exchange of money and therefore restricts the arena of work to paid employment.

Perhaps the best-known attempt to construct an alternative definition of work based upon social activity undertaken is the work of Gershuny and Pahl (1980), who argued that there is a need to distinguish between the formal and the informal economy (see Table 5.5)

Table 5.5 Four ways in which services may be obtained

Mode of provision	Manner of obtaining service	Who does work	Who pays (if anyone)	Principle upon which service is is obtained
Market	Commercial purchase	Paid employees	Consumer	Market exchange
State	State provision	Paid employees	State	Citizenship right
Communal	Personal connections	Neighbours or acquaintances	No money involved	Reciprocal obligation
Domestic	Household do-it-yourself	Members of household	No money involved	Family obligation

Source: Abercrombie and Ward *et al.* (1994), p. 95

1) Which of the four modes of provision identified here would be part of the arena of work according to an economic definition?

2) Which category identified by Gershuny and Pahl does not appear on this table (at least not overtly)?

3) Write out a copy of this table and include the missing category from Gershuny and Pahl and also the additional category suggested by Rosemary Deem (see pages 114-15).

4) You should now have a table with six categories of mode of provision. Use sociology textbooks, official statistics and economics textbooks to investigate the relative importance of each of these modes of provision in the economy in contemporary Britain. Write a report of about 1,500 words and present your findings to the rest of the class.

5) Divide the class into six groups and allocate one mode of provision to each group. Each group is then to investigate how the importance of this mode of provision has changed over the last twenty years and write a report of about 750 words. These reports should then be presented and discussed in class.

As we noted in Chapter 1, Gershuny and Pahl identified three important areas of the informal economy where work takes place. The first is the household economy, essentially meaning housework and childcare. Since this is unpaid it falls outside official conceptions of work, and those who work in the household economy – overwhelmingly women – are considered to be economically inactive. Ann Oakley's pioneering study of the sociology of housework challenged this view. In her research she compared housewives' feelings about housework with those expressed by male assembly-line car workers and found that the former experienced more monotony, more fragmentation and more speed in their work. Housework can therefore be seen as more alienating than the archetypal alienating male job. It also has to be remembered that, unlike the male car-workers, housewives get no monetary reward for this alienating and stressful job.

Similarly, the Legal & General insurance company calculated in 1993 that if the work done by housewives were paid for it would cost £348.75 per week (*Independent,* 3 February 1993). As many feminist sociologists have pointed out, the fact that this work – which is essential for the continued existence of society – is unpaid is a reflection of the oppression of women, and official definitions perpetuate this oppression.

The second area identified by Gershuny and Pahl is the black economy. This means work done in return for payment which is not declared in order to avoid paying tax on it. The administrators of unemployment benefit have always believed that some people who are registered as unemployed are in fact working in this black economy. A 1983 government estimate put the numbers involved as high as 8 per cent of those registered as unemployed.

Pahl (1984) conducted research on the Isle of Sheppey and found that the unemployed were in fact the *least* likely to be involved in the black economy because, for instance, they could not afford the equipment to set themselves up as a window-cleaner. He also argued that this area of the economy was in decline because of greater surveillance by tax and social security inspectors, because in the mid–1970s there was a decline in the numbers of self-employed (who have a history of under-reporting their income) and because there was a growth in Do-It-Yourself which reduced demand for people to undertake the small household tasks characteristic of the black economy.

In the 1990s self-employment is very much on the increase: between Winter 1992/3 and 1993/4 the numbers self-employed rose from 3,040,000 to 3,150,000, an increase of 3.6 per cent compared to a rise in the numbers employed of only 0.2 per cent in the same period (compare Figures 5.2 and 5.3). Pahl's findings in this respect may therefore now need revision.

Figure 5.2 Economic activity rate (seasonally adjusted)

Source: *Economic Trends*, July 1994, p. T38

Figure 5.3 Self-employed (seasonally adjusted)

Source: *Economic Trends*, July 1994, p. T38

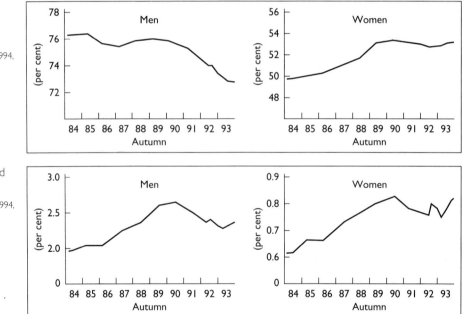

The growth of DIY also points to the difficulty of establishing a cast-iron division between the world of work and leisure, since DIY can arguably fit into both categories, which undermines the old assumption that work and leisure are polar opposites.

Deem (1988) has suggested another important area of the black economy which remains hidden for slightly different reasons. This is the area of work concerned with illegal activities such as burglary and drug-dealing. While they are not included in any official definition of employment, these activities clearly involve some effort (work) and are undertaken for financial gain.

The third area of work in the informal economy identified by Gershuny and Pahl is work in the communal economy. This essentially means voluntary work done for friends, neighbours or acquaintances, or indeed for charities which would have to be paid for if it were not provided in this way. This area is also of increasing importance due to the greater emphasis placed on charity and voluntary work as part of the government's reforms of the health service.

The alternative conceptual framework offered by these researchers has not yet been adopted by the government, and we are therefore unfortunately reliant on statistics that do not reflect a broad sociological understanding of what work is. This is a problem most sociologists face in using official statistics. There is little that one can do about it immediately except to be aware of the problem and treat official statistics with caution.

The remainder of this chapter is itself highly reliant on official statistics on unemployment and work, with all the consequent problems, but we will note some of the specific shortcomings as they come to light.

Recent trends in unemployment

For much of the post-Second World War period the vast majority of the industrialized countries attempted to attain full employment, and to varying degrees succeeded in achieving that aim. In the UK unemployment between 1959 and 1967 averaged 1.8 per cent per annum. However, by the early 1970s this picture was undergoing a fundamental change.

The return of mass unemployment

Figure 5.4 Claimant unemployment and job centre vacancies, UK

Source: Department of Employment, in *Social Trends* (1994), p. 55

In April 1994 the government's official unemployment statistics showed that there were 2,734,400 people classified as unemployed, representing 9.7 per cent of the workforce. This figure was down on the peak figure for recent years of 3,062,100, or 10.9 per cent of the workforce (see Figure 5.4). The re-emergence of mass unemployment, not only in the UK but across the industrialized world, has generated renewed debate about the causes of unemployment.

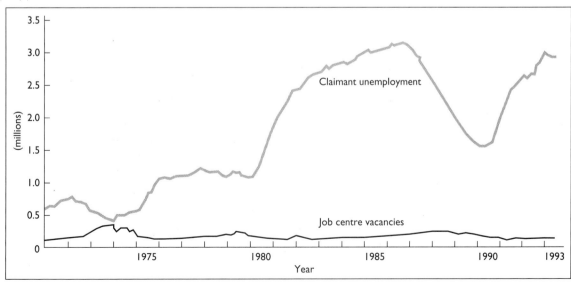

> *The statistics on unemployment and vacancies are released every month and will be reported in newspapers. Use these to update the information provided on Figure 5.5 and draw a more up-to-date picture of unemployment.*

The advanced industrial countries suffered a period of economic crisis, starting in the early 1970s, which led to a slowdown in the rate of economic growth. Figures for six industrial countries (France, Germany, Italy, Japan, the UK and the USA) show that during the period 1950–73 these economies grew at an average annual rate of 5.5 per cent, whereas the corresponding figures for 1973–9 and 1979–85 were 2.75 per cent and 2.0 per cent.

Alongside reduced economic growth there was a notable rise in the twin economic and social evils of unemployment and inflation. Table 5.6 shows the changing rates of all three indicators for the UK.

Table 5.6 Economic growth, inflation and unemployment in the UK, 1951–68 (annual averages)

	Government	Growth in GDP	Inflation	Unemployment
1951–64	Conservative	3.2	3.5	1.7
1964–70	Labour	2.4	5.2	2.0
1970–74	Conservative	2.4	11.7	3.1
1974–79	Labour	1.8	21.2	4.7
1979–88	Conservative	2.0	8.4	9.5

Source: Adapted from Bazan and Thirlwall (1989), p. 90

> *Update this table with the figures from 1988 onwards.*

High levels of inflation and/or unemployment have historically been associated with political and social instability. This is why unemployment forms an important part of the social analysis of society beyond its simple immediate impact on individuals and societies.

Economists, sociologists and politicians can, broadly speaking, be clustered into two camps when it comes to debating unemployment. One camp believes in the importance of state intervention in the economy to try to regulate its behaviour with the objectives of minimizing the extent of economic and social ills such as unemployment and inflation and maximizing economic growth; the other camp argues that such intervention, far from solving the emerging economic crisis, has been an important contributory factor in precipitating it. The latter camp, often known as the New Right, calls for a return to the free market and invokes the spirit of enterprise and competition as a way of solving the economic crisis, promoting economic growth and thereby reducing unemployment.

Another phenomenon that began to appear in the 1970s and accelerated in the 1980s was the rise of the global economy. The impact on many areas of industry of competition from the rest of the world has, it has been argued, contributed to the growth of unemployment in the advanced economies; a new international division of labour has emerged with the rise of the 'Newly Industrializing Countries' (NICs) such as the so-called Pacific Tigers of Hong Kong, Singapore, Taiwan and South Korea.

These changes have renewed uncertainty over the meaning, duration and nature of work and therefore of unemployment:

> The settled period of economic growth which was experienced in the UK in the 1950s has given way to a period of instability, an uncertainty over where the economic changes of the last few decades will lead ... The declining role of the British economy in world manufacturing raises the question of what its future international role will be; long-term increases in levels of unemployment and perhaps more particularly in part-time employment raise the question of how 'work' of all kinds should be distributed as we approach the end of the twentieth century. [Allen and Massey 1988, p. 1]

A study of long-term unemployment in Europe edited by Benoit-Guilbot and Gallie (1994) found that, while figures for overall unemployment have risen in similar proportions in the countries which make up the European Union and other advanced countries in the OECD (Organization for Economic Cooperation and Development, basically comprising the advanced industrial economies of the world), an examination of the extent of long-term unemployment reveals clear differences:

> What distinguishes Europe of the EU is the continuing length of unemployment. Once on the labour market job applicants appear to have enormous trouble finding or returning to work. The proportion of unemployed who remain so for a year or more is a lot higher than in the other OECD countries. [Benoit-Guilbot and Gallie 1994, p. 2]

While those who become unemployed in other countries seem to find other jobs within a year, and therefore long-term unemployment is only a small percentage of total unemployment, in the EU the long-term jobless represented between 41 per cent and 76 per cent of total unemployment in 1989.

This is combined with larger than average substitutions of labour with machinery, a move to a more capital-intensive form of production. In Britain, in particular, these factors are probably responsible for the large rise in the number of ex-manual workers in long-term unemployment.

Figure 5.5 Long-term versus short-term unemployed (males and females) in the UK

Source: *Guardian*, 8 June 1990

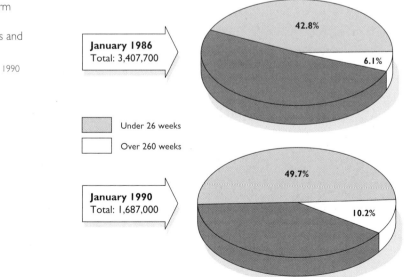

January 1986
Total: 3,407,700

42.8%

6.1%

Under 26 weeks

Over 260 weeks

January 1990
Total: 1,687,000

49.7%

10.2%

The Employment Gazette *(June 1994, Tables 2.6 and 2.7) provides the following figures for unemployment in April 1994:*

>   *Total unemployment: 2,734,400*
>   *Total unemployed for less than 26 weeks: 1,131,900*
>   *Total unemployed for more than 52 weeks: 1,045,600*
>   *Of which total unemployed for more than 260 weeks: 114,360*

1) *Draw up a pie-chart for April 1994 and compare it with the two in Figure 5.5.*
2) *Update this information with the latest figures available in the* Employment Gazette.

Types of unemployment

Economists break down the overall level of unemployment into several categories. The first, known as frictional unemployment, occurs during the process of transferring from one job to another, which may involve a short period of unemployment while waiting to start a new job. This type of unemployment is very short term and can be seen as an indicator of economic and technical change.

Table 5.7   Rates of unemployment, 1982–94 (annual averages)

	Unemployment total (Claimant count)	Unemployment rate (% of work force)
1982	2,916,900	10.9
1983	3,104,700	11.7
1984	3,159,800	11.7
1985	3,271,200	11.8
1986	3,289,100	11.8
1987	2,953,400	10.6
1988	2,370,400	8.4
1990	1,664,400	5.8
1991	2,291,900	8.0
1992	2,778,600	9.8
1993	2,919,200	10.4
1994*	2,734,400	9.7

*April only   Source: Compiled from *Employment Gazette*, various issues

A second type of unemployment is structural unemployment. This occurs when there are changes to the economic structure in the form of the decline of industries which previously formed an important part of the work environment. There are many examples of this type of unemployment in the UK. The shipbuilding industry, which used to employ large numbers of people in areas such as Clydeside and Tyneside, is now virtually non-existent. Another important example is coal mining. In 1955 there were 696 collieries employing 698,700 miners; by 1983 this had been reduced to 191 collieries employing 207,600 miners; and by 1993 there remained only 25 working collieries employing 23,000 miners.

The third major type of unemployment is cyclical unemployment. This derives from the notion of the business cycle and the ups and downs of economic performance. A booming economy will require more workers than one in recession, and this obviously affects the level of unemployment. In the UK, for example, in the last 15 years the economy appears to have gone through a complete cycle, starting with a large recession between 1980 and 1983 followed by an economic boom which reached its height in 1987–8 and then another recession starting in about 1990 which appeared to be coming to a slow end by late 1994.

The effect of the business cycle on unemployment can be gauged by looking at the unemployment rates for some of these years (see Table 5.7).

While a level of frictional unemployment will always occur and does not present much of a problem, the relative importance of the other two types of unemployment do have important implications. If the majority of those suffering unemployment do so as a result of cyclical factors, they might be expected to find work once the economy begins to recover. However, if structural unemployment is the most important factor and there are no new industries growing up that require large amounts of labour power, unemployment may well persist even if the economy as a whole experiences an economic boom.

Provide two concrete examples of each type of unemployment mentioned in this section.

Technological change and unemployment

One of the main debates taking place among economists and sociologists is the effect of the introduction of new technology on employment and therefore unemployment.

In his explanations of economic change and rising unemployment, Joseph Schumpeter (1939, 1943) relied heavily on notions of technological change and the social and organizational innovations that accompany them. He argued that such innovations

Table 5.8	Change of techno-economic paradigm	
	'Fordist' old	*ICT* new
Energy-intensive	Information-intensive
Design and engineering in 'drawing' offices	Computer-aided designs
Sequential design and production	Cncurrent engineering
Standardized	Customized
Rather stable product mix	Rapid changes in product mix
Dedicated plant and equipment	Flexible production systems
Automation	Systemation
Single firm	Networks
Hierarchical structures	Flat horizontal structures
Departmental	Integrated
Product with service	Service with products
Centralization	Distributed intelligence
Specialized skills	Multi-skilling
Government control and sometimes ownership	Government information, co-ordination and regulation
'Planning'	'Vision'

Source: Adapted from Perez (1990)

119

tend to come in clusters and are thus an important force for disequilibrium in the economy; in particular, they are the most important cause of cyclical unemployment. Other economists have argued in this vein that economic depressions arise when there is a mismatch between technological innovations and the social and institutional climate, whereas if they fit together they provide the basis for economic boom.

Graeme Salaman (1987) has pointed out that dire predictions of job loss have accompanied the introduction of information technology (IT), but that most of these have not come to pass. He believes that technological changes must be considered in their overall social context. There is little evidence to suggest that IT is systematically used to deskill workforces, but it does alter the balance of skills between different groups of workers.

Freeman and Soete (1994) surveyed the prospects of change into the twenty-first century arising from the increasing prevalence of computerization. According to these authors, IT and computerization will have the disequilibrium effects outlined by Schumpeter; Table 5.8 summarizes some of their predictions. Although the rapid progress in computer technology has greatly increased the number of jobs available in high-tech industries, the increased productivity resulting from the deployment of this technology has led to a decline in employment in manufacturing industry. IT has also enabled the widespread adoption of a number of time-saving innovations (which lead to savings on capital and labour). The growth and scope of these technologies has meant that service industries such as insurance, banking and other financial services, previously tied to locations near the customer, are becoming increasingly international in character.

> Many of the present fears about unemployment associated with technical change are strongly related to the increasingly international implications of computerized technical change. Whereas there is little doubt that there are many employment creation features associated with the emergence and further diffusion of information and communication technology, there are also good reasons to assume that such employment creation might occur increasingly in other countries far removed from the country of origin of such technologies ... what adds in particular to this international relocation process in manufacturing is the role of information and communication technologies in enabling increased international tradability of hitherto 'untradable' service activities. Yet it has been precisely those service activities which have until now provided most of the employment growth in the developed OECD countries. [Freeman and Soete 1994, p. 67]

For Freeman and Soete the only way mass unemployment can be averted is to develop more flexible forms of working which reduce the total number of hours employees work and share out the work left in a more capital-intensive economy. More systematic attention must be paid to improving the provision of education and technical training. Other benefits will flow from these new working patterns. For example, greater reliance on teleworking would reduce the need for business travel, reducing traffic jams and bringing other environmental benefits.

One of the obvious disadvantages of this model is that, unless these new flexible patterns are adopted mass unemployment will probably persist. Attempts to get the number of working hours reduced in recent years have been resisted by employers, and indeed there is evidence that working hours for some groups have actually increased. A beneficial outcome is therefore heavily reliant on employers agreeing to reduce working hours, and there is as yet little evidence that they are willing to do so.

The social distribution of unemployment

One of the key concerns of sociologists is the way the overall level of unemployment is distributed between different social groups.

Class divisions

Researchers have commonly found that unemployment is heavily structured by class. For instance, Michael White (1994, p. 34) reports that 'In Britain unemployment, especially long-term unemployment, is heavily concentrated among working-class occupations.' During the 1980s, about 80 per cent of men and 90 per cent of women in long-term unemployment came from a background in manual occupations.

He suggests that several factors may account for this situation. First, the period of notice given to manual workers is usually much shorter than that for non-manual workers. Second, manual workers are given relatively worse provision for ill-health by employers. Some white-collar workers may be able to retire early and so avoid technical unemployment, but this is less likely for manual workers who are more likely to face dismissal on grounds of ill-health. Manual workers are more likely to suffer ill-health arising from their work environment, so the overall effect is a clear differential in the experience of manual and non-manual workers.

A third point, according to White, is that employers mainly concentrate training on non-manual employees; manual employees are expected to gain experience by moving between jobs, which makes them more vulnerable to periods of unemployment between one job and the next, and their job prospects are worse than if they had certificate skills acquired through job training.

A fourth factor is the loss of jobs in manufacturing industry. Bazan and Thirlwall (1989) calculate that between 1966 and 1987 the number of jobs in manufacturing industry in the UK fell by 4 million. White provides figures showing that employment in manufacturing fell by 41.3 per cent between 1951 and 1987. It is important to realize that this does not mean that manual employment fell by the same amount (a common but mistaken assumption) for the simple reason that many of the jobs in the service sector are manual (for instance, car mechanics); nonetheless over the same period manual employment fell by 36.5 per cent. Sue Glyptis (1989) reported that in 1985 manufacturing industries accounted for 59 per cent of all redundancies, and these were strongly concentrated in traditional industries such as coal-mining and mechanical engineering.

Table 5.9   Change in employment in Great Britain, 1951-1987

	1951	1961	1966	1971	1981	1987
Manufacturing employment (millions)	8.7	9.0	9.2	8.6	6.1	5.1
Manual workers (millions)	14.5	14.0	14.4	13.2	11.1	9.2
Manufacturing as % of total	39	38	37	35	26	24
Manual as % of total	64	59	58	53	48	45

Source: *Benoit-Guilbot & Gallie, p48*

White adds a further consideration. The radical monetarist policies pursued by successive Conservative governments in the UK have not eradicated the country's economic problems, but they *have* been accompanied by sustained attacks on the rights of trade unions; countries such as Sweden, Norway and Austria which have strong trade unions have not suffered the levels of long-term unemployment seen in EU countries, including the UK.

Gender divisions

Official Department of Employment statistics indicate that there is a pronounced gender aspect to the social structuring of unemployment. In April 1994, 9.7 per cent of the workforce overall was registered as unemployed, but this constituted 13.2 per cent of the male workforce and 5.2 per cent of the female workforce. The actual numbers unemployed were 2,101,300 men and 633,100 women.

Several important factors need to be considered in relation to this issue. The first, and probably the most important, concerns the validity of the official figures. As we have seen, these are collected as a by-product of the administrative procedure of distributing the various benefits available to the unemployed. However, married women not eligible for a whole range of these benefits and therefore will not appear in the official statistics even though they might be looking for work and consider themselves unemployed.

The Beveridge report, which laid the foundations of the Welfare State, expressed a clear belief that the proper place for married women was in the home. The benefits system incorporated the assumption that there was a gendered division of labour; work was assumed to be a male arena, and benefits related to work (and the lack of it) were mainly available to men. Women were assumed to be dependants of their husbands and thus did not have independent entitlement on a par with males. Female unemployment has therefore been consistently under-reported. The official figure 'excludes many women who arguably should be counted, such as women who want work but do not register because they do not qualify for benefit' (Glyptis 1989, p.55). The extent of this under-reporting has been estimated in a number of research projects. Martin and Roberts (1984) found that 50 per cent of women seeking paid employment were not regarded as unemployed, and Sinfield (1981) found that 25 per cent of single women and 50 per cent of married women in his sample who described themselves as unemployed were not registered as such.

An indication of the importance of this can be seen by comparing the Labour Force Survey figures with the claimant count ones. The 1986 Labour force Survey identified 870,000 people who were unemployed under the ILO definition but who were not claiming benefit and therefore did not appear on the official UK unemployment figures. Two-thirds of these were women.

Sinfield has identified a silent reserve of people who simply disappear from the labour market. A significant proportion of these are married women, particularly those with children, who are not seeking employment and are not eligible for benefits. The differential gender effect of this can be seen from Table 5.8.

One of the recent administrative changes in the way statistics are collected has also affected the representation of women. Married women with children often seek part-time employment. Since October 1982 the publication of figures for those seeking

Figure 5.6 State of the labour market by gender

Source: Benoît-Guilbot and Gallie (1994) p23

— — population aged 15-64

—— in employment

▬▬ labour force

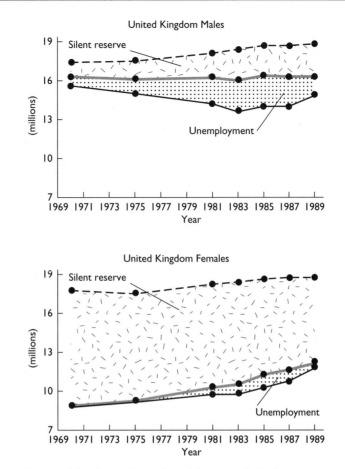

part-time work has been discontinued. It seems likely that women are a significant element of this group who now no longer appear. As the Unemployment Unit comment: 'Changes to the official unemployment count haven't had a uniform impact across the unemployed population. They have tended to affect women more than men – this is especially the case with married women and women single parents' (Taylor 1994, p. 2).

Jane Lewis (1993) notes that the UK is the only country in Europe where labour market participation by lone mothers is lower than that of married mothers. She provides comparative statistics for lone mothers with very young children (aged 0–4) showing that only 7 per cent of women in this category participate on a full-time basis in the UK, compared to 27 per cent in Germany and 44 per cent in France. Although rates for part-time participation are less unequal (UK 10 per cent, France 8 per cent and Germany 14 per cent), overall participation is very low. She also points out that the participation of lone mothers of children of all ages in the UK labour market had fallen in recent years. Forty-seven per cent of lone mothers were in paid work in 1977–9, but this figure had fallen to 39 per cent by 1986–8.

Thus the validity of official figures on unemployment is considerably more questionable in relation to women than men. Nonetheless the fact remains that more men are officially unemployed than women. The most likely explanation for this is the changing nature of employment in the UK. The 1990 Policy Studies Institute

(PSI) workplace survey found that the proportion of women employed in their overall sample was 38 per cent, while among workplaces established since 1984 the figure was 50 per cent and for those established since 1987 it was 55 per cent. The main reason for this was the increased proportion of part-time workers and the declining percentage of manual workers employed. The decline of manufacturing and the rise in service industries has shifted the balance of employment opportunities in the direction of areas traditionally occupied by women, as has the recent increase in flexibility leading to greater numbers of part-time jobs (see Figure 5.7).

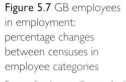

Figure 5.7 GB employees in employment: percentage changes between censuses in employee categories

Source: *Employment Gazette,* April 1993, p. 119

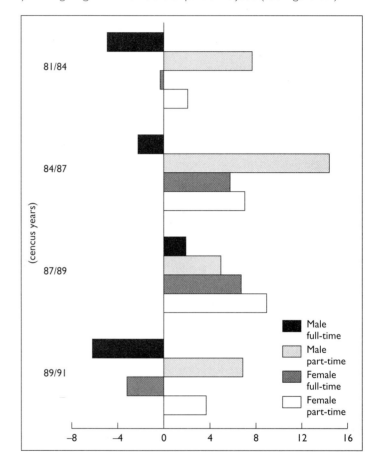

Write short reports on the gains and losses encountered by men and women over the four periods shown in figure 5.7.

This has led some to argue that women are displacing men in the job market. Women are certainly participating in paid employment in greater numbers, and this might have the effect of pushing men out. However, there is evidence that women are not simply gaining at the expense of men. Rapoport (1982) reported that between 1974 and 1977 male unemployment doubled while female unemployment quadrupled. Claire Callender (1992) provides more recent figures showing that between 1979 and 1986 male unemployment rose by 146 per cent and female unemployment by 276 per cent. As she points out, 'women's unemployment has at times risen at a much faster rate than men's although the absolute and percentage numbers for men remain higher' (p. 129).

Ethnicity

There is clear evidence that ethnic minorities are disproportionately likely to experience unemployment. Unemployment among white females in the 1982 PSI survey was 10 per cent while for Bangladeshi women it was 52 per cent. The equivalent figures for males were: whites, 13 per cent, and Bangladeshis, 29 per cent.

This division is a recent phenomenon. Simon Field (1986) reported that unemployment rates for ethnic minorities were about the same as for whites in 1974. This is perhaps not surprising since the main reason for mass immigration into this country in the 1950s and 1960s was a shortage of workers.

Figure 5.8 ILO unemployment rates by ethnic origin and sex, Great Britain

Economically active persons of working age; average spring 1989, 1990, 1991

Source: *Employment Gazette*, February 1993, p. 31

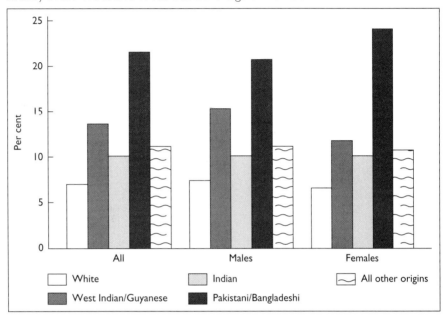

The onset of economic recession after 1974 changed everything. By the 1980s clear divisions had opened up. The greater propensity for ethnic minorities to become unemployed reflected a number of factors. The first is overt racism. A second is minority workers' position in the workforce. They were over-represented in the manual jobs that were hit hardest by the recession in the early 1980s. The 1982 PSI survey showed that Asians were twice as likely as whites to be in unskilled manual jobs, and West Indians three times as likely. This imbalance has been described as producing institutional racism, meaning that, even where overt racism is absent, the unequal employment structure produces further inequalities such as a greater likelihood of experiencing unemployment. The survey showed unemployment rates of 21.7% for Asians and 23.7% for West Indians compared to 12.9% for whites.

The City of Leicester has a larger than average proportion of ethnic minority citizens; the 1991 Census gave the proportion for Leicestershire overall as 11.1 per cent against a national average of 5.9 per cent. The councils in Leicester carried out a survey of the city in 1983 which exposed clear inequality along ethnic lines in relation to unemployment. Leicester's industrial base has historically been in the engineering and textile industries; these were badly hit during the recession of the early 1980s, increasing existing ethnic divisions in relation to unemployment.

Figures from the 1991 Census confirm that this pattern was still present across the country as a whole. Unemployment among Pakistanis and Bangladeshis, for instance, was three times as high as for whites. Among these groups women were also more likely than men to be unemployed, contrary to the general pattern. Figure 5.7 illustrates the pattern.

This growing division along ethnic lines has fed into the debate about whether ethnic minorities can be classified as an 'underclass' in the UK.

Age and unemployment

There appears to be a relationship between age and the likelihood of unemployment, which is high for young people and older people and lower for those in middle age. An unemployment profile by age therefore looks something like a 'U' on a diagram. Table 5.9 gives some figures calculated from the 1991 Census. The high levels of youth unemployment (even after excluding those on government training schemes such as YT) are especially obvious.

Table 5.9   Unemployment rates by age and sex, 1991

Age	Male	Fenale	All persons
All 16+	11.1	6.7	9.2
16	22.5	18.2	20.5
17	16.4	13.8	15.2
18	19.7	15.4	17.7
19	20.8	14.6	17.9
20	19.9	12.5	16.5
21–24	16.6	10.1	13.6
25–29	12.4	8.0	10.5
30–34	10.1	6.2	8.5
35–39	8.9	4.8	7.1
40–44	7.7	4.2	6.1
45–49	7.5	4.4	6.1
50–54	9.1	5.2	7.4
55–59	11.1	6.2	9.1
60–64	13.7	1.5	10.1
65–69	1.7	1.4	1.6
70–74	1.4	1.9	1.6
75+	2.7	5.2	3.6

Source: adapted from 1991 Census

Obtain a piece of graph paper and plot the figures from Table 5.9 onto a graph. Put age ranges on the horizontal axis and percentage unemployment on the vertical axis. Plot graphs for males, females and all persons using three differently coloured pens.
Summarize the patterns on this graph in a short report.

Dan Finn (1987) points out that in the 1960s the unemployment rate for young people was similar to that of other age groups, but between 1972 and 1977, while overall unemployment grew by 40 per cent, for those under 20 it rose by 120 per cent. This trend appears to have continued, so age is now a very important factor determining the likelihood of unemployment.

The explosion of youth unemployment has had a major impact on a number of areas of society. Some argued that the education system was not providing appropriate skills for the world of work. Accordingly a whole range of new training initiatives – from BTEC and GNVQ courses to the Youth Training (YT) schemes – was developed to provide vocational education and training. By the late 1980s approximately 70 per cent of 16 year olds were joining YTS (as it was then called).

However, there has been a critical debate about the effectiveness of these schemes. The proportion of YT trainees getting a job after finishing a course was 64 per cent in 1989–90 but fell to 53 per cent in 1990–91, and of those leaving in December 1991 it had fallen to 45 per cent. In July 1994 the figure stood at 47 per cent (*Employment News*, August 1994). (For further information on this debate, see Chapter 3 of Trowler, 1995.)

It seems that other factors besides training must be affecting levels of youth unemployment. This view is given more credibility when one considers the increasing extent of graduate unemployment (see Table 5.10). In 1993 it reached 15 per cent, compared to 1 per cent in Scandinavia and Japan.

Table 5.10 Graduate unemployment in the UK

Year	Average per cent	Graduate per cent
1987	10.0	6.9
1988	8.1	5.8
1989	6.3	5.2
1990	5.8	8.2
1991	8.1	11.5
1992	9.9	14.5

Source: *Observer*, 29 August 1993

The age group least at risk of facing unemployment appears to be those aged between 25 and 49; above that age (at least until the official retirement ages) unemployment rates again rise, albeit not to the levels suffered by the young. However, those unemployed who are aged 50+ tend to be unemployed for much longer periods than at earlier ages. Among the long-term unemployed (those unemployed for a year or more) figures for April 1994 show that 20 per cent of the unemployed in the 18–24 age group had been unemployed for more than a year. The equivalent figures for other age groups were 28.8 per cent for those aged 25–49 and 45.1 per cent for those aged 50+.

The Department of Employment estimates that up to 40 per cent of employers discriminate on the grounds of age, and during the wave of mass redundancies resulting from the recession of the late 1980s many employers seem to have persuaded older employees to take early retirement or simply made them redundant. The Carnegie Report into the Third Age supports this suggestion: 'Redundancy falls disproportionately on young workers and those aged 55–64: the redundancy rate for 55–59 year old men is 40 per cent higher than for 24–54 year olds, and for 60–64 year old men it is over twice as high' (Carnegie Trust 1993, p. 26).

In an article entitled 'The economy – retirement of unemployment?' (June 1991) Help the Aged argue: 'In 1945 a third of over 65s still worked, today the proportion is very much lower . . . With an ever increasing number of non-working elderly people in both the rich and poor regions of the world, many of our ideas about work, leisure and retirement will be challenged.'

In what ways do you think the trends identified here will challenge the concepts of work, leisure and retirement?

Geographical region

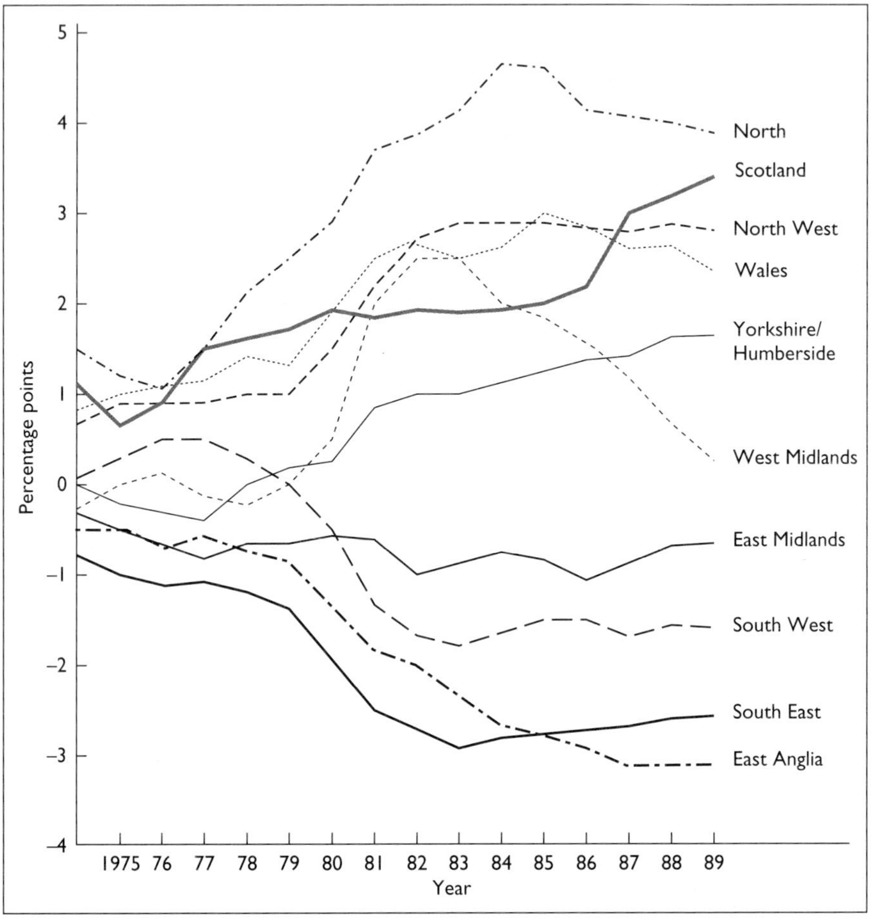

Figure 5.9 Regional unemployment disparities, 1974–89

The vertical axis shows the regional unemployment rate minus the national (UK) rate, expressed as a percentage point difference.

Source: Armstrong and Taylor (1990), p. 7

One of the main causes of unemployment has been the relative decline of manufacturing industry. This has an unequal regional impact because manufacturing industry is unequally distributed through the UK:

As the national unemployment rate increases, regional unemployment disparities tend to widen since a national recession has more serious effects on the north than in the south. This is partly the result of the fact that northern regions rely more heavily upon industries which are highly sensitive to fluctuations in national economic activity. Manufacturing industries, for example, are more sensitive to booms and slumps than are service industries. Since northern regions depend more heavily on manufacturing industries, they are consequently more severely affected by booms and slumps. [Armstrong and Taylor 1990, p. 5]

The recession of the early 1980s opened up a regional divide (illustrated in Figure 5.8), provoking much debate about the existence of a North–South divide. The phenomenon can be overstated because there was a substantial loss of manufacturing jobs in the South East (in Greater London in particular) as well as in the North; moreover the recession of the late 1980s and early 1990s seems to have reduced the regional disparities somewhat. Nonetheless regional disparities in unemployment are still significant, which means that national averages can be misleading.

Explanations of unemployment

Social democratic perspectives

Social democrats challenge the view that free markets, left to themselves, automatically attain equilibrium and thereby eliminate unemployment.

John Maynard Keynes (1936) argued that in a free-market economy there was more than one possible equilibrium position; therefore an economy might be in equilibrium, with no pressure to change, while there remained large numbers of unemployed people and other unemployed resources. He urged the government to use its powers to encourage investment and if necessary to invest directly in public expenditure. This would lead to an increase in economic activity and therefore a fall in unemployment. The Keynesian model thus places great emphasis on active government involvement to solve the problem of unemployment.

Keynes's ideas provided the intellectual background to British government policies to tackle with unemployment pursued between 1945 and 1976. This was the era of the mixed economy, when private enterprise and government acted in partnership to influence the economy.

The New Right

The distinguishing feature of New Right approaches to unemployment is the belief that free-market economies can work and achieve equilibrium. Left to themselves, such economies would ensure that demand and supply exactly matched each other, even in the labour market, and therefore there would be no unemployment. In reality, of course, this is not the case; therefore New Right thinkers have sought to explain the existence of unemployment as resulting from actions that stop the market mechanism working properly.

They point to a number of rigidities in the labour market that stop real wages falling in periods of unemployment. A fall in wages (the price of labour) would, according to the New Right, lead to an increase in demand for and a fall in the supply of labour and would therefore eliminate unemployment.

The key institutions held responsible for interrupting this process are the trade unions and the Welfare State. The New Right argue that trade unions contribute to the inflexibility of wages since they attempt to operate as monopolistic suppliers of labour. The Welfare State is said to be a contributor to the creation of a dependency culture, by which is meant that people without work can survive on state benefits and therefore reject jobs that offer less income than they can get from benefits. This further discourages a fall in the wage rate and saps the incentive to work.

As an example of this type of thinking, the New Right economist Von Mises argued: 'The point is not that the "unemployed" cannot find work, but that they are not willing to work at the wages they can get in the labour market for the particular work they are able and willing to perform' (quoted in Freeman and Soete 1994, p. 25).

New Right thinkers therefore argue that there is a need to cut back on the extent and availability of state benefits to discourage the creation of a dependency culture and encourage workers to take jobs at lower rates of pay and thereby solve the unemployment problem.

A more influential version of this argument was presented by Milton Friedman (1976, 1980), who claimed that the 'natural' level of unemployment could be reduced because it depended on the flexibility of wage levels and the level of state welfare benefits. If these could be lowered, the natural rate of unemployment would also fall as the unemployed became prepared to take up the jobs that were on offer. Increased government expenditure, as advocated by Keynesians, was therefore not a solution but was part of the problem as it fed into the system of benefits which kept the natural level of unemployment high. Instead government should concentrate on removing rigidities in the labour market and reducing the dependency of unemployed people on the state. This thinking can be seen to underpin the actions of the Conservative governments elected since 1979.

Using the information in this section, divide into two groups. One group is to research solutions to unemployment based on a Keynesian perspective, and the other to research solutions based on the New Right/monetarist perspective. Use the summaries outlined here as a basis but also use the economics section of your college library.

1) Write a report of about 1,500 words on each of the two approaches.
2) Hold a debate on the topic of the contemporary relevance of these two perspectives to unemployment.

Marxist perspectives

Marxists argue that it is capitalism itself which causes unemployment and that no amount of tinkering (as advocated by Keynes and social democratic thinkers) will be able to overcome the inevitable production of mass unemployment and poverty in a capitalist society.

Marx argued that the central dynamic of a capitalist economy is the cycle of booms and slumps which flows from the reduction of everything to calculations of profit and loss. Capitalists invest only when they feel it is profitable to do so. Once one invests, however, others have to follow or lose out in the competition for markets. This leads to crises of overproduction. Too much is being produced, and as a result prices fall and the goods become unprofitable to make. Some producers go bankrupt, and this creates unemployment. The survivors produce fewer goods, which drives prices up, while the increase in the numbers of unemployed reduces the pressure on wages to rise. Production therefore becomes profitable again. But this entices new producers into the market, and the cycle repeats itself. The solution is to abolish capitalism and base production upon people's needs rather than profit.

Marx described the unemployed as the reserve army of capitalism. Because of the unstable nature of production in capitalist societies, the capitalists need a group of workers who can be hired quickly in times of boom and dispensed with quickly in times of slump. The idea of a permanent layer of unemployed existing as a reserve pool of labour is the basis of later theories to the effect that the workforce can be split into a secure 'core' and a highly insecure 'periphery'. Workers in the periphery are said to suffer much more from unemployment, have poorer conditions and worse wage rates.

To some extent this is a rejection of Marx's argument that unemployment plays the role of disciplining the entire working class. Those who argue that we can now see a distinct core/periphery split in the workforce suggest that workers in the core are not really affected by the conditions in the periphery because there are two distinct labour markets. The implication is that the working class is split – not at all a united proletariat, ready to rise up and overthrow capitalism. Thus the core/periphery argument links into the wider debate about the real nature of the working class and whether it measures up to Marxist expectations about its role as the potential vanguard of a movement to overthrow capitalism.

Essay Questions

1) What is the difference between the formal and informal economies? (4 marks)

2) Briefly identify two activities which typically form part of the informal economy. Justify your choices. (4 marks)

3) Briefly comment on the problems of gaining accurate measures of unemployment. (7 marks)

4) Examine the view that the higher the levels of unemployment in the formal economy, the more the informal economy will flourish. (10 marks)

(Interboard Syllabus, Specimen Question Paper, 1994)

Structured Question

Item A

The claimant count and the Labour Force Survey count compared

The gap between the two measures exists because certain groups are classified as unemployed on one measure but not the other. In spring 1993 the gap represented the difference between 1 million claimants who were not unemployed according to the LFS (ILO) definition, and the 950,000 people who were unemployed on the ILO measure but who were not claiming benefits.

In spring 1993 the number of men unemployed according to the ILO measure (1.9 million) was less than the number of male claimants (2.2 million) while the number of ILO unemployed women (0.9 million) was greater than the number of female claimants (0.66 million). The large majority of men were unemployed on both measures, while for women the overlap was much smaller.

Source: Adapted from *Employment Gazette,* October 1993, p. 457

Item B

Application of IT certainly has implications for employment, as it substitutes capital for labour and accelerates the shift from manufacturing to services, though it also opens up new jobs and creates new skills. However, numerous studies of the impact of IT confirm the general impression that the predicted huge levels of IT-generated unemployment have not materialized. A study by Northcott and Rogers in 1984 found that of factories using IT, over two-thirds reported no change in their employment as a result, and if there was a change it was a small one.

Source: Salaman (1987), p. 32

Item C

To date, microtechnology has probably had a limited impact on available employment; it has, in the short run, created as many jobs as it has destroyed. Current unemployment rates are primarily due to other causes. However, little of this technology is yet in use in Britain, owing partly to low levels of investment and partly to worker resistance. When it becomes widespread – which may take a few years yet – it might be expected to have a massive impact. Because it tends towards greater ease of centralized control through improved communication, it will almost certainly reduce discretion at work, even where it does not abolish jobs altogether. We tend to be pessimistic, but it seems entirely safe to predict that the new technology will not reduce unemployment.

Source: Abercrombie, Warde *et al.* (1994), p. 112

Item D

Looking at the position in 1989, it appears to be an approximate rule of thumb that there are 2 unemployed males for every unemployed female for unemployment durations of up to one year,

but beyond that period the ratio rises to 7:3. This 2:1 ratio also holds approximately true for the 18–24 age group irrespective of duration, but in the 25–49 age group the male–female ratio for those unemployed in excess of 52 weeks is 80:20. However, for those aged over 50 the ratio is approximately 75:25 irrespective of duration. The most notable conclusions are thus that young males are twice as likely to be unemployed as young females, and older males three times as likely to be unemployed as older females no matter how long they have been unemployed. However, long-term unemployment amongst the middle-age group is very much a male phenomenon.

Source: McCormick (1990), p. 222

1) Identify the difference in the number of men calculated as unemployed between the claimant count and the International Labour Office (ILO) measure in Spring 1993 (Item A). (**1 mark**)

2) Suggest two examples of new jobs opened up by the introduction of IT (Item B). (**2 marks**)

3) Describe in your own words the interaction between age and gender in the social distribution of unemployment as outlined in Item C. (**4 marks**)

4) Using information from the items and elsewhere, evaluate whether the argument put forward in Item C that microtechnology has 'created as many jobs as it has destroyed' is still supported by sociological evidence. (**8 marks**)

5) Using any material you are familiar with, assess the extent to which the differential patterns of unemployment outlined in Item D can be explained by the measures of unemployment primarily used in the UK as outlined in Item A. (**10 marks**)

Coursework suggestions

Use data from the 1991 Census to investigate the social distribution of unemployment in the area in which you live. The information is broken down into local council areas so you will be able to

analyse differences within your locality. Investigate the differences between Census areas in your locality and the extent to which the patterns of unemployment in these areas conform to or differ from the national trends in unemployment.

Use sociological accounts of the causes and distribution of unemployment to account for any such differences and provide a detailed summary of the key causes of unemployment in your locality. Do they indicate that unemployment in your area is largely cyclical or structural in

character? Explain the implications of this distinction.

Devise a questionnaire to test the awareness of unemployed people in your area of the actual causes and likely extent of unemployment as revealed in your survey. Administer the questionnaire and suggest reasons for any discrepancies you find.

Bibliography

Abercrombie, N., Warde, A. *et al.* (1994) *Contemporary British Society,* 2nd edn, Cambridge: Polity

Allen, J. and Massey, D. (1988) *The Economy in Question,* London: Sage

Armstrong, H. and Taylor, J. (1990) *Regional Economics,* London: Heinemann

Bazan, S. and Thirlwall, T. (1989) *Deindustrialization,* London: Heinemann

Benoit-Guilbot, O. and Gallie, D. (eds) (1994) *Long-term Unemployment,* London: Pinter

Callender, C. (1992) 'Redundancy, unemployment and poverty', in Glendenning, C. and Millar, J. (eds.) *Women and Poverty in Britain: The 1990s,* Hemel Hempstead: Harvester-Wheatsheaf

Carnegie Trust (1993) *Life, Work and Livelihood in the Third Age: The Carnegie Inquiry into the Third Age,* London: Carnegie UK Trust

Convery, P. (1994) *Reforming the Unemployment Count,* Working Brief, London: Unemployment Unit and Youthaid

Field, S. (1986) 'Trends in racial inequality', *Social Studies Review,* March

Finn, D. (1987) *Training without Jobs,* London: Macmillan

Freeman, C. and Soete, L. (1994) *Work for All or Mass Unemployment,* London: Pinter

Friedman, M. (1976) *Unemployment versus Inflation?,* London: Institute of Economic Affairs

—— (1980) *Free to Choose,* Harmondsworth: Penguin

Gershuny, J. and Pahl, R. (1980) 'Britain in the decade of the three economies', *New Society,* 3 January

Glyptis, S. (1989) *Leisure and Unemployment,* Milton Keynes: Open University Press

Keynes, J. M. (1936) *The General Theory of Employment, Interest and Money,* London: Macmillan

Lewis, J. (1993) 'Women, work, families and social policies in Europe', in Lewis, J. (ed.) *Women and Social Policies in Europe: Work, Family and the State,* Aldershot: Edward Elgar

McCormick, B. (1990) 'The labour market', in Curwen, P. (ed.) *Understanding the British Economy,* London: Macmillan

Martin, J. and Roberts, C. (1984) *Women and Unemployment: A Lifetime Perspective,* London: HMSO

Marx, K. 'Wage, labour and capital' and 'Preface to a contribution to the critique of political economy', in *Selected Works,* London: Lawrence & Wishart (1968)

Pahl, R. (1984) *Divisions of Labour,* Oxford: Blackwell

Rapoport, R. (1982) *Unemployment and the Family,* London: Family Welfare Association

Salaman, G. (1987) 'Information Technology and the debate about work', *Social Studies Review,* May

Schumpeter, J. (1939) *Business Cycles,* New York: McGraw Hill

—— (1943) *Capitalism, Socialism and Democracy,* 6th edn, London: Unwin (1987)

Sinfield, A. (1981) *What Unemployment Means,* Oxford: Martin Robertson

Taylor, D. (1990) *Creative Accounting: An Unemployment Unit Briefing,* London: Unemployment Unit and Youthaid

Trowler, P (1995) *Investigating Education and Training,* London: Collins Educational

White, M. (1994) 'Unemployment and employment relations in Britain', in Benoit-Guilbot and Gallie (1994)

6   The effects of unemployment

The effects of unemployment can be considered in several ways. First, we can distinguish between the economic, social and political effects of unemployment. Second, we can consider the effects on individuals and households as well as the overall effect on society. It is important to differentiate these levels because the distribution of unemployment is very uneven.

Although it is possible to distinguish between these different effects, unemployment is not usually experienced in the fragmented way such a schema implies, so we also need to consider the overall impact of unemployment on individuals and society.

1) *Before you read this chapter, and working in groups, think up as many effects of unemployment as you can.*
2) *Write a short sentence on how each item you have identified has an effect on people and/or society.*
3) *Present your findings to the rest of the class and make sure each group has a comprehensive list. Add on effects identified in this chapter if they do not form part of your list.*
4) *Using this list, construct a spider diagram to show the links between unemployment and other areas of society and sociology.*

The effects on individuals

Income

The first noticeable effect of being unemployed is a fall in the net income available to either individuals or households.

As we saw in the last chapter, the New Right believes that the Welfare State has undermined the efficient operation of the market and created a 'dependency culture'. A commonsense version of this attitude is the idea that people can live quite happily on state benefits; and there is a more serious academic argument to the effect that people's income does not drastically fall as a result of being unemployed.

As an example of this type of analysis, in July 1983 the *Economist* magazine claimed that in November of that year a British father of two on unemployment benefit would get about 84 per cent of the net spending power he would enjoy on average male manual earnings. The implication was that there was not enough of an incentive for such a person to attempt to find a job, and thus high levels of state benefit were indeed feeding the 'dependency culture'.

This argument was contested by John Micklewright (1985), who pointed out that the *Economist* had made several assumptions in calculating its figure, chiefly that the man's wife was not in work and the household therefore had no other source of income, and secondly that the children were both over 10 and therefore the family was receiving child benefit at the highest level. These were unrealistic assumptions because only about 25 per cent of unemployed males found themselves in such a position. Rather more typical, covering 33 per cent of unemployed males, would be a single man with no children. A man in that position would receive state unemployment benefits equivalent not to 84 per cent but to 27 per cent of the average male manual wage.

Heady and Smyth (1989) carried out a large-scale longitudinal survey which followed 2,925 unemployed main family earners over a fifteen-month period during 1983–4. They concluded that there was a sudden and drastic drop in disposable income as a result of becoming unemployed. Three months after becoming unemployed from a previously full-time job, net income was 59 per cent of the previous level. They also noted that there was a further slight deterioration after about a year, although this was largely restricted to the elderly.

Commenting on this survey, Duncan Gallie (1994, p. 122) has noted: 'the view that welfare benefits provided a level of support that eradicated the financial benefits of employment has little empirical support . . . The severe financial effects of unemployment take place relatively early on and, in this respect, the long-term unemployed do not form a distinctive group.'

Find out the current levels of benefits for the unemployed available from the Departments of Employment and Social Security. How does the amount available compare to (a) a student grant, (b) average earnings?

Psychological distress

In contemporary society, work is not only a source of income but also an important source of personal status and social identity. If people are asked to describe themselves they will often do so with reference to their job and employment status. This aspect of identity is of course denied to the unemployed.

The experience of unemployment has often been associated with both increased ill-health and falling levels of self-esteem and other indicators of psychological distress. A study by Payne *et al.* (1984) found that unemployment consistently increased levels of psychological distress among men, and a similar study by Warr and Jackson (1985) showed that there was a large decline in psychological distress once people returned to employment. Further evidence on this question is provided by the research conducted by Gallie and Vogler as part of a large-scale research project into unemployment and social change (Gallie, Marsh and Vogler 1994). The ratings for psychological stress for various groups are shown in Table 6.1. The higher the score the greater the psychological distress.

Another indicator of psychological stress is suicide and attempted suicide. Steven Platt (quoted in Harris 1984) calculated that men who are unemployed for less than six months are six times more likely to attempt suicide than employed men, and those unemployed for over a year are nineteen times more likely. One of the problems with this finding, however, is that attempted suicide is higher in social class 5

Table 6.1 Psychological distress scores by sex and partnership status

	Self-employed	Employed	Unemployed	Non-active
Men				
All	3.24	3.27	4.30	4.00
In partnerships	3.17	3.23	4.40	3.81
Single	3.71	3.47	4.12	4.50
Women				
All	3.07	3.49	4.26	3.72
In partnerships	3.04	3.43	4.05	3.27
Single	3.25	3.76	4.51	3.74

Source: Gallie, Marsh and Vogler, 1994, p. 26

than other classes anyway, so class rather than unemployment might be the causal factor.

> *Suggest ways in which research might be done to distinguish the 'class effect' from the 'unemployment effect' in relation to suicide and attempted suicide.*

Much research in this area links the psychological stress to the financial problems caused by unemployment, as in the work of Fraser. While the financial problems caused by unemployment undoubtedly contribute to psychological stress, the work of Marie Jahoda, originally in Marienthal in Austria (Jahoda, Lazersfeld and Zeisel 1972), suggests that a more important source of the psychological stress associated with unemployment is the loss of social routines associated with work, which seem to provide a source of personal stability; Jahoda cites the imposition of a time structure, the extension of social relationships, regular activity and a sense of collective purpose and identity. While other activities could provide these, her argument is that in modern industrialized societies work and the experience of work are central to their provision.

As part of a large-scale study on unemployment in the UK, Jonathan Gershuny (1994) set out to test the 'Jahoda thesis'. His findings provide some support for the notion that there are significant differences between the unemployed and the employed in relation to access to the sources of personal stability that Jahoda identified (see Table 6.2, on page 137), though he is not convinced that these are crucial in causing the psychological harm associated with unemployment.

> 1) *Among which of the 'Jahoda items' shown in this table was there the greatest difference between the employed and the unemployed?*
> 2) *Write a short report on any significant gender differences you can see in this table.*

Gershuny also found a slight gender difference in his research. This, it is argued, can be accounted for by the effects of the highly gendered domestic division of labour. Loss of employment may lighten the burden of work that women have to do; or the domestic arena, housework and caring for others may provide an alternative basis for a general sense of well-being. However, as Gershuny himself points out, 'there is also evidence, at least for women, that high levels of work in these areas may give rise to

Table 6.2

Jahoda items	% agree Self-employed	Employed	Unemployed	Non-active
Men				
Time on hands	9	10	58	39
Meet range of people	69	59	42	44
Doing something useful	69	62	36	44
Responsibilities at particular time	83	77	51	53
Feel respected	59	49	43	50
Women				
Time on hands	17	8	31	19
Meet range of people	69	66	40	38
Doing something useful	66	69	56	51
Responsibilities at particular time	90	83	75	74
Feel respected	59	51	37	43

Source: Adapted from *Household and Community Survey*, 1987 in Gallie, Marsh and Vogler, p 217

considerable dissatisfaction (e.g. Oakley 1974). Thus ... a countervailing Oakley effect might be set against the Jahoda effect' (Gershuny 1994, p. 229). Some women might feel that they have indeed contributed useful activity but may still be dissatisfied about the social arrangements in which housework and domestic care take place.

Another explanation for the damaging psychological effects of unemployment on men is offered by Brendan Burchell (1994). He argues that the crucial factor is insecurity. His research found that psychological distress was a characteristic not only of the unemployed but also of those in employment but on short-term contracts or in other flexible work situations. These two groups' scores for psychological distress were similar but both were markedly different from those in stable full-time employment. An implication of this finding is that the extent to which there is a psychological improvement when an unemployed person finds a job will be affected by the type of job. If it is short term or in other ways insecure there will be little improvement in psychological well-being. However, Burchell detected a gender difference here, because improvements in women's well-being, unlike men's, was not crucially affected by the level of security the job offered. This links into the different gender roles which place more emphasis on the male as the breadwinner.

In an article on changing patterns of work (Guardian, 28 October 1994), Will Hutton made the following comments:

'If more than half the working population had full-time, tenured jobs 20 years ago, now the proportion has fallen to barely a third. Even if you include those self-employed who are secure and the part-timers who actively want to work part-time, barely more than half the working population are working in conditions that earlier generations would recognize as secure employment. The rest have been plunged into a maelstrom of uncertainty, and conditions that 19th-century factory workers would have recognized.'

What will be the effect on levels of psychological distress if this trend continues if (a) Jahoda is correct, (b) Burchell is correct?

Physical health

There is a clear link between unemployment and ill-health, but it might be argued that the direction of causation is the reverse of what is often assumed. Martyn Harris (1984) suggested: 'while a lot of unemployed people may be unhealthy, it could be a predisposition to illness which made them unemployed in the first place'. This view has been called the social selection model of ill-health and was investigated as part of the Black Report investigation of 1980. The evidence of this research suggested that social selection is less important than cultural/behavioural and social structural factors in determining patterns of ill-health.

Harris reported that a survey of 10,000 children conducted by the Department of Health and Social Security in 1981–2 found that two-year-old children of the long-term unemployed were up to an inch shorter than other children. Similarly, according to Alistair Graham (1985) a report in 1971 indicated that families living on welfare benefits were more than twice as likely to have medical problems. The unemployed are likely to be a large part of such a group.

An American researcher, Harvey Brenner, investigated the link between ill-health and economic cycles (a cycle might be from slump to boom to slump, as in the UK in the 1980s and early 1990s). He found that societies which experienced an increase in unemployment of 1 million over five years were likely to have 50,000 more deaths from general illness, 167,000 more deaths from heart disease and 63,900 more admissions to psychiatric hospitals (Brenner 1979).

Information relating to the UK appears to back up this picture. According to the *Observer* (27 September 1992) the British Regional Heart Survey, based on studies of 253 British towns over ten years, found that those who were unemployed at any time during the five years prior to the research were more than one and a half times as likely to die in the next five years as employed men. In relation to morbidity as opposed to mortality, the Office of Health Economics published statistics showing that the number of prescriptions issued on Merseyside was 9.7 per person in 1991 compared with 6.9 per person in the South West Thames Regional Health Authority. The respective unemployment rates in these two areas was 12.5 per cent and 4.2 per cent.

Gallie and Vogler report that information from the 1987 Household and Community Survey shows that the link between unemployment and poor health is backed up by measures of self-rated physical health. These show that the unemployed consistently rate their health worse than those in secure employment. Another indication of the health effects of employment status is the use of health services, such as visits to GP and hospitals. Gallie and Vogler's findings on these issues are shown in Table 6.3 on p139. They also show that, in relation to health differences, the degree of job security seems to be as important as pay levels for those in employment.

Although it is difficult to disentangle the many possible reasons for this link, notably whether it is due to the greater prevalence of unemployment among manual workers who suffer poorer heath anyway, or whether it is due to the physical and psychological effects of stress due to financial hardship which is again not restricted to the unemployed, the available evidence does suggest that unemployment has very negative effects on individuals' health.

Table 6.3 GP visits in the last twelve months

Labour market experience	Whole sample	Men	Women
Mean (Average)	4.5	3.2	5.9
Insecure non-employed	10.1	7.5	10.7
Secure non-employed	8.1	8.0	8.1
Unemployed	6.7	5.9	7.8
Secure low-paid	3.8	2.8	4.2
Insecure low-paid	3.5	2.3	4.6
Secure higher-paid	2.9	2.5	4.0
Insecure higher-paid	2.7	2.4	4.1
Self-employed	2.4	2.3	3.2
Significance	0.001	0.001	0.001

Hospital outpatient visits in the last three years

Labour market experience	Whole sample	Men	Women
Mean (Average)	3.6	3	4.2
Insecure non-employed	8.2	5.1	8.9
Secure non-employed	5.3	10.4	4.3
Unemployed	5.2	4.5	6.0
Insecure low-paid	3.2	2.0	4.3
Secure low-paid	3.1	2.4	3.3
Self-employed	2.7	2.4	4.4
Secure higher-paid	2.6	2.5	2.7
Insecure higher-paid	2.4	2.0	4.2
Significance	0.001	0.001	0.001

Source: Gallie, Marsh and Vogler, 1994, p. 316

Effects on households

Households are composed of individuals, so clearly all the effects identified above will be present in households with unemployed individuals in them. However, we can also analyse the effect of unemployment on the quality and type of social interaction between individuals in households.

One interesting area of research is the way unemployment affects relationships between couples. This can be looked at in a number of ways. The British Social Attitudes Survey of 1991 showed that although a majority of people in couple households felt that most domestic tasks should be shared equally, in none of the tasks investigated was there actual equality of division in domestic labour (see Table 6.4). This suggests that the conventional domestic division of labour with men as the breadwinners and women as housewives is very much a continuing phenomenon. Investigators have therefore looked at what happens when this pattern is disrupted by the unemployment of men in such relationships.

Lydia Morris (1990) found in a study of financial management in households that

Table 6.4 Who does the chores?

	Done mainly by man	Done mainly by woman	Shared equally
Shopping	8	45	47
Evening meal	9	70	20
Evening dishes	28	33	37
Cleaning	4	68	27
Washing and ironing	3	84	12
Repairing equipment	82	6	10
Money and bills	31	40	28

The contrast between doctrine and practice: % of respondents in couple households saying:

	Should share equally	Do share equally
Shopping	74	47
Evening meal	54	20
Evening dishes	75	37
Cleaning	60	27
Washing and ironing	36	12
Repairing equipment	29	10
Money and bills	64	28

Source: Guardian, 18 November 1992

when income was low, such as when the man was unemployed, there was a tendency for financial management to become the responsibility of the woman, thus modifying the 'conventional' pattern.

However, in relation to domestic labour overall, Pahl's study of the Isle of Sheppey (Pahl 1984) found that the clearly gendered domestic division of labour was altered very little as a result of male employment; it *was* affected by the employment status of the women in the households they studied, though even when the woman was working full-time she still undertook the majority of domestic tasks.

In a survey of unemployment in six areas of the UK, Gallie, Gershuny and Vogler (1994) found little change in the financial management arrangements in households where the male became unemployed. There was some evidence of a modification of the domestic division of labour in such circumstances, with unemployed males increasing their participation, but the researchers stress that this was a modest increase and did not approach anything like equal sharing. This change was most likely when the woman was in paid employment, whereas if the woman was not employed a more traditional patterns remained.

This leads into a consideration of a second household effect. One of the most interesting findings in this area is that if a man becomes unemployed the chances of his partner becoming unemployed also appear to increase. Harris (1984) found that while nationally about 60 per cent of wives had a paid job, only 30–35 per cent of wives of unemployed men were employed, and for men who were long-term unemployed the figure for wives in paid employment fell to 10–15 per cent.

Research by Martin and Roberts (1984) also noted such a relationship. They found that 62 per cent of wives with working husbands were in paid employment whereas for those with unemployed husbands the figure fell to 33 per cent.

Davies, Elias and Penn (1994), too, discovered the effect, though it was less marked in their sample. They suggest three basic explanations for it. First, it can be due to the workings of the welfare benefit system. This is because, where the man is unemployed, the benefits given to a couple are reduced pound for pound by any of the woman's earnings over a very low threshold. It may therefore be quite rational for both partners to avoid employment in this situation. Davies, Elias and Penn estimate that about 10–20% of the cases they examined could be explained in this way.

> *Is this still true of the benefits system? Investigate the extent to which this problem still exists by referring to leaflets produced by the Department for Social Security.*

Second, wives of unemployed men may be reluctant to work due to the negative effect this would have on male esteem. This is linked to conventional gender roles and has been called the 'macho' explanation. Third, since unemployment is unequally distributed around the UK, partners of men in areas with high unemployment may simply not be able to get a job.

A further effect of unemployment on households concerns its impact on marriages. Richard Lampard's (1994) research on this area concluded that those who suffered pre-marital unemployment had significantly increased chances of experiencing the failure of their marriage. For those suffering post-marital unemployment he found that a bout of unemployment in one year increased the chances of the marriage failing in the next year by 70 per cent.

There is evidence, however, that this relationship might result from other factors. Poverty and financial stress have been found to be a major cause of the break-up of marriages, and Haskey (1984) found that divorce rates for unemployed men were similar to those for unskilled male workers. It is therefore difficult to disentangle the precise effect of unemployment, but the social circumstances that usually accompany it (although not exclusive to the unemployed) do appear to place much greater stress on marriages, leading to a higher rate of marriage break-up.

Lampard (1994) makes the interesting suggestion that the link between unemployment and marital break-up might be a two-way one. He found that some individuals experienced unemployment which seemed to be a direct result of the break-up of their marriage, and that in general the risk of unemployment appeared to be greater for those whose marriage had broken up.

> *You can locate figures for unemployment over the past 20 years from information in this book and from official statistics such as* Economic Trends *and* Social Trends.. *You can also locate information on the divorce rate in recent years from* Social Trends.
>
> *Look at the patterns in both over recent years and see if your findings justify the idea that increased unemployment leads to an increased chance of marriage failure.*

The social activities of households

One of the most often quoted findings is that unemployment leads to social withdrawal and increased social isolation. This view is outlined by Sue Glyptis (1989), who points out: 'Financial hardship forces household economies to be made, and leisure activities are early sacrifices ... For most people unemployment is boring. Time hangs heavily, the more so the longer they have been out of work ... There is a loss of social contacts, a loss of confidence and a sense of isolation' (p. 91). Younger people and women may suffer less from this problem than other groups among the unemployed, but nonetheless the overall effect on social interaction seems very negative.

Reporting their research on unemployment and social change, Gallie, Gershuny and Vogler (1994) suggest, however, that the difference between the unemployed and the employed may have been over-emphasized: 'the overall leisure activity levels of the unemployed were very similar to those of the employed' (p. 245). This conclusion is based on the evidence summarized in Table 6.5. However, they go on to break down the concept of leisure further and find that the unemployed tend to engage more in visiting other people at home or other activities that do not cost money and are less likely to engage in activities that involve expenditure such as visiting the pub or playing sport. They also find that there is an increase in 'passive leisure' such as sleeping longer and watching TV or listening to the radio.

Table 6.5 Leisure activities by employment status, men (N = 1.503) (weighted index)

Activity	Self-employed	Employed	Unemployed	Non-active
Library	0.07	0.13	0.16	0.29
Swim	0.09	0.12	0.09	0.09
Play sport	0.35	0.37	0.28	0.22
Watch sport	0.26	0.31	0.32	0.29
Theatre	0.04	0.04	0.02	0.05
Cinema	0.05	0.05	0.05	0.04
Pub	0.62	0.57	0.54	0.42
Church	0.12	0.12	0.13	0.12
Visit	0.45	0.49	0.60	0.46
Entertain	0.44	0.42	0.54	0.47
Garden	0.47	0.50	0.38	0.46
TV	0.96	0.96	0.95	0.96
Read book	0.70	0.75	0.65	0.75
Walk	0.43	0.154	0.65	0.59
Leisure group	0.15	0.14	0.09	0.14
Evening class	0.02	0.06	0.03	0.06
Overall activity index	5.27	5.57	5.46	5.50

Source: Gallie, Gershuny and Vogler (1994), p. 245

They conclude that because they are less involved in leisure activities which incur expenditure, the unemployed suffer a reduction in their social network. Using what they call a 'sociability index', they argue that 'the sociability index discriminated more sharply between those with a job and those without than had been the case for the activity index. Among both men and women, the employed and the self-employed had markedly higher scores than the unemployed' (p. 251).

The unemployed are also much more likely than the employed to have large numbers of unemployed people in their social network. The significance of this is that forms of social support which exist among friends, who might help each other out, are less available to the unemployed.

The effect of unemployment on society as a whole

All of the above effects of unemployment will in aggregate have an effect on society. For example, it has been shown that the unemployed suffer higher levels of ill-health. It follows that periods of mass unemployment will lead to increases in demand on the National Health Service.

Unemployment has several effects at the macro-societal level in addition to those we have noted at the individual and household levels. The most obvious immediate economic effect is the cost of unemployment benefit. The unemployed will also contribute less in taxation revenue than they would if they were employed. These two components might be called the direct cost of unemployment. Fraser and Sinfield calculated these costs as totalling £20 billion in 1984/5, which represents £6,600 per unemployed person (quoted in Maunder *et al.* 1987, p. 179). This clearly affects society as a whole as this is money that could have been spent elsewhere.

There is also the indirect cost of unemployment, namely the loss of the goods and services that the unemployed would have produced had they been employed. This is a considerable cost. Nigel Proctor (1987, p. 11) estimates the total cost of unemployment in the UK in 1986, when there were 3.5 million unemployed, at £55 billion. This was composed of £5 billion in unemployment benefits, £10 billion in lost tax revenue and £40 billion in lost production. It represented 18.5 per cent of the value of the entire economic production of the UK in 1986. In other words, without unemployment our standard of living would have been 18.5 per cent higher. This clearly has a cumulative effect since it is a cost that recurs every year. Unemployment therefore leads to an overall lowering of the standards of living. As a society we are poorer as a consequence of unemployment.

Unemployment also has negative social effects. Research conducted by David Dickinson (1994) showed an important link between unemployment and crime. While Dickinson emphasizes that unemployment cannot explain all crime or all rises in crime (since the crime rate rose while there was full employment in the 1960s and early 1970s), nonetheless he argues that there appears to be a relationship between the rate of unemployment among young males and the number of criminal offences. Figure 6.1 plots the relationship.

Figures produced by Northumbria police and quoted by Dickinson also seem to show some link between the two, with the percentage of crimes involving the unemployed rising as unemployment rises (see Table 6.6). Dickinson concludes that allowing mass unemployment to continue, particularly among young men, may contribute to the creation of criminals for the future and rising crime rates in the present.

> 'One argument put forward against the idea that unemployment is a source of crime, is that recorded crime has been rising since 1954 – a period that includes the full employment years of the postwar era . . . That crime rose when we had

Figure 6.1 Recorded crime and unemployment, England and Wales, 1971–91

Source: Dickinson, 1994

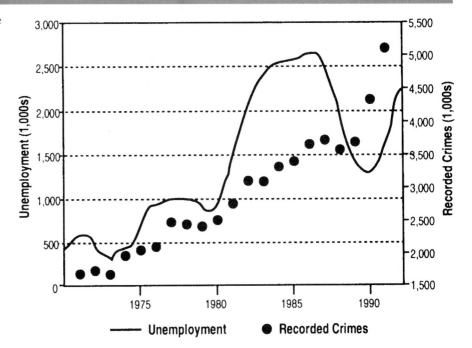

—— **Unemployment**   ● **Recorded Crimes**

Table 6.6   Employment status of offenders recorded by Northumberland Police

Year	1975	1976	1977	1978	1979
% of crimes involving unemployed persons	26	30	38	38	49
Unemployment rate %, North of England (registered count)	5.3	7.3	7.9	8.8	12.1

Source: Dickinson, 1994

full employment tells us that we should not attribute crime to a single cause . . . No claim should be made that there is a simple relationship between unemployment and crime: clearly other factors are also responsible. Nevertheless, unemployment must be regarded as a major factor motivating crime' (Dickinson 1994, pp. 20–1).

1) In what ways do Dickinson's research findings indicate that unemployment is a 'major factor motivating crime'?
2) What other causes of crime might be involved?
3) How important do you think unemployment is as a cause of crime in contemporary Britain?

Another social effect of mass unemployment is the growth of political protests about the issue. Mass unemployment, particularly among the young, can be seen as a major factor underlying the urban riots of the 1980s. A survey conducted by Gallie, Marsh and Vogler (1994) certainly found that the unemployed tended to have more collectivist political views than other groups. This would clearly bring them into conflict with the prevailing ideology of the government.

Evidence from the past shows that periods of sustained mass unemployment can bring political instability to the whole system. The experience of mass unemployment in the 1930s was followed by the rise of fascism in Italy and Germany and the consequent abominations visited on the world by those regimes. Parallels have been drawn between the 1990s and the 1930s, and there appears to be some cause for concern. Mass unemployment is again an important phenomenon across Europe (not least in Eastern Europe), and there has also been a rise in fascist activity in the 1990s.

Structured question

Item A

Unemployment also affected the extent to which people were satisfied with their family lives. The evidence here suggests a difference in the experiences of unemployed men and unemployed women. Satisfaction with family life was markedly lower among unemployed men than among those that were employed, even where unemployment had lasted for less than six months. Moreover, the longer the time that men had been unemployed, the greater their dissatisfaction.

Among women, in contrast, those unemployed for less than six months showed higher levels of satisfaction with family life than women in employment, and satisfaction was even greater among those unemployed for six to twelve months. It was only among women unemployed for more than twelve months that satisfaction declines.

Source: Gallie (1994), p. 127

Item B

It has been recognized that a whole series of consequences may emerge from unemployment, not all of them negative, as early redundancy can be an opportunity to embark upon a different type of work or may be a release from unsatisfactory work. However, the main effects of unemployment seem to have been disruption of family life and even destruction of individual lives. The loss of employment highlights the importance of work for an individual's status and welfare, although it should not be assumed that the experience of work is always a pleasant one.

Source: Lawson (1993), pp. 102–3

Item C

On the one hand, the movement from manufacturing to service employment was explained as a historical shift from industrial to post-industrial society. Equally, the changes in the organization of work and employment were variously interpreted as a move from Fordist to post-Fordist practices; or as the replacement of mass production with flexible specialization. In this, unfortunately, critical traditions which once emphasized the damaging effect of work upon workers gave way to those which celebrated the enriching aspects of employment. These were regularly contrasted with the debilitating experience of unemployment. In this way, the major division in society became understood as that between those with and those without work.

Source: Beynon (1992), p. 175

Item D

A report by Stone and Schlamp in 1971 indicated that families living on welfare benefits are more than twice as likely to have medical problems and that those on benefit had the highest percentage of illness. Less money therefore does no mean less unhealthy living – quite the reverse. It leads rather to stress and anxiety with all the accompanying dangers to mental and physical health.

The difficulties of unemployment run deeper than financial worry and depend on the meaning of employment. It is evident that people do not just work for money. Thousands of people would be better off on the dole than in work, yet they continue to work.

Employment is the main source of creativity and mastery, it is the main opportunity for social interaction, the main provider of temporal structure, and it is a major contributor to identity.

Source: Adapted from Graham (1985)

1) How long did women have to be unemployed before they experienced a decline in satisfaction with family life, according to the author of Item A? **(1 mark)**

2) The author if Item B suggests that the effects of unemployment may not all be negative. Suggest one positive and one negative effect of unemployment and explain the likely effect of each. **(4 marks)**

3) Briefly describe in your own words the changes in thinking about employment according to the author of Item C. **(2 marks)**

4) Evaluate the arguments sociologists have offered in relation to the differential experiences of unemployment by men and women as argued by the author of Item A. **(7 marks)**

5) Using material from the items and elsewhere, assess the extent to which sociological evidence and arguments support the statement in Item D that 'employment is the main source of creativity and mastery, it is the main opportunity for social interaction, the main provider of temporal structure, and it is a major contributor to identity'. **(11 marks)**

Coursework suggestions

Take one of the areas investigated in this chapter on the effects of unemployment or another you have found mentioned in literature on the subject, and investigate in detail the extent to which there is evidence of a a causal connection between unemployment and this factor, or simply a correlation caused by some common third factor.

Effects you might wish to consider include: poverty, ill-health, divorce, suicide, more satisfaction from family life, changes in leisure activities.

Bibliography

Beynon, H. (1992) 'The end of the industrial worker?', in Abercrombie, N. and Warde, A. *Social Change in Contemporary Britain*, Cambridge: Polity

Black Report (1980) *Inequalities in Health: Report on a Research Working Group*, London: DHSS

Brenner, B.H. (1979) 'Mortality and the national economy', *Lancet 2*, 15 September, pp. 568–73

Burchell, B. (1994) 'The effects of labour market position, job insecurity, and unemployment on psychological health', in Gallie, Marsh and Vogler (1994)

Davies, R.B., Elias, P. and Penn, R. (1994) 'The relationship between a husband's unemployment and his wife's participation in the labour force', in Gallie, Marsh and Vogler (1994)

Dickinson, D. (1994) 'Criminal benefits', *New Statesman and Society*, 14 January

Economist (1983) 'Tory paternalism keeps getting in the way', *Economist*, 9 July

Gallie, D. (1994) 'Social Consequences of long-term unemployment in Britain', in Benoit-Guilbot, O. and Gallie, D. (eds), *Long-Term Unemployment*, London: Pinter

Gallie, D., Gershuny, J. and Vogler, C. (1994) 'The household and social networks', in Gallie, Marsh and Vogler (1994)

Gallie, D., Marsh, C. and Vogler, C. (eds) (1994) *Social Change and the Experience of Unemployment*, Oxford: Oxford University Press

Gershuny, J. (1994) 'The psychological consequences of unemployment: an assessment of the Jahoda thesis', in Gallie, Marsh and Vogler (1994)

Glyptis, S. (1989) *Leisure and Unemployment*, Milton Keynes: Open University Press

Graham, A. (1985) 'Bearing the weight of unemployment', *Community Care,* 7 March

Harris, M. (1984) 'How unemployment affects people', *New Society,* 19 January

Haskey, J. (1984) 'Social class and socio-economic differences in divorce in England and Wales', *Population Studies,* No. 38, pp. 419–38

Heady, P. and Smyth, M. (1989) *Living Standards During Unemployment,* London: HMSO

Jahoda, M., Lazersfeld, P. and Zeisel, H. (1972) *Marienthal: The Sociography of an Unemployed Community,* London: Tavistock

Lampard, R. (1994) 'An examination of the relationship between marital dissolution and unemployment', in Gallie, Marsh and Vogler (1994)

Lawson, T. (1993) *Sociology for A-Level: A Skills-based Approach,* London: Collins Educational

Martin, J. and Roberts, C. (1984) *Women and Employment: A Lifetime Perspective,* London: HMSO

Maunder, P., Myers, D., Wall, N. and Miller, R.L. (1987) *Economics Explained,* London: Collins Educational

Micklewright, J. (1985) 'Fiction versus fact: unemployment benefits in Britain', *National Westminster Bank Quarterly Review,* May

Morris, L. (1990) *The Workings of the Household,* Cambridge: Polity

Oakley, A. (1974) *The Sociology of Housework,* Oxford: Martin Robertson

Pahl, R. (1984) *Divisions of Labour,* Oxford: Blackwell

Payne, R.L., Warr, P.B. and Hartley, J. (1984) 'Social class and psychological ill-health during unemployment', *Sociology of Health and Illness,* Vol. 6, pp. 154–75

Proctor, N. (1987) *The UK Economy: An Integrated Approach,* Bromborough: Checkmate Gold

Warr, P. and Jackson, P. (1985) 'Factors influencing the psychological impact of prolonged unemployment and of re-employment', *Psychological Medicine,* No. 15, pp. 795–807

7 Theories of leisure: towards a leisure society?

Leisure: the link with work

Much early writing on the sociology of leisure adopted a rather unproblematic definition of leisure which contrasted it with time spent in work. The sociology of leisure therefore essentially grew out of the sociology of work, and work was seen as the central influence on the experience of leisure. As Green *et al.* (1990) point out: 'It is no accident that leisure should emerge as an area for study within the context of social science perspectives on industry . . . The most cursory analysis of leisure studies in their historical context readily reveals this as the background to leisure conceptualised as compensation for the privations endured at work' (p. 11).

> Look up as many definitions of leisure as you can find. Use dictionaries, sociology books and books for courses on sport and leisure.
> Discuss in groups which of the definitions you have located is the most useful. Are they mainly concerned with differentiating leisure from work, or do they spell out the actual content of leisure?

This view is reflected in the theory of the growth of a leisure society. In simple terms, this theory implies an almost automatic evolution from pre-industrial times, when there was no distinction between work and leisure – and thus it is virtually assumed that leisure did not exist – to the industrial revolution and the advent of industrial society, when much greater productivity allowed for the creation of free time and the modern concept of leisure; the progressive enlargement of leisure time and the declining importance of work are said to be ushering in the post-industrial society, where leisure will be allocated more time and will become more central to people's lives.

This chapter will consider the ways in which the study of leisure has moved from being an adjunct to that of work, through the notion of the growth of a leisure society, to more recent theories which stress the important elements of inequality in terms of access to and participation in leisure. It will end with a consideration of some examples of more recent theoretical approaches to the study of leisure in society.

Towards the 'leisure society'?

Technological advances in production have for some time been said to offer the possibility of creating a leisure society. For example John Maynard Keynes, writing in the 1930s, envisaged a society where fifteen hours of work per week would meet societal needs, leaving more time available for the satisfaction of non-economic ends, such as leisure, culture and enjoyment.

Another optimistic prediction of the leisure society was offered by J. Neulinger: 'Once a society has reached a certain minimum of material, that is, economic well-being, other domains of life begin to take on increasing importance. There is little doubt that many of the so-called post-industrial societies have entered that stage' (quoted in Clarke and Critcher 1985, p. 2).

These predictions received added impetus in the 1980s, when the negative environmental impacts of untrammelled expansion in industrial production came to the forefront of political debate. Some writers now look to labour-saving technology, together with a reduced emphasis on the accumulation of material wealth as a measure of the quality of life, to save us from ecological disaster as well as liberating us from repetitive and unsatisfying work and giving us more time for leisure.

However, the thesis that a 'leisure society' is evolving has attracted a number of criticisms. One line of attack questions its accuracy by considering in detail the reality of life in historical and contemporary societies and the differences between them.

E.P. Thompson (1993) discusses the implications of the shift from the pre-industrial system of work, in which production was organized around achieving a certain number of tasks and the time taken to do this was not considered the most important detail, to a system based on clock time which arose with the growth of industrial capitalism and the factory system in the nineteenth century. This changeover introduced the distinction between work time and free time, giving rise to the mistaken belief that the industrial revolution brought into being leisure itself. In reality, according to Thompson, the different forms of work discipline led to different notions about the relationship between work and life:

> A community in which task-orientation is common appears to show the least demarcation between 'work' and 'life'. Social intercourse and labour are intermingled – the working day lengthens or contracts according to the task – and there is no great sense of conflict between labour and 'passing the time of day' ... As soon as actual hands are employed the shift from task-orientation to timed labour is marked. It is true that the timing of work can be done independently of any time-piece [but] the computation is difficult, and dependent on many variables. Clearly a straightforward time-measurement was more convenient.
> This measurement embodies a simple relationship. Those who are employed experience a distinction between their employer's time and their 'own' time, and the employer must use the time of his labour, and see it is not wasted. [Thompson 1993, pp. 358–9]

'Leisure' therefore existed before industrial times even though there was no clearly demarcated time devoted to it. Thompson also recounts how workers resisted the attempts to remove their leisure that accompanied the introduction of time-orientation and work discipline by celebrating 'Saint Monday', in other words absenting themselves from work to compensate for the long working hours.

Thompson contends that the growth of industrial capitalism, far from leading to the creation of leisure, had the opposite effect. Clarke and Critcher agree: 'It is simply inadequate to suggest that industrialization created leisure, which has subsequently grown to today's level. In fact, industrialization in Britain began by destroying leisure' (1985, pp. 48–9). The lives of working-class people were increasingly regulated by the bourgeoisie as a way of instilling work discipline in the factories. Popular working-class leisure activities, particularly those involving drink, were rigorously suppressed.

Marxists such as Clarke and Critcher and E.P. Thompson thus reject the idea that the future automatically holds the promise of increased leisure. They also hold that leisure is not an arena characterized simply by personal choice and freedom: it is subject to the same constraints that bear down upon other arenas of social life, though these constraints can be resisted.

In what ways are leisure activities regulated today? Make a list of the ways in which legal regulation affects the leisure pursuits of members of your class.

Drawing on historical data, the radical sociologist Mike O'Donnell writes in a similar vein:

> Technological progress has not yet 'liberated' people from work and introduced the 'new age of leisure' some had predicted. Of course, most people do have much more leisure time than they did 150 years ago but not very much more than they did 50 years ago. Work, paid and/or domestic, still dominates the weekdays of the majority of adults aged 16–65 and still provides most of them with their core identity. [O'Donnell 1992, p. 266]

Kenneth Roberts (1986) also states that the reduction in work time in industry was typically from 70 hours to 54 hours between 1850 and 1918, followed by a further reduction of only about three hours from the 1940s to the 1970s (quoted in Haralambos and Holborn 1995, p. 265).

An examination of recent figures on the amount of free time people have tends to confirm this viewpoint. Indeed in recent years, when government thinking in the UK has been dominated by the New Right's emphasis on the free market and greater productivity, there have been sharp reductions in people's free time. Figures from the Henley Centre for Forecasting show that the amount of free time available in an average week fell by 1.9 per cent between 1990/91 and 1992/3 for full-time employed males (see Tables 7.1 and 7.2). The equivalent figures for other groups are:

Table 7.1 Time use in a typical week, by employment status and sex, 1990–91

| | Full-time employees | | Part-time employees | | |
	Males	Females	Females	Housewives	Retired
Weekly hours spent on:					
Employment and travel	48.3	42.6	20.9	0.3	0.7
Essential activities	24.1	39.6	52.1	58.4	33.0
Sleep	49.0	49.0	49.0	49.0	49.0
Free time	46.6	36.8	46.0	60.3	85.3
Free time per weekday	4.5	3.3	5.4	8.4	11.6
Free time per weekend day	12.1	10.3	9.5	9.3	13.6

1. Travel to and from place of work.
2. Essential domestic work and personal care, including essential shopping, child care, cooking, personal hygiene and appearance.
3. An average of 7 hours sleep per night is assumed.

Source: Henley Centre for Forecasting, in *Social Trends* (1992), Table 10.2

Table 7.2   Time use in a typical week, by employment status and sex, 1992–93   *Hours*

	Full-time employees Males	Females	Part-time female employees	Housewives	Retired Males	Females
Weekly hours spent on:						
Employment and travel	47.1	42.2	20.8	0.4	0.5	0.6
Essential cooking, shopping and housework	13.0	25.5	32.5	38.1	17.0	33.0
Essential child care, personal hygiene and other shopping	13.2	20.0	25.2	29.4	10.0	14.0
Sleep	49.0	49.0	49.0	49.0	49.0	49.0
Free time	45.7	31.4	40.6	51.1	91.5	71.4
Free time per weekday	5.0	3.0	4.7	6.6	12.8	9.7
Free time per weekend day	10.3	8.2	8.5	9.0	13.8	11.5

1. Travel to and from place of work.
2. Seven hours per night.

Source: Henley Centre for Forecasting, in *Social Trends* (1994), Table 10.2

Full-time employed females	–14.6 per cent
Part-time employed females	–11.7 per cent
Housewives	–15.2 per cent
Retired people	–4.5 per cent.

1) Explain how the percentage changes in free time outlined here can be calculated from the figures provided in Tables 7.1 and 7.2.
2) Obtain the most up-to-date figures on time use (they are reported most years in Social Trends) and write a short report updating the changes in the availability of free time for the various social groups identified.

These figures do not suggest a move towards a leisure society. By 1995 the average working week in the UK was 43.4 hours. The Henley Centre predicts that free time will further decline from 39 to 36 per cent of total time over the next few years (quoted in the *Independent*, 6 May 1995).

1) To what extent does the evidence in Tables 7.1 and 7.2 undermine notions of movement towards a leisure society?
2) In what ways might this evidence help to justify the need for a sociological approach to the study of leisure?

The growth of leisure studies

Despite the contested nature of the argument about the growth of the leisure society, there has been a massive growth in leisure studies and to some extent this has also spurred the growth of the sociology of leisure.

From a sociological point of view the central problem with much of the leisure studies literature is that it appears to view leisure almost in isolation from the rest of society. One of the implications of the notion of a leisure society has been to reduce the importance attached to work in such studies as leisure is assumed to replace work as the central life interest. Moreover the very concept of leisure studies implies a separation between the two spheres.

Sociologists have made a number of criticisms of this approach. For example Roberts (1978, 1981) calls such research 'recreation research', by which he means the market research undertaken by leisure industries plus the various government surveys that chart people's use of public recreation facilities such as the General Household Survey. (For a summary and discussion of the limitations of this approach, see SSRC/Sports Council 1978.)

Roberts argues that such research presents very simplistic pictures of leisure divorced from other aspects of life and ignores both the fact that most leisure activities take place outside consciously provided outlets for recreation (and therefore cannot explain the 'big five' leisure activities of watching television, drinking alcohol, smoking tobacco, betting and making love), and also the motivations of people undertaking leisure. He argues therefore that a sociological approach is necessary:

> We have mountains of data on how leisure is spent, very little of it collected primarily for social scientists' purposes . . . The main problem is not a shortage of information but how to interpret the evidence and decide what the statistics mean. Sociology's standard complaint is that, having been produced primarily at the behest of the leisure industries with their own problems in mind, the data often fail to address questions that sociologists want to pose. [Roberts 1981, p. 5]

1) *What problems might emerge in attempting to measure whether the activities mentioned above are still the 'big five'?*
2) *Try to find out how much time and/or money people spent on these five activities for the most recent period you can.*

Roberts also comments: 'There are limits to how widely the influence of leisure is spreading throughout the social structure. Work and politics are two areas of life where its impact is slight and, while this remains so, talk of a leisure society is ill-advised' (quoted in Haralambos and Holborn 1995, p. 265).

Clarke and Critcher (1985) note that talk of the growth of a leisure society tends to reappear every time we go through a period of mass unemployment: 'Leisure has an uncanny habit of becoming a matter for public debate when large numbers are suddenly left with a lot of "time on their hands"' (p. 2). From this perspective leisure studies could be seen as a way to ensure that the unemployed use their time 'wisely' and do not engage in other, less desirable activities such as rioting or crime that might result from 'idleness'.

Most sociologists thus tend to be critical of the possibility of analysing leisure without reference to other factors in society. However, they disagree among themselves about precisely how leisure is tied into the rest of society and about the relative importance of the various other social factors that affect leisure and leisure participation.

The sociological analysis of leisure

The earliest work in the sociology of leisure was concerned to locate leisure in a social context and to consider the elements of the social structure that were most influential upon the experience of leisure.

Stanley Parker: leisure and work

Probably the most influential early piece of research to illustrate the important link between work and leisure was undertaken by Stanley Parker.

Parker (1976, 1983) argued that work is central to life in industrial society and that the work/leisure distinction which arises is an important difference from pre-industrial society. The categories he developed have been influential in the presentation of official statistics on time usage. He distinguished between work, work obligations, non-work obligations, time spent on physiological needs and leisure which is time left over when all the above have been fulfilled.

Table 7.3 Types of work-leisure relationship and associated variables (individual level)

Work-leisure relationship variables	Extension	Opposition	Neutrality
Content of work and leisure	similar	deliberately different	usually different
Demarcation of spheres	weak	strong	average
Central life interest	work	–	non-work
Imprint left by work on leisure	marked	marked	not marked
Work variables			
Autonomy in work situation	high	–	low
Use of abilities (how far extended)	fully ('stretched')	uneven ('damaged')	little or no ('bored')
Involvement	moral	alienative	calculative
Work colleagues	include some close friends	–	include no close friends
Work encroachment on leisure	high	low	low
Typical occupations	social workers (especially residential)	'extreme' (mining, fishing)	routine clerical and manual
Non-work variables			
Educational level	high	low	medium
Duration of leisure	short irregular	long	
Main function of leisure	continuation of personal development	recuperation	entertainment

Source: Parker (1983), p. 89

Parker argued that leisure is shaped by the reaction to work. This line of reasoning has given rise to a well-known trilogy of patterns in which leisure is said to develop in reaction to different work experiences (see Table 7.3). In occupations that allow some degree of job satisfaction, for example in the professionals but also in manual craft work, according to Parker, leisure is an extension of work and the division between work and leisure is blurred (the extension pattern). In contrast, occupations such as car assembly that are endured and felt to be oppressive produce a pattern where work and leisure are viewed as polar opposites (the opposition pattern).

Parker's third pattern, the neutrality pattern, is the predominant one. Here work has only a weak effect on leisure. It is not seen as personally degrading or damaging, as in the opposition pattern, but leisure rather than work remains the central source of enjoyment and the two spheres are largely independent. Leisure is often family-centred. Work is simply a means to an end: it provides the money to pay for leisure. Parker argues that this pattern is characteristic of the large range of white-collar occupations below the professional level. The bank clerk is his key example.

The centrality of paid work in this analysis has been criticized. Some have argued that other factors, notably family structures, are more important than work in determining people's leisure activities. This is essentially the position of writers such as the Rapoports and Wilmott and Young (see below).

A more thoroughgoing criticism of Parker's work is that it only really applies to the lifestyle of one section of society, namely male full-time workers. Feminist writers have argued that it is not applicable to the position of women who are full-time housewives; the gender relationships involved in domestic labour cannot be derived from an analysis centred on paid work.

A further criticism is that Parker ignores the influence of social class relationships and instead talks about occupations. Class lifestyles are more than simply the reflections of particular occupations, yet Parker lumps together different class lifestyles – such as those of doctors and craft workers – in the same pattern.

The final key criticism of Parker is that he tends to view the influence of work on leisure patterns in a rather deterministic way. Clarke and Critcher (1985) allege that this is an example of functionalism, which downplays human action: 'it fails to allow adequately for human agency and tends to reduce social behaviour to the level of a cultural reflex, in this case to the influence of work' (p. 20).

Young and Willmott: leisure and the family

Young and Willmott (1961) see the changing family structure as the crucial element affecting patterns of leisure. They argue that the evolution of the family has gone through three stages. Stage One families were predominant until the nineteenth century when the family was primarily a productive unit. Stage Two families arose as a result of industrialization and the growth of factories, which moved production away from families, leading to a disrupted family life. By the beginning of the twentieth century Stage Three families had emerged. Families were unified again but based around consumption rather than production. The relevant change so far as leisure is concerned is the transformation of the family from a unit of production to a unit of consumption. The three key elements of Stage Three, which Young and Wilmott identify as emerging at the beginning of the twentieth century among the middle classes and later spreading to the working class, are:

- the privatized, home-centred nature of the contemporary family,

- the shift from an extended to a nuclear-type family, and

- the breaking down of role segregation between males and females within the family.

The modern 'symmetrical family' involves both partners engaging in paid work outside the home and sharing domestic tasks. This notion of change starting at the top of the class structure and spreading downwards is given the name of the 'Principle of Stratified Diffusion'.

Table 7.4 Conjugal roles

Joint conjugal role	Segregated conjugal role
Husband and wife share tasks and activities	Husband and wife have different tasks and interests
Dispersed network where people known to the family may not be known to each other.	Highly connected network where people known to the family also know each other.
Husband and wife have similar interests.	Husband and wife have separate interests.
Typical of middle class families.	Typical of working class families.

Source: Joseph (1986), *Sociology for Everyone*, Cambridge: Polity

---

Explain in your own words the 'Principle of Stratified Diffusion'. If this process is occurring, would the direction of change be from left to right or right to left in Table 7.4?

Young and Willmott point out that their respondents saw leisure as the opposite of work and stressed freedom and pleasure as important components of leisure. They point to the increasing amount of time spent in leisure activities centred on the home and the family. Although they did find class differences in patterns of leisure participation, the most important factor was the difference between owning or not owning a car. Working-class car owners were more like the middle class in their leisure patterns, and car ownership is therefore seen as an example of the Principle of Stratified Diffusion. While overall this is an optimistic picture of the future of leisure, Young and Willmott accept that gender is an important factor governing the nature and extent of leisure. Social contacts outside the family are far more restricted for women than men.

Young and Willmott's work has been much criticized, mainly for its assertion that domestic labour is becoming more of a shared responsibility between partners. Ann Oakley (1974) claims that this conclusion was based on a very imprecise definition of men helping in the home and on the findings of one question in their research. She maintains that domestic labour is still highly gendered as women are expected to carry the major burden of housework. This clearly has implications for the amount of leisure time available for women.

The methodology of Young and Willmott's study has also come in for general criticism. It has been argued that the wording of the questions used left a lot to be desired and tended to stimulate predictable and superficial responses. Another problem is that the sample was skewed towards middle-class families in the South East and may therefore not be generally applicable. Moreover a large number of young single people in their sample were reported as not contactable. Their leisure activities, and those of other people whose lives do not conform to the cornflake packet image of the family, are unlikely to be explained by reference to the family-centred symmetrical family.

Perhaps Young and Willmott would not be worried about allegations that their sample was unrepresentative since they see the middle-class families they did contact as the model for others in the future. However, the recent increase in the numbers of households that do not conform to this pattern calls this line of reasoning into question, and critics have also contested the notion that the middle class is the vanguard and model for other groups.

The Rapoports: leisure and the life cycle

An alternative model of leisure centring on the family has been offered by Rapoport and Rapoport (1975). They argue that the key determinant of leisure patterns is the life cycle. Their model connects changes in the arenas of work, family and leisure and explores the ways in which they are connected.

There are four key stages of the life cycle arising from psycho-biological maturation processes, according to the Rapoports:

- The first they consider is the adolescent stage (13–19 year olds) where the central life preoccupation is exploration and the quest for personal identity. There is a desire for new experiences in all areas of life such as the family, school and leisure.

- In the second stage, young adulthood (19–25), the concern moves from personal identity to social identity. The key interest is the establishment of sexual relationships, sometimes leading to marriage. Becoming part of a couple is therefore the most important element, and this frames other areas of life. The Rapoports point to the problems that arise from this privatization of leisure for young women as it may impose restrictions that do not apply to males. Talking about an engaged couple they comment:

> Thus a young woman narrows her range of interests to those which are courtship-orientated . . . her pre-engagement activities are no longer suit-able because they involve going with girls to places where there are unattached men . . . This pattern continues after marriage. The woman depends on her husband to take her out and is in many ways physically constrained . . . male groups' activities are much less exclusively courtship-orientated . . . They can therefore sustain some involvement in activities like sport, unlike their females who do not. [Rapoport and Rapoport 1975, p. 125]

- Next comes the establishment stage, covering most of adult life (25–55). Here the central preoccupation is life investments in the form either of material possessions or of children. Leisure often becomes child-centred, and childcare may become the exclusive focus for the woman. This period away from the labour market may lead to problems of adjustment later on when children have grown up and women wish to work again.

- In later years (55+) leisure becomes more home-centred and often related to grandchildren. However, variations may arise due to factors such as health and income.

The Rapoports argue that, although it is not the only factor responsible for leisure patterns, the life cycle is crucial to an understanding of patterns of leisure. Their work also consistently links leisure to other sphere of life.

The key criticism of their work is that it exhibits a form of biological determinism. Their life cycle stages are characterized principally by changes of a biological or physiological nature. They argue, for instance, that adolescence is characterized by developmental processes that are biologically rooted. Important biological changes clearly do take place then, but many sociologists have also argued that the key features of this and indeed the other stages are socially constructed rather than biologically determined. For instance, the average age at which women give birth does not appear to be biologically determined but reflects the changing social construction of the family, marriage and women's place in society. Equally, it seems difficult to sustain any proposition that retirement ages (either 60 or 65) are biologically determined. Ageing is thus more than a biological inevitability, and the meaning of this process is shaped by social factors.

Explain the meaning of the phrase 'biological determinism'.

Kenneth Roberts: a pluralist perspective

Roberts (1978) is critical of theories that try to explain leisure and leisure patterns by reference to a single predominant factor such as work, class or family structure. He argues that we need to recognize the importance of the choices individuals make. These may be socially structured, but they nonetheless still involve free choice.

Commercial leisure providers may well try to manipulate the choices people make, but at the end of the day people are still able to choose among the alternatives on offer. The multiplicity of observable patterns of leisure participation are the result of these choices, made under the influence of a plurality of factors such as work, class and occupation, but no one of these factors – or others such as gender, education or the life cycle – can be presented as the dominant factor explaining all leisure patterns.

Clarke and Critcher: a neo-Marxist account

John Clarke and Chas Critcher (1985) have developed an account of leisure that draws heavily upon the notions developed by cultural studies. They argue that leisure is a social process and that, rather than being seen as a reflection of either work or the family, it needs to be considered in the context of the social structure as a whole.

Theirs is a broadly Marxist approach, concerned with developing a theory and analysis of the totality of economic, social, political and ideological processes. However, they are neo-Marxist in their emphasis on the active process of cultural creation: 'If societies are made by humans, under conditions imposed upon them, they are nonetheless made' (p. 45).

They argue that existing theories of leisure are inadequate since they tend either to focus on a single area of the social structure or to portray people as largely passive.

Their critique of pluralism, on the other hand, is that it ignores the structural constraints within which choices about leisure are made. They hold that the sociology of leisure should be concerned with the dual context of constraint and creation that shapes leisure and culture in contemporary society.

> *Draw up a table to provide a summary of the classical sociological approaches to leisure that are briefly outlined here. You will find more detail on these in any sociology textbook.*
>
> *The headings you should include are: Name of researcher, Date of research, Central factor affecting leisure patterns, Central findings, Criticisms. You may wish to add further headings of your own.*

Patterns of participation

One of the concerns of the sociology of leisure has been to consider how leisure as a growing element of society appears to be distributed in ways remarkably familiar to sociologists concerned with other areas. Inequalities in participation place a question mark over theories that suggest the extent of leisure people engage in is merely a matter of personal choice.

Torkildsen (1986) lists a total of 46 factors that affect leisure choice. His full list, reproduced in Table 7.5, is divided into the three categories of personal, social and circumstantial and opportunity factors.

Table 7.5 Influences on leisure participation

Personal	*Social and circumstantial*	*Opportunity factors*
Age	Occupation	Resources available
Stage in life cycle	Income	Facilities – type and
Gender	Disposable income	quality
Marital status	Material wealth and	Awareness
Dependants and ages	goods	Perception of
Will and purpose in life	Car ownership and	opportunities
Personal obligations	mobility	Recreation services
Resourcefulness	Time available	Distribution of facilities
Leisure perceptions	Duties and obligations	Access and location
Attitudes and	Home and social	Choice of activities
motivation	environment	Transport
Interests and	Friends and peer	Costs: before, during
preoccupations	groups	after
Skill and ability –	Social roles and	Management: policy
physical, social and	contacts	and support
intellectual	Environment factors	Marketing
Personality and	Mass leisure factors	Programming
confidence	Education and	Organization and
Culture born into	attainment	leadership
Upbringing and	Population factors	Social accessibility
background	Cultural factors	Political policies

Source: Torkildsen (1986) p 91

1) *In groups, try to provide an example of how each of these factors might affect participation in leisure activities.*
2) *Do you agree with the classifications offered here, in particular the distinction between personal and social factors?*

This section will examine the evidence on participation in leisure activities and its structuring by social divisions, some of which are familiar to sociologists, such as class, gender, ethnicity and age. One of the major problems in this area pointed out by Sue Glyptis (1989) concerns the sample sizes in the main survey referred to. Since virtually all leisure activities considered singly are minority activities, the small sample size of the General Household Survey (in 1983 it was 19,050 adults) can lead to representativeness problems. In that year, for example, the survey found fewer than 50 participants in hockey, ice skating, fencing, wrestling and boxing. We need to be aware of this problem, but in the absence of other reliable data there is little we can do about it.

Social class

Torkildsen reports that 'it is generally considered that social class, as determined by occupation, is the most influential factor in determining recreational participation'

Table 7.6 Participation in indoor sports, games and physical activities: by socio-economic group, 1990

Great Britain　　　　　　　　　　　　　　　　　　　　　　　　　　　　　　*Percentages and numbers*

	Professional	Employers and managers	Intermediate and junior non-manual	Skilled manual and own account non-professional	Semi skilled manual and personal service	Unskilled manual	All groups[1]
Percentage in each group participating in activity in the 4 weeks before interview							
Snooker, pool, billiards	14	13	10	19	12	8	14
Swimming	19	13	15	9	9	5	12
Keep fit, yoga	11	10	17	6	9	6	12
Darts	5	6	5	11	7	6	7
Weightlifting, training	7	5	4	5	3	2	5
Tenpin bowls, skittles	5	4	4	3	3	1	4
Badminton	5	3	4	2	1	1	3
Squash	9	5	2	2	1	1	3
Soccer	4	2	1	2	1	1	2
Table tennis	2	2	2	1	1	1	2
Carpet bowls	1	2	1	1	1	1	1
Self-defence	1	1	1	1	–	–	1
Ice skating	1	–	1	–	1	–	1
Basketball	–	–	–	–	–	–	1
Sample size (= 100%) (numbers)	680	2,355	5,666	3,602	3,302	970	17,574

1. Includes full-time students, members of the Armed forces, people who have never worked, and inadequately described occupations.

Source: *Social Trends* (1993), p. 146

Table 7.7 Participation in outdoor sports, games and physical activities, by socio-economic group, 1990

Great Britain   *Percentages and numbers*

	Professional	Employers and managers	Intermediate and junior non-manual	Skilled manual and own account non-professional	Semi skilled manual and personal service	Unskilled manual	All groups[1]
Percentage in each group participating in activity in the 4 weeks before interview							
Walking	51	45	43	40	35	31	41
Cycling	13	8	9	9	9	8	9
Golf	13	10	4	5	2	1	5
Running (ncluding jogging, etc.)	11	6	5	4	3	2	5
Swimming	8	5	4	4	2	2	4
Soccer	6	3	3	5	2	2	4
Tennis	4	3	2	1	1	1	2
Fishing	3	2	1	3	2	2	2
Lawn bowls	1	2	1	2	1	1	1
Water sports (excluding sailing)	3	2	1	1	–	–	1
Cricket	2	1	1	1	–	–	1
Horse riding	1	1	1	1	1	–	1
Field sports	1	2	–	1	–	–	1
Sailing	3	1	1	1	–	–	1
Hockey	1	1	1	–	–	–	1
Sample size (= 100%) (numbers)	680	2,355	5,666	3,602	3,302	970	17,574

1. Includes full-time students, members of the Armed forces, people who have never worked, and inadequately described occupations.

Source: *Social Trends* (1993), p. 147

(p. 96). On the basis of evidence from the General Household survey, he finds that the effect is greatest in relation to participation in outdoor sports, with a participation rate of about 50 per cent for professional workers, falling to 20 per cent for unskilled manual workers.

Glyptis notes similar differences in relation to indoor sport (with 34 per cent participation by professional workers and 15 per cent for unskilled manual), open-air outings (23 per cent professional, less than 11 per cent unskilled manual) and entertainment (28 per cent professional, 9 per cent unskilled manual). She argues that key factors are inequalities in income and discrepancies in the pattern of car ownership. The Countryside Commission also found that car owners were three times as likely as non-car owners to visit the countryside.

1) *To what extent do Tables 7.6 and 7.7 (reported in* Social Trends, *but originally derived from data collected as part of the General Household Survey) confirm the points made by Glyptis on the basis of earlier information from the General Household Survey?*

2) *Make a list of any changes between the period reported by Glyptis and these figures for 1990.*

3) *Are there any activities in 1990 which do not present a clear social class trend in terms of participation constantly rising or declining throughout the social class scale?*

Which sports show the greatest level of differential involvement by social class, and which show the least?

Differential incomes can clearly explain some of the discrepancies in terms of leisure participation by social class. However, other writers, taking a neo-Marxist position, have also pointed to the greater amount of social control exercised over traditional working-class leisure activities. Clarke and Critcher note that the introduction of the Poor Law Amendment Act of 1834 had effects on leisure as well as work. Street football, street entertainers and other street-based forms of leisure were banned as a result of the 1835 Highways Act. However, perhaps the best example of class bias is the 1835 Cruelty to Animals Act. In order to avoid disrupting the hunting and shooting activities of the upper classes, this legislation was confined to domestic animals. Ian Henry comments: 'Animal baiting, throwing at cocks and the holding of public cockfights were all banned although the hunting, shooting and fishing of the middle classes were left intact, providing good evidence of the selective nature of the establishments' opprobrium for cruel sports' (Henry 1993, pp. 7–8). All neo-Marxist writers are, however, at pains to point out that attempts to reduce leisure outlets for workers with the explicit aim of encouraging greater work discipline were resisted by the workers in numerous ways.

Much contemporary leisure is based on commercial outlets, so the dominant form of choice is consumer choice. Clarke and Critcher point out that this kind of choice is dependent on access to hard cash: 'The much-vaunted democracy of the marketplace (where rational individuals exercise their free choices) rests on the rather less democratic foundations of the profoundly unequal distribution of wealth and income' (1986, p. 96). This observation has become even more relevant as the New Right governments of the 1980s and 1990s have raised these inequalities to new heights.

Control of leisure is now in the hands of large entertainment conglomerates, and the concentration of ownership is greatest in the area of home-based leisure, which has grown in recent years.

Consult books on the leisure industry to investigate the extent to which commercial leisure provision is concentrated in the hands of large conglomerates. Make a list of the names of these conglomerates and which areas of the leisure industry they operate in.

The expansion of business sponsorship also threatens to subordinate leisure activities to the profit motive. Clarke and Critcher note that those who have argued most loudly about the need to keep 'politics' out of sport have been only too willing to let commercial interests in – yet these interests can influence sport at least as much as the feared political activists. To take one instance, during the 1994 soccer World Cup players were required to play in unbearable midday temperatures to satisfy the requirements of the television companies.

Another contemporary example of the commercial control of leisure is the increased regulation of public space in the 1990s. The growth of shopping malls (see Figure 7.1) has reduced the amount of available public space since these developments are private property and usually impose stringent restrictions on the type of activity permitted within them.

Figure 7.1 Private development proposals around London, 1987

Source: *New Society,* 8 May 1987

Major out-of-town, drive-in shopping and leisure centres proposed in Greater London, beside the M25 motorway or near to it.	
	Site Area
1 Waterdale Park, Bricket Wood, St Albans. Town and City Properties.	80 acres
2 Runnymede Centre, Wraysbury, Berks. ARC Properties.	80 acres
3 Hewitts Park, Chelsfield, Orpington, Kent. Prudential Assurance Co.	500 acres
4 Blue Water Park, Swanscombe, Kent. Blue Circle Property Holdings.	330 acres
5 Lakeside, Grays, Thurrocks, Essex. Capital and Counties PLC.	123 acres
6 Royal Docks, Greater London. Rosehaugh Stanhope PLC.	250 acres
7 Leybourne Grange, Nr Maidstone, Kent. New Ideal Developments Ltd.	420 acres
8 Sandon Springs, Luton, Beds. Blue Circle Property Holdings.	355 acres
9 Elmbridge Mall, Hook, Kingston-upon-Thames. London and Edinburgh Trust.	54 acres

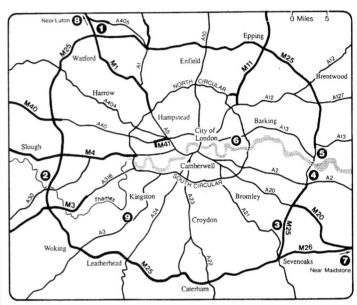

How do you think most people travel to these places? How might this lead to unequal distribution of access to them?

The Criminal Justice and Public Order Act 1994 includes several provisions placing controls on leisure activities including rave parties, seemingly with the aim of protecting private property and privacy in general.

Social class is clearly related to occupation, so the effects of unemployment are relevant here. Glyptis studied 60 unemployed people in Nottingham who were a sub-sample of a larger study on leisure. She acknowledges that they are not representative of unemployed people in general and that the sample size is very small; nonetheless, detailed information about their activities reveals different patterns of behaviour, which she groups into the following categories:

- The home-bound unemployed. These people were mostly young, aged 16–24, and more men than women. They spent between 17 and 33 hours a week on leisure, all but a few hours indoors, and passed a significant amount of time alone or with their immediate family only. The women spent less time on leisure than the men.

- The outward-bound unemployed. Again young males predominated, though there was a greater mix of age groups here. This group spent between 27 per cent and

65 per cent of their leisure time out of the home and therefore spent more leisure time with their friends.

- The busy unemployed. These tended to be older men in their fifties, often with working wives whose job seemed to provide a structure and routine for the household.

Figures 7.2 and 7.3 summarize case studies of two of these leisure types.

Figure 7.2 A home-bound unemployed man

Source: Glyptis (1989), p. 114

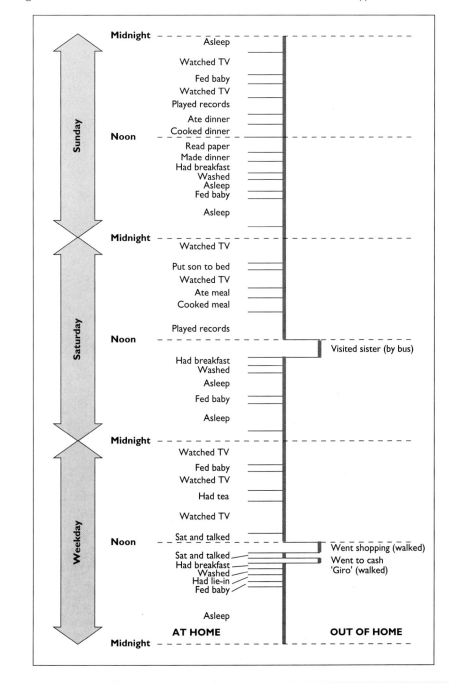

Figure 7.3 An outward-bound unemployed man

Source: Glyptis (1989), p. 119

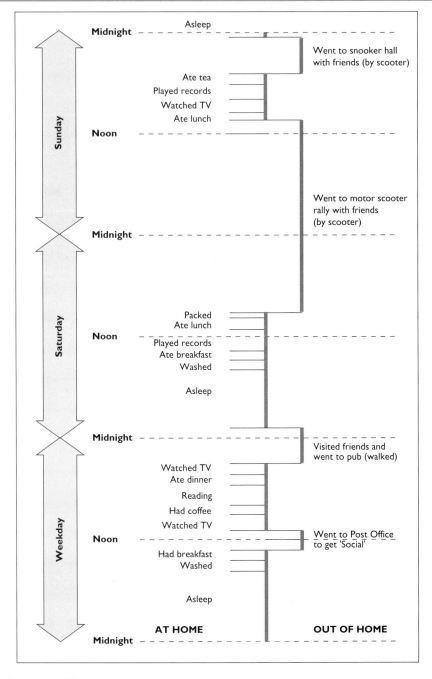

Gender and leisure

Gender is an important factor not only in terms of the time available for leisure but in terms of the type of leisure activities undertaken.

Rosemary Deem (1988, 1990) has pointed to the way in which the patriarchal structures of society constrain the amount of leisure time available for women. The key social relation responsible for this is the continued highly gendered domestic division of labour.

> *Explain the meaning of this statement in your own words. Try to provide examples of how the household may constrain the leisure time and facilities available for women.*

While there is some evidence that household tasks are shared more equally if the woman is in full-time as opposed to part-time paid employment, she will almost certainly not be fully compensated for the extra hours of work she is putting in. The net result is that the free time per weekday available to women in full-time paid employment in 1991–2 was 3.3 hours compared to 4.8 hours for males in full-time paid employment. Even women in part-time paid employment only enjoyed 4.7 hours free time per weekday (see Figure 7.4).

Figure 7.4 Free time in a typical week, by sex and employment status, 1992–3

Source: *Social Trends* (1994), p. 129

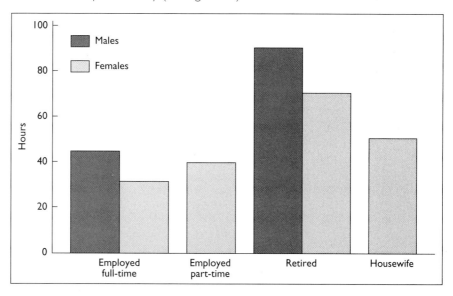

There is also evidence from the official statistics that patterns of domestic labour (particularly in relation to childcare) are becoming more rather than less gendered over time. The care of sick children was mainly done by men in 1 per cent of cases in 1984, rising to 2 per cent in 1987. However, the percentage of households where this responsibility fell mainly on women rose from 63 per cent in 1984 to 67 per cent in 1987. The net result was that the percentage of households where this task was shared equally fell from 35 per cent in 1984 to 30 per cent in 1987 (*Social Trends* 1990).

The classification of domestic labour activities undertaken by women in the household as leisure in government surveys until quite recently also served to fuel the debate about the privatization of leisure. It was argued that leisure lifestyles were becoming more home-centred, but examination of the data reveals that much of what is classified as leisure for women sounds remarkably like housework. For example, the 1977 General Household Survey recorded needlework/knitting as a frequent social/cultural activity for women. A similar phenomenon can be seen in relation to the mainly male pastime of DIY. Here more than anywhere, the increasing popularity of the notion of unpaid work in the household has caused a re-evaluation of the meaning of the terms work and leisure.

> Social Trends (1990) includes the following as social and cultural activities:

Activity	Percentage participating		
	All males	All females	All persons
House repairs/DIY	54	27	39
Needlework/knitting/dressmaking	3	49	27

1) Look up more recent copies of Social Trends to see if there have been changes to the patterns shown here.
2) Do you think these activities should be classified as leisure or work?
3) What effect might changes in participation in these activities have on the extent of work and leisure?

Thus leisure participation is clearly affected by gender: 'The continuing responsibilities of most women for household work and the care of dependants, whether in conjunction with paid employment or not, have been shown ... to have a considerable impact on the constraints, leisure time, leisure values and leisure experiences of women' (Deem 1990, p. 139). Deem's research in Milton Keynes also pointed to the impact of more general patriarchal relations in affecting leisure. She found that many women were constrained from engaging in certain activities unaccompanied by men because of fears of sexual harassment either at the location of the leisure activity of during the journey to and from it. For Deem this was evidence of the way men's control over women's sexuality constrains their leisure choices.

A similar piece of research in Sheffield conducted by Green, Hebron and Woodward (1990) also found that women were strongly discouraged or prevented from attending certain leisure facilities (notably pubs and discos) by the attitude of their male partners, presumably their concern was that other men would be present in such places.

The area of leisure where there appears to be the greatest gender disparity is that of sport. Glyptis reports that participation in outdoor sport by men is about 150 per cent of that of women, and for indoor sports it is about 200 per cent that of women (see Table 7.8). Men are also twice as likely as women to be spectators at sports events:

Table 7.8 Participation in sports, games and physical activities (percentage taking part in the four weeks prior to interview)

		Men	Women
At least one outdoor activity, excluding walking	1977	23	8
	1980	24	9
	1983	25	10
At least one outdoor activity, including walking	1977	35	21
	1980	37	24
	1983	39	24
At least one indoor activity	1977	31	13
	1980	32	15
	1983	33	18

Source: Glyptis (1989), p. 99

> Sports participation, in particular, runs counter to social expectations of women ... Girls are expected to play with dolls, do needlework, play netball and help around the house; boys are expected to play rugby and football, and do woodwork and car maintenance. A few forms of sport are generally seen as a legitimate interest for women, such as horse riding, aerobics and keep fit; others, such as football, remain suspect. [Glyptis 1989, pp. 99–100]

The General Household Survey also shows that there are clear differences in terms of other outdoor leisure activities undertaken by men and women. Women are more likely to visit the theatre or go dancing, whereas men are much more likely to go out for a drink and engage in sport. The only activity consistently engaged in equally by both sexes is going out for a meal, which is perhaps not surprising since this is an activity most often engaged in by couples.

Women's leisure activities as such are much more likely to be centred on the home, though, as we have noted, there is the problem of delineating what is leisure and what is work in activities such as looking after children and cooking.

Many other social divisions interact with gender in the leisure patterns of women. One factor often forgotten is age. This is important in relation to women and leisure because the majority of the elderly population is female. As Green *et al.* (1990) point out, 'the experience of many elderly women is widowhood and the end of their "couple" relationship on which so much leisure activity is predicated' (p. 82). They point out that older women therefore tend to have very different patterns of leisure activity than younger women. However, younger women still experience more restrictions than young men. Gendered norms about sexual activity mean that the leisure activities of young women are more likely to be more heavily policed by parents than are those of young men.

Christine Griffin, in a study of work, leisure and cultural resistance among young women aged 14–18 entitled *Typical Girls* (1985), began by considering whether the model of youth subcultures developed in relation to males was appropriate for the study of adolescent females. She concluded that divisions such as 'the lads' and 'the earoles', developed by Paul Willis in his study *Learning to Labour* (1977) could not easily be applied to young girls because of the different patterns of friendship and socializing. The fact that she found that most friendship groups were single sex also underlines the importance of gender among this age group.

Young women did not go around in gangs but socialized with one or two best friends. Young women's forms of resistance to the perceived acceptable routes into jobs did not coincide with friendship groups as they did for males in Willis's study. Griffin argues that while their reactions to and resistance towards their perceived place in the labour market may be important for boys, girls face the additional and cross-cutting pressures of the marriage market. Getting involved in a steady relationship tended to lead to isolation from other female friends for young girls, while boys still kept up contact with their male friends in such situations. Girls might thus suffer isolation in a future marriage, but Griffin notes that they devised strategies of resistance to help ensure they maintained contact with their female friends. Nonetheless this does point to the possible ways in which the process of becoming part of a couple can have different effects upon men and women in terms of their circle of friends, who are important partners in future leisure activities.

Find a recent copy of statistics on leisure participation by gender in Social Trends *or the* General Household Survey. *Write a short report on the extent to which participation is affected by gender.*

Are there any significant modifications to the conclusions outlined here that you feel need to be made in the light of your findings?

Ethnicity

Ethnic minorities are less well off on average than the white population, so they suffer proportionately more severely from the restrictions on access to leisure facilities imposed by the shortage of money. In addition, fear of racism and racist attacks further deters some members of ethnic minority communities from participation in leisure activities.

These are two of the reasons that 'despite the influence of assimilationist policy over provision, the signs are that the social networks of people of different ethnic groups have always remained relatively segregated, particularly in the sphere of leisure' (Kew, quoted in Glyptis 1989, p. 104). Another reason is that culture has an important influence on leisure pursuits, and there is a clear connection between culture and ethnicity. Many studies have focused on ethnic cultural lifestyles as a form of activity which can be classed both as leisure and as an assertion of identity, and therefore also a form of resistance in the face of racial disadvantage and discrimination.

Cultural activities are emphasized in the writings of those associated with the Centre for Contemporary Cultural Studies, based at Birmingham University. This group has used Gramsci's notion of hegemony, which stresses the importance of ideological and cultural struggle, to develop a new theory of sub-cultures in society as potential sources of resistance to dominant ideas. In their book *Resistance Through Rituals* they argue that youth sub-cultures 'win space for the young, cultural space in the neighbourhood and institutions, real time for leisure and recreation, actual room on the street or street-corner' (Hall and Jefferson 1976). This view of sub-cultures can be applied to the resistance of ethnic minorities to racism in society. Paul Gilroy (1992) argues that cultural politics based in the community is an important form of resistance in black communities in contemporary Britain. Leisure and cultural activities are therefore also political acts.

Mike Davis (1990) argues that gangs such as the Crips and the Bloods sprang up in Los Angeles in the 1960s as an expression of Black resistance to the notorious racism of the Los Angeles Police Department at the time. They filled the gap left by the destruction of more avowedly political groups, notably the Black Panthers, in the wake of the Watts riots.

Brian Cross (1993) traces a link between the emergence of these groups and the later emergence of the musical styles which are classed under the heading of rap. In a series of interviews with leading rap artists he explores the social and political commentary in the work of groups such as Public Enemy, Run DMC, NWA and rap artists such as Ice Cube and Easy E. This style of cultural expression has aroused controversy, however, not only for its anti-racist message but also for the attitude towards women and gays expressed in the lyrics of some rap artists.

Studies of Afro-Caribbean communities in the UK, such as Ken Pryce's study of Bristol (1979), have also emphasized the way in which cultural styles emerge as a

Figure 7.5 Lifestyle map showing the impact of 'slave labour' and 'shit-work' on the lifestyles of West Indians in Bristol

Source: Haywood *et al.* (1989), p. 40

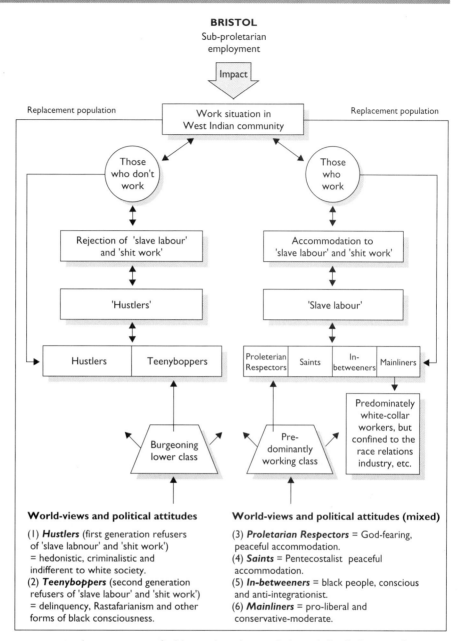

response to the structures of white society that exclude and discriminate against them (see Figure 7.5).

O'Donnell (1991) has suggested that British Asians tend more towards separatism than do Afro-Caribbeans, a contention supported by Dahya (1973), who found that Pakistanis in the UK are concentrated together in inner-city areas. However, unlike earlier writers who portrayed this concentration as a result of racial discrimination, Dahya argues that it is an active choice undertaken to defend their ethnic cultural identities.

Another example of Asian culture that harks back to traditional roots in the Punjab but also recognizes the position of young Asians in modern industrial Britain is the increasingly popular Bhangra music. What started out as dance music to celebrate the gathering of the crop in the rural areas of the Punjab has become a mass-produced modern musical form for British Asians. Young people in Asian families, finding themselves constrained from visiting evening discos, evolved the all-dayer, a form of gathering in which Bhangra music flourished.

1) *What elements of culture might be important in affecting differential participation in various leisure activities by ethnic group? Make a list of the possible factors involved and explain how they might affect leisure participation.*

2) *What evidence can you find in musical styles developed by ethnic minorities in the UK and the USA for the idea that such forms of sub-culture might act as a form of resistance to racism? Make a list of examples included in this section and from your own knowledge of contemporary musical styles.*

Age

As one might expect, active participation in various sports falls off with increasing age (see Table 7.9). Meanwhile other leisure activities, particularly home-based activities such as gardening and DIY, are more likely to form part of the leisure lifestyle of the middle-aged and the older generations. Activities such as watching TV and reading do not appear to be particularly influenced by age.

Table 7.9 Participation in the most popular sports, games and physical activities, by age, 1990

Great Britain — *Percentages and numbers*

	16–19	20–24	25–29	30–44	45–59	60–69	70 and over	All aged 16 and over	Median age of participants
Percentage in each group participating in each activity in the 12 months before interview									
Walking	72	70	73	73	69	61	37	65	41
Swimming	70	65	63	58	35	20	6	42	34
Snooker, poll, billiards	56	46	37	25	13	7	3	22	29
Keep fit, yoga	31	35	31	23	14	9	5	19	33
Cycling	41	23	22	22	13	8	4	17	35
Darts	29	26	21	15	10	4	2	13	31
Golf	21	19	18	15	11	7	2	12	35
Tenpin bowls, skittles	26	26	19	15	7	2	1	11	30
Running, jogging	30	20	18	13	3	1	–	9	28
Soccer	33	23	18	9	2	–	–	9	25
Weightlifting, training	27	24	20	10	3	–	–	9	27
Badminton	32	18	13	10	4	1	–	9	27
Tennis	29	16	11	9	3	1	–	7	27
Squash	15	15	15	8	2	–	–	6	27
Fishing	11	7	8	8	6	3	1	6	36

Source: *Social Trends* (1993), Table 10.25

The young and the retired both have more time available for leisure pursuits than other groups, but there is more commercial provision for the young since they have larger disposable incomes. Music and fashion for teenagers have been growing steadily in importance since the 1950s.

 Use the information contained in Table 7.9 to assess the importance of age as a factor in determining participation in leisure activities.

Explaining the inequalities in participation

The early studies in the sociology of leisure attempted to locate the crucial factors determining patterns of leisure participation. We have examined these factors in the last section. More recent theories have attempted to locate leisure within an overall theory of society, and in so doing they touch on one of the most common divisions in sociology, namely that between social structural theories and social action theories.

In a comprehensive survey of recent theories of leisure, Haywood *et al.* (1989) summarize these two approaches. According to the social structural approach, leisure is determined by the power of society over the individual; the forms of leisure function to preserve the existing social order by controlling and coercing the individual's leisure 'choices'. In contrast, the social action perspective tends to view leisure as the result of individual choices made in relative freedom; leisure is thus a relatively autonomous sphere of society free from the constraints characteristic of other spheres of society.

There have been attempts to overcome this dualism by developing theories that take account of both the social structuring of leisure and the individual actions of leisure participants and leisure providers. We will look at two such attempts.

Pierre Bourdieu: cultural capital and cultural competence

One of the more recent influential accounts of the social structuring of participation in leisure is to be found in the work of Pierre Bourdieu. He has produced a comprehensive theory of leisure participation in his book *Distinction: A Social Critique of the Judgement of Taste* (1984).

For Bourdieu, the choices we make about the leisure we engage in are not totally free from structural constraints. He acknowledges that social factors such as our income, our age, our gender and the cost of various leisure pursuits constrain our leisure choices, but argues that nonetheless, when these have been taken into account, there are still a variety of possible leisure activities we might engage in. He wants to explain what influences our choices in this situation. This moves the analysis away from the sort of economic constraints found in Marxist versions of theories of leisure and into the arena of cultural choices.

Bourdieu's explanation for the differences and inequalities in leisure pursuits even within the area of free choice rests upon the notions of cultural capital and cultural competence that are needed to engage in certain leisure activities. He argues that our childhood experiences and upbringing in a particular family and class background create a 'habitus', a set of unconscious tastes, perceptions and preferences which provide the basis for the cultural capital and cultural competencies we have as adults.

The concept of cultural capital is central to the work of Bourdieu. He argues that while our upbringings provide the basis for a variety of cultural styles, none of which is inherently superior, the dominant class can use its power to impose its own view of what is best on the rest of society. Members of this class therefore have the ability to use their power derived from capital (money) to create cultural capital for themselves, by defining their own particular cultural styles as superior. Bourdieu particularly argues that this process can be seen in the education system. However, the idea is also applicable to leisure, since style and taste are crucial differentiating criteria for leisure involvement, producing consistent and interdependent preferences through all our leisure activities.

We make our choices about leisure activities partly in relation to other people's choices. Those who prefer high culture often do so because this form of leisure confers social distinction, since others are excluded from this arena because they do not possess the necessary cultural competence to appreciate it. The choice is therefore mainly about differentiating ourselves from others, so according to Bourdieu cultural tastes are also about distaste for others:

> Our tastes do indeed express us or betray us more than our judgements, in politics for example. And perhaps nothing is harder to bear than other people's 'bad' taste. Aesthetic intolerance can be terribly violent. Tastes are inseparable from distastes: aversion to different lifestyles is perhaps one of the strongest barriers between the classes. [Bourdieu 1993, p. 104]

Bourdieu's theory explores new terrain in that it attempts to provide an explanation of the leisure choices people make in terms of a whole theory of socialization and social differentiation.

Bourdieu and Passeron (1977) identified the education system as a key agency of cultural reproduction. Use your textbooks to research their ideas on education and write a short report explaining how these provide a link between the sociology of education and the sociology of leisure.

Norbert Elias and figurational sociology

Another attempt to go beyond the structure/action dichotomy characteristic of so much work in leisure theory and indeed sociology in general has been made by Norbert Elias, who has developed what he calls 'figurational sociology' (Elias 1978).

Figurations are the things that bind us together, the whole array of complex interdependencies that create networks of people. Individual actions and choices, according to Elias, can only be analysed by reference to the set of networks or figurations in which they are situated. All such figurations have power; the key question is how that power and the resources that go with it are distributed within the figuration in which an individual is located.

In modern-day society the systems of interdependence that a relationship or involvement includes are becoming more and more complex. Elias argues that if power is shared between the participants in a figuration, the outcome of the interplay of individual interests is unlikely to be dictated by any one individual and is therefore not likely to be anticipated by any of the individuals involved. Haywood *et al.* summarize this thought:

Elias's enduring contribution to understanding leisure activities is therefore to suggest that explanations of individual *actions*, whether as providers or consumers, can only be explained by reference to the chains of interdependency within which such action takes place. Moreover, social *structures* are to be understood not as an abstract entity, but as networks of actors. Hence the idea of figurations is an explanation both of individual action and of social structure. [Haywood *et al.* 1989, p. 287]

Elias shares with Freud and the later Frankfurt School an interest in the development of civilization. Specific and complicated historical circumstances ('figurations') result in the development of a self demarcated from society and also notions of bodily self-restraint. Over time there is a shift from societies in which behaviour is restrained by others to ones characterized by self-restraint. Social behaviour becomes more subtle and there is a growing concern with concepts of civilized behaviour, and in consequence people come to act in a restrained way even when alone.

Elias applies this theory to the development of society in general; for example, he cites the change from unrestrained killing in the feudal era to the regulated conduct of civilized armies subject to the Geneva convention. However, perhaps the most famous application of Elias's notion has been Eric Dunning's work on the development of sport and leisure (Dunning 1971; Dunning and Sheard 1979). He argues that sport has evolved from folk games, in which there were high levels of violence and unwritten rules, into highly organized rituals with clearly outlined rules of behaviour (see Table 7.10).

Table 7.10 Characteristics of folk games and modern sporting games (after Dunning)

Folk games	Modern sporting games
High toleration of physical violence; open and spontaneous 'battle-excitement'	Low toleration of physical violence; controlled and sublimated 'battle-excitement'
Simple unwritten rules transmitted orally	Formal, codified rules transmitted through bureaucratic channels
Regional variations in rules, equipment	International standardisation of rules, equipment
No precise space and time boundaries or numbers of participants	Precise space and time boundaries, or numbers of participants
Emphasis on force as opposed to skill	Emphasis on skill as opposed to force
Little division of labour (role differentiation) amongst players	High division of labour (role differentiation) amongst players
Playing and spectating roles loosely distinguished	Playing and spectating roles strictly separate

Source: Haywood *et al.* (1989), p. 292

Critics of Elias's work suggest that he is merely offering a new form of evolutionary theory, more complex but still similar to the earlier functionalist theories of the evolution of complex societies. For example, Anthony Giddens (1984) argues that Elias tends to view the civilizations of Western Europe as superior to the oral cultures studied by anthropologists. However, the anthropologists' studies show that these societies are highly complex, and to conclude from the evidence of spontaneous behaviour that they lack moral prohibitions is simply wrong. Once the notion of 'uncivilized' societies is rejected the picture of evolution proposed in Elias's *The Civilizing Process* begins to break down.

A second criticism, raised by Helmut Kuzmics (1988), is that in the modern world there has been no shortage of barbarism. The behaviour of the Nazis, for instance, not only tends to undermine the evolutionary idea but also calls into question the importance attached to the idea of civilization itself, since the Nazi leadership generally had good table manners and listened to classical music. The explanation for their barbaric behaviour therefore has to be sought elsewhere, for example in the logic of capitalist production.

Supporters of Elias reply, however, that his theory does not present evolution in a simple linear fashion, and although it has similarities with Weber's theory of rationalization, Elias was aware of the dark side of this process.

1) *How might the notion of the growth of civilization and the development of self-restraint be applied to sport and leisure?*
2) *Do you agree that leisure has become more civilized as time progresses? How might Clarke and Critcher feel about this argument?*

Conclusion

The sociology of leisure started out as an adjunct to the sociology of work but has now become important in its own right. Combined with cultural studies, it becomes a very wide-ranging investigation into the consumption behaviours apparent in modern societies.

The relative importance of production and consumption in contemporary society is at the heart of many of the current debates and developments in social theory. This issue will be considered in more depth in Chapter 8.

Structured question

Item A

In Britain and other Western societies there exists a variety of taste publics that possess contrasting interests generated by their different circumstances . . . In recreation and other sphere the public uses its leisure to nurture life styles that supply experiences which the individuals concerned seek and value . . . This is the reality of modern leisure, and theories which fail to spotlight this aspect of reality prove only their own need of revision.

Source: Adapted from Roberts (1978), p. 86

Item B

The probability of practising the different sports depends, to a different degree for each sport, primarily on economic capital and secondarily on cultural capital and spare time; it does so through the affinity between the ethical and aesthetic dispositions associated with a particular position in the social space and the profits which, on the basis of these dispositions, appear to be offered by the various sports.

Source: Bourdieu (1993), p. 129

Item C

As society has become more postmodern, leisure has moved from having had a mass basis towards being more individualized in the composition of pursuits. This has increased the opportunity for individuals to choose how to spend their leisure time. One of the contradictions involved in this change is that leisure itself has become dependent on large-scale organizations rather than individual autonomy and this has allowed the range of leisure pursuits to expand. But, at the same time, leisure provision has become more standardized as the leisure industries offer similar leisure products.

This can be seen in one of the more popular leisure activities – shopping. While the range of goods available in the shops has increased enormously and many products have come within the financial reach of employed people, the growth of national chain stores has meant that the same products are available throughout the country at standardized prices. This leads to the contradictory situation that individual choice increases, while national choice becomes restricted.

Source: Lawson (1993), pp. 103–4

Item D

Gender as a social division in leisure does not simply produce the effect that women have less time than men and are less mobile; it redefines time and space for women as compared with men. Women are expected – and come themselves to expect – to participate in those leisure activities defined as appropriate for women, at those times and in those places compatible with established female roles. All these are severe enough limitations on the access to and enjoyment of leisure. But there is more, for the inferior status of women's leisure has as its obverse the superiority of men's interests within leisure.

Coursework suggestions

Investigate in detail the social divisions in participation in a leisure activity of your choice. Outline these divisions and if possible conduct

Throughout our discussion, we have tended to show how leisure reflects social divisions ultimately rooted outside leisure itself. In so far as leisure is dependent on the social organization of work and family life, this is a valid approach. Leisure however does more than simply reflect social divisions. It 'realizes' them, becoming one of the powerful means by which social divisions receive expression and validation. This double relationship is evident in the case of gender. The quantitative and qualitative differences between male and female are first of all an extension of the sexual division of labour within society as a whole. They are also secondly ways in which the dominant definitions of what it means to be male or female are enforced and confirmed. Leisure 'celebrates' gender differences.

Source: Clarke and Critcher (1985), pp. 160–1

1) Identify the sociological perspective adopted by the author of Item A. **(1 mark)**

2) Explain the meaning of the term 'cultural capital' (Item B) and explain the role that it plays in Bourdieu's explanation of leisure pursuits. **(4 marks)**

3) Suggest one other leisure activity where the contradictory effects outlined in Item C may be applicable. **(1 mark)**

4) The author of Item C argues that 'as society has become more postmodern, leisure has moved from having had a mass basis towards being more individualized in the composition of pursuits'. To what extent is this view of leisure supported by sociological evidence? **(9 marks)**

5) Using material from the items and elsewhere, assess the arguments for and against the assertion in Item D that 'leisure reflects social divisions ultimately rooted outside leisure itself'. **(10 marks)**

interviews with participants in this leisure activity in your area. Use these interviews to investigate both the actuality of social divisions in

participation and also whether the participants themselves are aware of these divisions.
Analyse your data using the theories of leisure offered by sociologists. Include the work both of older theories of leisure such as Parker and Roberts as well as the newer theories of Bourdieu and Elias. Evaluate the relative usefulness of these theories in explaining your data. Remember, testing theories requires that you have a detailed knowledge of them before you ask any questions.

Bibliography

Bourdieu, P. (1984) *Distinction: A Social Critique of the Judgement of Taste*, London: Routledge

—— (1993) *Sociology in Question,* London: Sage

—— and Passeron, J. (1977) *Reproduction in Education, Society and Culture,* London: Sage

Clarke, J. and Critcher, C. (1985) *The Devil Makes Work,* London, Macmillan

Cross, B. (1993) *It's Not About a Salary: Rap, Race and Resistance in Los Angeles*, London: Verso

Dahya, B. (1973) 'Pakistanis in Britain: transients or settlers?', *Race*, Vol. 14, No. 3, January

Davis, M. (1990) *City of Quartz: Excavating the Future of Los Angeles,* London: Verso

Deem, R. (1988) *Work, Unemployment and Leisure*, London: Routledge

—— (1990) 'Women and leisure – all work and no play?', *Social Studies Review*, Vol. 5, No. 4, March

Dunning, E. (ed.) (1971) *The Sociology of Sport,* London: Frank Cass

—— and Sheard, K. (1979) *Barbarians, Gentlemen and Players,* London: Martin Robertson

Elias, N. (1978) *The Civilising Process*, Oxford: Blackwell

Green, E., Hebron, S. and Woodward, D. (1990) *Women's Leisure, What Leisure?*, London: Macmillan

Giddens, A. (1984) *The Constitution of Society,* Cambridge: Polity

Gilroy, P. (1992) *There Ain't No Black in the Union Jack,* London: Routledge

Glyptis, S. (1989) *Leisure and Unemployment,* Milton Keynes: Open University Press

Griffin, C. (1985) *Typical Girls? Young Women from School to the Job Market,* London: Routledge

Hall, S. and Jefferson, T. (eds) (1976) *Resistance Through Rituals,* London: Hutchison

Haralambos, M. and Holborn, M. (1995) *Sociology: Themes and Perspectives*, 4th edn, London: Collins Educational

Haywood, L. *et al.* (1989) *Understanding Leisure,* Cheltenham: Stanley Thornes

Henry, I. (1993) *The Politics of Leisure Policy,* London: Macmillan

Joseph, M. (1986) *Sociology for Everyone*, Cambridge: Polity

Kusmics, H. (1988) 'The civilizing process', in Keane, J. (ed.) *Civil Society and the State,* London: Verso

Lawson, T. (1993) *Sociology for A-Level: A Skills-based Approach*, London: Collins Educational

Oakley, A. (1974) *The Sociology of Housework,* Oxford: Martin Robertson

O'Donnell, M. (1991) *Race and Ethnicity*, London: Longman

—— (1992) *A New Introduction to Sociology*, 3rd edn, Walton-on-Thames: Nelson

Parker, S. (1976) *The Sociology of Leisure,* London: Allen & Unwin

—— (1983) *Leisure and Work,* London: Allen & Unwin

Pryce, K. (1979) *Endless Pressure*, Harmondsworth: Penguin

Rapoport, R. and Rapoport, R. (1975) *Leisure and the Family Life Cycle,* London: Routledge & Kegan Paul

Roberts, K. (1978) *Contemporary Society and the Growth of Leisure,* London: Longman

—— (1981) *Leisure,* 2nd edn, London: Longman

—— (1986) 'Leisure', in Haralambos, M. (ed.) *Developments in Sociology*, Vol. 2, Ormskirk: Causeway Press

Social Science Research Council/Sports Council (1978) *Report of the Joint Working Party on Recreation Research,* London: SSRC/SC

Thompson, E.P. (1993) *Customs in Common,* Harmondsworth: Penguin

Torkildsen, G. (1986) *Leisure and Recreation Management,* 2nd edn, London: Chapman & Hall

Willis, P. (1977) *Learning to Labour*, Farnborough: Saxon House

Young, M. and Willmott, P. (1961) *The Symmetrical Family*, Harmondsworth: Penguin

From production to consumption? Postmodernism, leisure, culture and society

Eclecticism is the degree zero of contemporary general culture: one listens to reggae, watches a Western, eats McDonalds food for lunch and local cuisine for dinner, wears Paris perfume in Tokyo and 'retro' clothes in Hong Kong; knowledge is a matter for TV games.

J.P. Lyotard, *The Postmodern Condition*, p. 76

How many of the above activities have you engaged in? How many are you likely to engage in?

It is interesting to consider why the topics of work and leisure are linked as they are in the current syllabuses (and consequently in this book). Perhaps this reflects the views predominant in sociology at the time the syllabuses were written, which might be summarized as centring on the key importance of the sphere of production in the construction of social identity. Connected with this is the importance of class as an explanatory device. Despite enormous differences and debates over exactly what class is, it is certainly concerned in some way with work, occupations, jobs and incomes, that is, the sphere of production.

1) Why was production central to the classical sociologists?
2) To what extent was class an important concept in the work of Weber, Marx and Durkheim?

This position has often been treated with scepticism or downright hostility in recent times. It has been denounced as an example of economic determinism, seeking to explain the whole of social life in terms of essentially economic activities. For instance, Mark Poster (1988) argues that the work of Jean Baudrillard is significant precisely because it 'shatters the existing foundations for critical social theory, showing how the privilege they give to labour and their rationalist epistemologies are inadequate for the analysis of the media and other new social activities' (p. 8).

The attempt to produce total theories of society was rejected by pluralist thinkers and later by the postmodernists.

There is an excellent summary of the ideas associated with postmodernism in Social Studies Review, *September 1990, and a more detailed review of postmodernism and culture in* Sociology Review, *April 1992. Jones (1993) also explains some of the theoretical bases of this trend in social thought. Obtain*

> *copies of these works and write a 500-word report on the postmodernists'
> rejection of total theories of society. Which theorists does this rejection target?*

In response to these types of criticism, which hit the Marxist view of society hardest, neo-Marxists developed theories that explained society as consisting of a number of elements, notably the economic, the social, the political and the cultural or ideological. The link between these elements is not direct. Other spheres of society have 'relative autonomy' from the economic, and must be considered as realities in themselves. The most important examples of this approach are found in the theories of the Frankfurt School and the works of Antonio Gramsci and Louis Althusser. All were concerned to consider why the key (production-defined) entity in Marxist theory, namely the working class, did not appear to be fulfilling the role laid out for it in Marxist theory. Their explanations centred largely on the cultural and ideological spheres.

Theories of culture and ideology

The Frankfurt School and Critical Theory

During the 1930s a group of Marxist-influenced writers, including Max Horkheimer, Theodor Adorno and Herbert Marcuse, who became known collectively as the Frankfurt School, developed what they termed Critical Theory (see Arato and Gebhardt 1978 or Held 1980). They explained the rise of Fascism and the failure of the working class to wage a determined fight against capitalism by arguing that the ruling class bound the working class to capitalism through its control of the culture industry, which promotes the idea of consumption as the most important activity in life.

Insofar as this strategy is successful – and writers in the Frankfurt tradition believed that it was largely successful – the working class is incorporated into capitalism through the pursuit of leisure goods and the consumption of popular culture. The workers are deluded into becoming passive creatures who believe they are free because the mass culture industry creates, and then satisfies, an endless succession of false needs. Leisure and culture become trivial and superficial, and people become incapable of critical thought. By providing the illusion of freedom, capitalism maintains its repressive hold over the working class. (For more on mass culture and the views of the Frankfurt School, see Trowler 1991.)

Gramsci and hegemony

A second Marxist view which also emphasized the realm of ideas and culture stems from the work of the Italian Communist theoretician Antonio Gramsci. Gramsci (1971) argued that the continued rule of the capitalists was to be explained in terms of their hegemony, by which he meant their dominance over the ideas and culture of society. The implication of this was that what occurred in the superstructure of society (the realm of society other than the economy) could itself have an impact and was not automatically determined by changes in the economic base.

The ruling class could only retain control insofar as it retained the consent of the working class in society. This was not guaranteed, because people might see through the dominant ideas. Economic crises did not inevitably lead to socialism, however.

Ideological and cultural struggle was necessary to break down the capitalists' hegemony if socialist change was to be achieved.

During the 1970s and 1980s Gramsci's ideas became highly influential within the British Communist Party (CPGB), and indeed other Communist Parties, and the journal of the CPGB, *Marxism Today*, vigorously promoted the need for cultural struggle. These ideas were also taken up by a group of academics associated with the Centre for Contemporary Cultural Studies at Birmingham University. These writers rejected the pessimistic analysis of the Frankfurt School about the effects of the rise of mass culture and instead developed Gramsci's notion of dual consciousness to argue that cultural struggle can sometimes be a form of resistance against capitalism. This notion can perhaps best be seen in their book, *Resistance Through Rituals* (Hall and Jefferson 1976).

However, the legacy of both Gramsci and the Frankfurt School was a belief in the need to take culture seriously as a relatively autonomous sphere of society. This fuelled the rise of cultural studies and arguments about whether popular culture was a form of indoctrination of the masses (as the Frankfurt School broadly argued) or a possible basis for cultural resistance (as followers of Antonio Gramsci inclined to believe).

Either way, culture lay at the centre of analysis. Ultimately this was to lead to the argument that culture and, importantly, the consumption of the images and signs produced by popular culture have become the central basis of social identities. Angela McRobbie (1992), for instance, has argued:

> Today, the social relationships and social movements which breathe life into society cannot be mapped with the predictability which sociologists used to look for. Such a search is doomed to fail in a situation where, for example, rapidly changing patterns of consumption offer a better sense of social identity than the old markers of occupation or class.

The emphasis on consumption and culture as a source of identity is also a central element in the set of ideas known as postmodernism.

> The centrality of class as a basis for identity has been challenged by Lash and Urry. They argue that economic and cultural changes have dislodged class as a key identity for the majority of the population . . . Bryan Turner has also highlighted the importance of status groups rather than classes (Clarke and Saunders 1991, p. 19).

Discuss the following questions:

1) What economic and cultural changes might Lash and Urry be referring to?
2) How would these dislodge class?
3) What basis of identity might replace class?
4) How might different styles of consumption act as a basis for identity?

As we will explore in more detail in a later section, the postmodernists reacted against the belief that science provided access to 'the truth' and that scientific knowledge could be used to improve society. In this context, it is important to note that sociology as a discipline is based on essentially modernist premises. That is why the postmodernist reaction against modernism has had such an impact on sociology.

Postmodernism was originally developed as a view of culture. However, it has had an impact far wider than its origins in art and architecture, notably through the influence of post-structuralism on sociology. The origins of this movement lay with the writings of the structuralists, and in particular Louis Althusser.

Louis Althusser and structuralism

Louis Althusser was a member of the French Communist Party, but a fierce critic of economic determinism (Althusser 1966, 1971; Althusser and Balibar 1970). He was an admirer of Mao Zedong, and his sympathies led him to emphasize the notion of cultural revolution rather than stressing the centrality of the working class. He combined these views with a structuralist analysis of language to develop the highly influential brand of Marxism known as Structuralist Marxism.

Structuralism has long been an influential element in French social thought. Its most important origin is probably the attempt by Ferdinand de Saussure (1974) to explain the basis of language. Saussure denied that there is any necessary link between an object and the word we use to refer to it. The sound 'dog', for instance, is not in any way inherently linked to the object 'dog'. This is important since individuals cannot develop a language in isolation – they have to adopt the prevailing meanings which were constructed before they were born. The power of human beings to consciously understand and shape their world is lessened since they have to make use of a structure of language that is determined outside their individual actions. This has important implications for social analysis, as Jones (1993) explains:

> If all this is so, then the importance of individual thought and conscious-
> ness, so central to action sociology, is minimal; language determines these
> thoughts and it is language we must explain . . .

> The reason for using the term 'structuralism' to refer to these ideas about
> language and its role in social life is thus clear. As with other structural
> theories such as Functionalism and Althusserian Marxism, the individual
> actor, agent or subject is irrelevant. The origin of social life lies in structur-
> al influences beyond the actor.

Thus structuralism 'decentred' the subject. Thus it pushed Marxism further and further away from any link to the working class, and served to intensify the importance given to notions of culture and ideology.

From structuralism to post-structuralism

A key problem arises from Althusser's attempt to retain some notion of science (the ability to know the world) but to distance himself from social action type theories which see humans as actively creating the world.

He tried to resolve this problem by introducing the notion of ideological state apparatuses; by this he meant that people engage in practices already mapped out for them which have the effect of maintaining the present economic structure. This presents a picture similar to the Frankfurt School of a strongly duped set of individuals. However, Althusser wanted to argue that we recognize this to some extent, which suggests that we are more than unsocialized individuals wholly determined by the structures of society. Yet the structuralist account tends to contradict this.

This dilemma leads to two possible choices. Althusser could keep his structuralist account of history, but to be consistent he would then have to eliminate the notion that subjects can recognize their situation. This is the position that leads to post-structuralism and the argument that it is impossible to have any knowledge of a real world and therefore any way of distinguishing between reality and illusion.

The alternative is to retain the conception of the subject able to arrive at an understanding of the world, but this requires the abandonment of the structuralist approach. This is essentially the route provided by Gramsci with his notion of dual consciousness. This still allows for a notion of ideology and therefore an explanation of why popular culture is an important element in explaining society, but it also includes a strong notion of people being able to understand the world through their everyday experiences which contribute to the struggle for hegemony.

The theory of language developed by Saussure talked of two elements, the signifier (sound-images) and the signified (object), which through their relationship created the meaning of language. Saussure himself gave no priority to the signifier or the signified; in contrast, the move to post-structuralism is precisely about assigning such a priority. Post-structuralists argue that the signifier has primacy over the signified. This leads to the final elimination of any meaning of language outside of itself. There is no link between language and the 'real' world. As Derrida (1976, p. 158) put it, 'there is nothing outside the text', meaning that it is not possible to compare language to an external reality. If a theory does not describe the real world, then the only alternative is that the theory itself creates the objects it describes.

Foucault (1970, 1972, 1980) argued that forms of thinking are like languages in that they provide us with a way to describe the world, but that these ways of thinking ('discourses') effectively create people's identity in that they constrain us to think in certain ways. We cannot test these theories out by seeing how they describe the world since the world is simply a construct of the particular way of thinking or discourse. Nor can there be any way of judging between different theories, since they are the creations of different discourses. Hence Foucault rejected the modernist notion that scientific investigation and rational thought will allow us to know the world and distinguish truth from falsehood.

Postmodernism

Out of the transformation from structuralism to post-structuralism come a number of key themes which underlie much of today's cultural analysis.

Postmodernists, following Foucault, reject the idea that it is possible to know the world in the sense that scientific explanation claims. The post-structuralist theory of language breaks the link between knowledge and reality which is the basis of science. Knowledge is held to create its own reality. We can only rely on aesthetic judgement, which does not admit of notions of truth and falsehood.

 The originators of sociology, and positivism in particular, looked to rationality and the scientific method as the basis of an understanding of human society. Postmodernism largely rejects this, and instead argues that explanations of human behaviour should mainly rest on aesthetics.

1) Look up the meaning of the term 'aesthetics' in a dictionary and consider the

implications of this postmodernist position for the meaning and methods employed by sociologists.

2) How do you think we should base our understanding of human behaviour?

Postmodernists place great emphasis on a plurality of factors in explaining phenomena and reject any attempt to provide all-embracing theories. For instance, Lyotard (1984, p. xxiii) states: 'I define postmodernism as incredulity towards metanarratives . . . Thus the society of the future falls less within the province of a Newtonian anthropology (such as structuralism or systems theory) than a pragmatics of language particles. There are many different language games – a heterogeneity of elements.'

Implications for the study of culture

Obscure theories about the meaning of language may seem a little out of place in discussing leisure and cultural habits, but their importance lies in the fact that language is the ultimate basis of all culture and therefore social activities, and language is inherently social.

This is the underlying reason why post-structuralism is important to our subject. Its more proximate importance lies in its effect on Marxist-inspired theories of culture. At their heart lay the working class (either as a victim of mass culture or as the creator through cultural practices of resistance to this mass culture). Post-structuralism rejects this approach entirely. The idea of progress itself is thrown out, along with the possibility of knowing the world. The old theories, insofar as they are based on the modernist conception of rational scientific investigation, are held to be not a solution, but part of the problem, and if they are acted on they lead to authoritarian outcomes.

The post-structuralist alternative – to make judgements based on aesthetic criteria which do not claim to be scientific – owes a great deal to Nietzsche. This point is made clearly by David Harvey when he states:

'after Nietzsche's intervention, it was no longer possible to accord Enlightenment reason a privileged status in the definition of the eternal and immutable essence of human nature. To the degree that Nietzsche has led the way in placing aesthetics above science, rationality and politics, so the exploration of aesthetic experience – "beyond good and evil" – became powerful means to establish a new mythology as to what the eternal and immutable might be about.' (Harvey, 1989, p. 18)

The critique of rationality and the Enlightenment combined with the emphasis on difference from post-structuralist theory fitted in with the critique of production centred class analysis which it was argued excluded certain groups. This certainly helped post-modernist ideas to gain an appeal. For example, Catherine Belsey explains how it might be seen as an ally of feminism:

'the Enlightenment commitment to truth and reason, we can now see, has meant historically a single truth and a single rationality, which have conspired in practice to legitimate the subordination of black people, the non-Western world, women.. . . None of these groups has any political interest in clinging to the values which have consistently undervalued them. The plurality of the post-modern, by contrast, discredits suprematism on the part of any single group. It celebrates difference of all kinds, but divorces difference from power. Post-modernism is in all these senses the ally of feminism'. (Belsey, 1991, p. 262 quoted in Norris, 1993, p. 287)

The denial of scientific rational reasoning does not however have universal appeal. Alex Callinicos argues that it represents a: 'depoliticization of radical theory, and its aestheticization, so that the critique of bourgeois society was transformed into striking a knowing, ironic attitude towards both the defenders of status quo and those still benighted enough to wish to overthrow it'. (Callinicos, 1995, p. 180)

In summary, therefore the post-modernist rejection of scientific rationality has led to a shake-up of sociological thinking precisely because sociology was born out of this movement. The growth of aesthetic theories deriving ultimately from the work of Nietzsche has found a ready reception in sociology due to the common link back to Nietzsche found in post-structuralist thinking which was already influential in sociology and secondly the writings of Max Weber, whose account of power and bureaucracy certainly owes a lot to Nietzsche.

Varieties of postmodernist theories

Michel Foucault

Probably the most influential theorist who is often put into the category of postmodernist thinking is Michel Foucault. He developed Nietzsche's theme that power underlies all social relationships and applied it to the modernist notion of rationality. He argued that science is simply a new form of domination which creates its own discourse of concepts and ideas to justify its domination.

For Foucault, doctrines that look to science and rationality for solutions to the problems of the world are part of the problem themselves. Instead we need to engage in resistance at a local level. Meanings are constructed by the collection of related events or discourses, which themselves are never fixed in their meaning. This is essentially an anarchist position, in which resistance is limited to small issues (because to go further threatens to invoke a metanarrative which will lead to totalitarianism), and the paradigm is the modelling of the body (Foucault 1979–86). Foucault's notion of the body as a locus of resistance to the structures of power/knowledge has been the inspiration for much contemporary work on the sociology of culture.

What differentiates Foucault from other thinkers in this tradition is that he 'does talk about an external world, an "extra-discursive" order, the institutional structure out of which discourses develop' (Craib 1992, p. 186). So ultimately there *is* a link between knowledge and reality, albeit mediated by the plurality of discourses. When he looks at the effects of the growth of rationality and institutional order, Foucault's work invites comparisons with Weber, although it lacks Weber's ultimate optimism.

Jean Baudrillard

Baudrillard is the sociologist who perhaps takes the implications of postmodernism to their greatest extremes. He argues that the analysis of society provided by Marx needs to be amended because the transformations he outlined rest on a more fundamental transformation, namely the transformation of simulations (see Poster

1988). He argues that society and the production of commodities within it have progressed through a number of stages, from copying the real object, through reproducing it in the stage of consumer capitalism, to the stage where in postmodern society production is based on a copy of a copy of a copy and the notion of reality is left far behind.

In the postmodern world 'reality' is entirely constructed through the mass media, whose values are determined by consumer demand, which in turn is so profoundly affected by advertising that it is impossible to distinguish what is real from what is not. This Baudrillard describes as 'hyperreality'. The search for truth is at best pointless, and at worst would lead to the creation of a totalitarian nightmare. Truth is simply a product of consensus values manufactured by the mass media, and science is no more than a label attached to some currently popular ideas.

Baudrillard goes on to suggest that the only form of resistance we can take in this situation is apathy or indifference to the truth. This 'refusal of truth' might lead to a stage where the techniques of mass indoctrination no longer work, not because the masses can see through it (because such an idea depends on a notion of truth) but because they simply do not care any longer.

The implication of this notion is effectively that one should treat the consumer culture which grew up in the 1980s as a joke, as a game, but one should not try to analyse it in relation to notions of truth. Dick Hebdidge (1989, quoted in Norris, 1990, p.141) provides the following account of what this entails:

> It is no longer possible for us to see through the appearance of, for instance, a 'free market' to the structuring 'real relations' beneath (e.g. class conflict and the expropriation by capital of surplus value). Instead signs begin increasingly to take on a life of their own referring not to a real world outside themselves but to their own 'reality' – the system that produces signs.

The basis of identity and therefore culture has, on this view, shifted from the system of production (social class), through various phases associated with non-production spheres (gender, ethnicity, nationality), to consumption. Goods and services are consumed not simply for their uses (since this would imply an opposition between useful and useless, which depends on some objective theory to distinguish between them) but also because of their symbolic or stylistic value.

The modernist idea of knowledgeable subjects gaining control of the objects in the natural world (which underlay sociology as well as other disciplines) has now been abandoned; Baudrillard believes that the reverse has occurred, since human subjects are now under the control of the objects of the hyperreal world we occupy. The boundaries and distinctions characteristic of the modern world have now imploded, allowing no distinction between truth and untruth. The answer is to take everything to excess: 'a system is abolished only by pushing it into hyperlogic, by forcing it into an excessive practice which is equivalent to a brutal amortization. "You want us to consume – OK, let's consume always more, and anything whatsoever, for any useless and absurd purpose" (quoted in Best and Kellner 1991, p. 131). There are no alternatives to the existing situation since all possibilities have been exhausted. All we can do is to play with images and models of the body, as Michael Jackson did by progressively making his skin whiter, and as transsexuals and transvestites do. We are now in the 'time of transvestism'.

It is easy to see why Baudrillard is considered rather extreme in his views. However, others have taken up the notion of a transfer of identity from production to consumption. Neo-Weberians, for example, are engaged in an argument about whether class analysis is useful any more. John Goldthorpe and Gordon Marshall (1992) argue it is, but Ray Pahl (1989, p. 718) maintains: 'The emphasis has shifted from groups to individuals, from classes to categories and from producers to consumers.'

In more post-modernist vein, the work of the various authors grouped around the New Times project have moved from an attempted reconstruction of Marxism which retained a notion of class, though divested of its economistic distortions, into the territory of post-Marxism centred on the politics of consumption and style. In this mix the centrality of leisure and culture in the formation of identity is given a very different meaning to that provided by the central identity of social class provided by modernist production-centred theories such as Marxism. Consumption floats free of any meaning, notions of truth are irrelevant, and we distinguish ourselves and build our identity through the consumption of signs.

Optimistic postmodernism

Some people have sensed that the pessimism inherent in many versions of postmodernism leads to a dead end, and there have therefore been attempts to sift through the postmodern analysis to see what is useful and what needs amending.

Scott Lash and John Urry, who at one time suggested that we now live in a post-Fordist economy and a postmodern society because of the fantastic increase in the velocity of commodity production (Lash and Urry 1987), have more recently argued that postmodernism may be seen not as a critique of modernism but as its exaggeration (Lash and Urry 1994). The image of a world out of control is as much a part of modernism as of postmodernism. What has happened is that the pace has intensified:

> This faster circulation of objects is the stuff of 'consumer capitalism'. With an ever quickening turnover, objects as well as cultural artefacts become disposable and depleted of meaning. Some of these objects, such as computers, television sets, VCRs and hi-fis, produce many more cultural artefacts or signs ('signifiers') than people can cope with. People are bombarded with signifiers and increasingly become incapable of attaching 'signifieds' or meanings to them. [pp. 2–3]

This vision leads in the direction of the pessimistic excesses of postmodernism; Lash and Urry contend that there is a way out through the reinsertion into analysis of a conception of subjectivity that was stripped out of cultural analysis by the adoption of the structuralist idea of the death of the subject. They argue that Bourdieu's (1984) concept of aesthetic reflexivity offers the possibility of embracing a 'we' to replace the 'I' which dominated in the free-market 1980s.

Postmodernism, culture and leisure

This chapter has tried to show how the development of ideas which have been characterized as postmodernism has shifted the emphasis of explanation away from production towards consumption and that this provides distinctive analyses of leisure and culture. In ways which appear very similar to the conservative 'end of ideology' thesis and the post-industrial society thesis of Daniel Bell (1974), postmodernism has promoted the idea that we live in a time when fundamental changes are taking place which alter the myriad forms of social structure and social intercourse that we engage in.

> *A number of different approaches are taken by sociologists influenced by postmodern ideas. As you work through the remainder of this chapter, make notes on the differences between the 'New Times' type of analysis based on the concept of post-Fordism and the work of Lash and Urry.*

One version of postmodernism, which centres on economic changes in society, points towards the decreasing importance of industrial work and the increasing centrality of service industries, including the leisure industries. The implication of this is that the old theories of society which were essentially based around an understanding of work and the sphere of production need to be replaced by thinking which places much greater emphasis on the sphere of consumption.

A second view operating within the broad ambit of postmodernism places less emphasis on economic changes and much more on how culture has changed.

We will examine one example of each of these approaches.

Ian Henry: the politics of leisure policy

In relation to the emphasis on economic changes, perhaps the most detailed examination of leisure is the work of Ian Henry (1993). He argues that the move from a Fordist to a post-Fordist economy has had profound implications for the provision of leisure facilities:

> In the form of the Thatcherite Conservative governments of the 1980s, a group of actors existed which sought to foster not only the restructuring of the British economy, but also the social and political culture of Britain; and explanation of leisure policy since the mid–1980s must take account of the nature and success (or failure) of such changes. [p. 173]

The basis of the Fordist system of production and regulation was the provision of mass production. This required mass consumption to sustain it. In relation to leisure this involved the provision of leisure facilities by the Welfare State and the expansion of local government. Examples of such expansion include the creation of bodies to promote forms of leisure such as the National Parks Commission (formed in 1949 but incorporated into the Countryside Commission after 1968), the Arts Council (1946) and the Sports Council (1965).

The central thrust underlying these developments was the idea of providing greater access to leisure in one form or another. This received a large boost with the expansion of local government leisure departments from the early 1970s onwards.

However, by the late 1970s the emergence of economic crisis placed a strain on this

Fordist arrangement and threatened the continued mass consumption which provided a market for the mass production on which it was based. Post-Fordism therefore emerged in the form of New Right strategies to deal with the economic crisis. The key implication for leisure was increasing control over and cutbacks in local government provision and a shift from seeing greater access to leisure as a strategic aim to using leisure policy as a form of social control.

 What do you understand by the idea of leisure and leisure provision as a form of social control? How convincing do you find this notion?

Thus Henry notes the way in which provision for leisure became more targeted in inner-city areas. This was based on the reasoning that better leisure facilities would reduce vandalism, hooliganism and social unrest, despite the fact that there is little evidence for this idea.

The key criterion of leisure policy thus shifted from social concerns to economic concerns (a wish to avoid the costs associated with social unrest). This shift was also reinforced by the emphasis on reducing costs in the free-market economics promoted by the Conservative governments. Commercial leisure activities were given priority over facilities provided by local government, which were progressively squeezed of funds during the 1980s. Even expenditure in the inner cities was cut back towards the end of the 1980s, as Table 8.1 indicates.

Table 8.1 Inner area programme expenditure, 1987–90 (£m)

	1987/8	1988/9	1989/90
Sport and recreation	20.7	19.3	12.2
Community centres	18.3	13.1	10.2
Health	12.2	11.6	11.9
Education	9.2	6.4	4.7
All social objectives	83.3	66.7	56.6
Housing objectives	24.4	24.6	24.6
Environmental objectives	49.1	46.1	44.3
Economic objectives	100.5	115.6	120.5

Source: Henry 1993, p 73

 Henry argues that the funding of sport, culture and leisure moved from criteria based on aesthetics and promotion of access for all to criteria based on economic considerations more in line with the free-market business philosophy of the New Right.

1) What evidence do you find in this table to support such an assertion?
2) Which areas of expenditure were cut the most over the period covered?
3) Use figures from Economic Trends *or* Social Trends *to work out how other areas of government expenditure changed over the period shown. Are the changes in leisure funding in the inner cities in line with these changes, or not?*

It is important to note that there was some resistance to these cutbacks, and that there were attempts by Labour-controlled councils such as the Greater London

Council (GLC) to widen access to traditional culture. It is this greater concern with cultural politics that lies behind the notion of a New Left.

Table 8.2   Per capitum revenue expenditure estimates for sport and recreation by English local authorities for 1982–3, 1984–5 and 1988–9

	1982–3					1984–5					1988–9*				
	Mean	Std. Devn.	Min.	Max.	N	Mean	Std. Devn.	Min.	Max.	N	Mean	Std. Devn.	Min.	Max.	N
All London boroughs (LBs)	16.0	8.6	5.6	44.5	32	17.0	8.6	8.3	40.1	25	22.6	7.5	13.8	45.8	22
Labour-controlled LBs	19.9	9.0	9.5	44.5	15	26.5	7.9	16.0	40.1	7	24.7	5.5	17.5	33.2	6
Conservative-controlled LBs	11.1	3.8	5.6	19.2	16	12.0	3.3	8.3	18.1	15	21.2	5.8	13.8	32.4	10
All metropolitan districts (MDs)	11.6	3.2	6.1	19.3	36	13.8	4.4	7.0	24.7	33	19.9	7.3	9.9	44.4	32
Labour-controlled MDs	12.0	3.2	7.6	19.3	26	15.0	4.8	8.0	24.7	21	20.9	7.9	10.5	44.4	24
Conservative-controlled MDs	9.7	1.9	6.1	11.6	6	11.2	2.5	7.0	13.1	5	10.56	--	--	--	1
All non-MDs	7.1	4.7	0.0	37.2	291	8.9	5.5	−0.2	3.8	285	12.8	7.6	0.3	42.4	263
Labour-controlled NMDs	11.6	4.8	3.8	27.2	55	15.4	6.8	2.3	33.8	52	22.0	8.1	6.8	42.4	42
Conservative-controlled NMDs	6.5	4.2	0.1	37.2	148	7.6	3.6	−0.2	18.8	137	10.9	5.7	0.3	28.3	131

* Expenditure levels for 1984–5 and 1988–9 are artificially low because of the failure of some authorities, particularly those threatened with rate-capping, to declare details of their expenditure. London boroughs and metropolitan districts include expenditure on items 'inherited' from the metropolitan counties and the GLC which were abolished in 1986.   Source: Henry 1993, p 94

1) *Write a report comparing the funding of leisure in Conservative-controlled and Labour-controlled boroughs and how these changed over the period concerned.*
2) *Which figures might be emphasized by Labour politicians, and which by Conservative politicians?*

Henry's analysis highlights the social and political context in which leisure and leisure opportunities develop. However, it ultimately rests on the proposition that economic changes are reflected in the rest of society, albeit not automatically. This has been the focus of criticism of the idea that we have witnessed a transformation from Fordism to post-Fordism.

John Urry: the tourist gaze

An alternative approach within the broad heading of postmodernist analysis is offered by writers who still talk of the transformation from Fordism to post-Fordism but concentrate more on cultural changes and their impact on consumption and leisure. An example of such an analysis is the work of John Urry (1990) on the growth and changing nature of tourism:

> The emphasis on the quality of the social interaction between producers and consumers of tourist services means that developments in the industry

are not explicable simply in terms of 'economic' developments … it is also necessary to examine a range of cultural changes which transform people's expectations about what they wish to gaze upon, what significance should be attached to that gaze, and what effects this will have upon the providers of the relevant tourist services. [p. 41]

Figure 8.1 The scientific study of holidays?

Source: *Guardian*, 25 August, 1990

While Urry's analysis of tourism clearly shows the influence of the ideas of Pierre Bordieu, he also makes use of ideas developed by Foucault in connection with the development of institutions and professionals in the areas of health and criminality, and also Baudrillard's idea that we now live in a world where it is not possible to distinguish between the true and the false, between the authentic and the inauthentic. Urry believes Baudrillard's contention is applicable to tourism since package tourism does not provide a genuine experience of the world you visit but instead a series of contrived events in artificially created environments.

> *What do you think is meant by 'artificially created environments'? List examples of such environments in the world of tourism. Obtain copies of tourist brochures from a travel agent and see if you can identify any examples which might fit into the category of artificially created environment.*

Urry argues that tourists themselves are aware of this inauthenticity; he explains the popularity of tourism in terms of its difference from the normal routine of work and home. He thinks we are now in a period that might be called 'post-tourist' because people have given up the search for authentic experiences of the world they visit and instead simply join in the games created out of artificiality.

Critical perspectives

Despite the proliferation of texts devoted to postmodernism, there are those who believe that culture and leisure are still understandable in terms of a modernist analysis.

Some, like Habermas (the heir to the Frankfurt School tradition) argue that although we live in post-industrial society, we are still capable of analysing society on the basis of the development of rationality. Modernism is an unfinished project, and we need to complete it (Habermas 1984, 1987).

Other writers argue that we need to locate the consumption of goods within an analysis that also looks at their production and how this production structures consumption. Paul Manning (1993), for example, argues that we should remember the culture industry is one of the most concentrated in the world and that those who control it can therefore exercise a large degree of control over consumption:

> Production factors limit the range of consumption options. In other words, certain commodities become available for consumption but others do not, and the manner in which commodities become available is likely to shape the way in which they are consumed and the meanings attached to them by the consumers! Try going into any record shop and asking for a record rather than a CD without being made to feel like a dinosaur. [p. 21]

The figure below shows deliveries (not the same as production) of various forms of musical recording. It could be argued that the decline in vinyl was due to consumer demand or alternatively it could be due to a drop in production following producer decisions not entirely related to consumer demand.

Figure 8.2 Trade deliveries of LPs, cassettes, compact discs and singles

Source: *Social Trends* (1994), p. 132

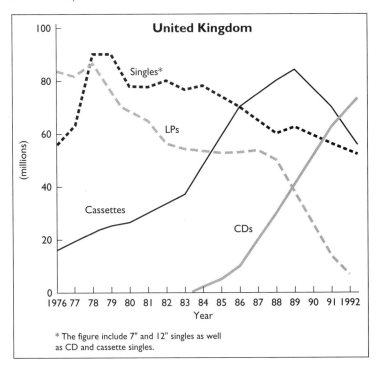

* The figure include 7" and 12" singles as well as CD and cassette singles.

1) To what extent does Figure 8.2 support Paul Manning's assertion about the importance of production limiting consumer choice?
2) What is the significance for consumers of the shift from LPs and cassettes to CDs?
3) What is the significance for the producers of the shift from LPs and cassettes to CDs?

A key element in decisions about production remains the profit motive. This point is central since capitalism, whatever form it takes, is concerned with profit above all. If we still live in capitalist rather than a 'post-capitalist' society, the forms of culture are still linked to the production of commodities and there is therefore still a link to the arena of production. Changes in the economy still have important implications and should feature in the debate about the changing nature of society.

In this vein some writers have attempted to analyse postmodernism itself as arising from the changing circumstances which some classes experienced as a result of the economic changes of the 1980s:

> The discourse of postmodernism is best seen as the product of a socially mobile intelligentsia in a climate dominated by the retreat of the Western labour movement and the 'overconsumptionist' dynamic of capitalism in the Reagan–Thatcher era. From this perspective the term 'postmodern' would seem to be a floating signifier by means of which this intelligentsia has sought to articulate its political disillusionment and its aspiration to a consumption-oriented lifestyle. [Callinicos 1989, p. 171]

1) Explain in your own words the point Callinicos is making here.
2) Consider how a postmodernist might respond to this critical and controversial statement. Assume you are a postmodernist and write a short reply of about 200 words.

Paul Hirst (1989) has also pointed out that the argument that we live in 'New Times' comes 'close to celebrating Conservative economic success' and is therefore a strange position for ex-Marxists to be taking.

The similarity between some postmodernist themes and those of capitalism is made even clearer by Terry Eagleton:

> It is not difficult ... to see a relation between the philosophy of J.L. Austin and IBM, or between the various neo-Nietzscheanisms of a post-structuralist epoch and Standard Oil. It is not surprising that classical models of truth and cognition are increasingly out of favour in a society where what matters is whether you deliver the commercial or rhetorical goals. Whether among discourse theorists or the Institute of Directors, the goal is no longer truth but performativity, not reason but power. The CBI are in this sense spontaneous post-structuralists to a man, utterly disenchanted (did they but know it) with epistemological realism and the correspondence theory of truth. [Eagleton 1986, quoted in Connor 1989, p. 41]

One further critique of the post-Fordist variant of postmodernism is that it is itself an example of technological determinism, much more so than any brand of Marxism. In an attempt to avoid this criticism, David Harvey (1989) writes of the growth of 'flexible accumulation' to stress the partial and variegated nature of the changes we have witnessed. He agrees that changes have taken place, particularly in the sphere of production where there has been a massive acceleration of the production process, and this has created fragmentation and insecurity in the cultural sphere. What distinguishes Harvey is that he sees this as a process we can understand and analyse, rather than dismissing any such attempt as pointless or dangerous.

Is postmodernism true?

This question appears to be becoming more and more central to more and more areas of sociology.

We have examined some of the themes that characterize the postmodernist approach to leisure and cultural studies, so you can hopefully begin to evaluate this question yourself.

But there is one final problem with the postmodernist analysis: the logical fallacy that any doctrine which declares that there are no truths must find itself included in that statement. If postmodernism is true, the postmodernist idea that there are no truths cannot be true.

Structured question

Item A

Advertisers aim at classless society

Carat Research today released details of its *media*GRAPHICS segmentation system which goes some way towards replacing social class as a method of categorizing the UK population for advertising purposes.

*media*GRAPHICS uses the notion that the amounts and types of newspapers and magazines people read and television they watch give a clear indication of their attitudes and lifestyle. In other words *you are what you read or watch*.

Said Phil Gullen, Managing Director at Carat Research, '*media*GRAPHICS works not only because people choose their media to fit in with their attitudes and lifestyle but also because what they read or watch then helps develop these attitudes and give further ideas on how to live their lives.'

This means that the *media*GRAPHICS group you belong to gives in many cases a better indication of the products you are likely to consume and the activities you are likely to take part in than social class – the advertisers'

traditional segmentation system – which is based (mostly) on the jobs people do.

Carat's *media*GRAPHICS groups are:

media GRAPHIC group Key characteristics	% of UK adult population	Key characteristics
M1 Broadsheet Browsers	9%	Read a lot of quality newspapers but don't watch much ITV
M2 Media Hermits	13%	Don't read many newspapers or magazines and don't watch much ITV
M3 Maggies	16%	Read a lot of women's magazines but not newspapers
M4 Telly Addicts	20%	Watch a lot of ITV but don't read much
M5 Media Junkies	15%	Read a lot of newspapers and magazines
M6 Tabloids Not Telly	9%	Read a lot of popular newspapers and don't watch much ITV
M7 Popular Masses	18%	Read a lot of popular newspapers and watch a lot of ITV

Source: TGI/Carat Research

Item B

Pierre Bourdieu's work on status differentials in different spheres of consumption – from food to art, from sport to clothing – was actually conceived as . . . an 'endeavour to rethink Max Weber's opposition between class and status'. This is really what an informed sociological study of leisure as consumption must do . . . Mike Featherstone's recent review of 'perspectives on consumer culture' cites Bourdieu and others on how goods are used to 'mark social differences and act as communicators'. We buy our way in to appealing subjectivities and accessible identities and yet, as Featherstone put it . . . we should bear in mind that the consumer industries have always marketed goods in ways which conceal their mass produced origins and emphasize their individuality . . . This is the central paradox of contemporary consumer culture; its constructedness, and its simultaneous openness to interpretation and the symbolic work which Paul Willis stresses so strongly.

The importance of the study of leisure as a major element of consumer culture is incontestable, though still at times disputed. For people in advanced capitalist economies work not just to survive, but to live in particular ways and to display the evidence of their success and status. Much of this goes on in the marketplace and places the individual consumer in a creative but often unequal tension with the cultural industry – the classic lone punter often up against the anonymous yet omnipotent producer . . . But the consumer trends in the areas of leisure expansion of the 1980s are undeniable. As Sharon Zukin argues, the area of consumption can no longer be relegated to a passive or residual role in any analysis of the market economy.

Source: Adapted from Tomlinson (1991)

1) Which category forms the largest grouping in the segmentation system outlined in item A? **(1 mark)**

2) Explain in your own words what the author of item B sees as 'the central paradox of contemporary consumer culture'. **(4 marks)**

3) Illustrating your answer with reference to item A, suggest ways in which 'we buy our way into appealing subjectivities and accessible identities' (item B). **(3 marks)**

4) How far would sociologists agree with the view that a segmentation system based on patterns of consumption 'goes some way towards replacing social class as a method of categorizing the UK population' (item A)? **(8 marks)**

5) Using information from the items and elsewhere, evaluate the claim that 'the area of consumption can no longer be relegated to a passive or residual role in any analysis of the market economy' (item B). **(9 marks)**

Bibliography

Althusser, L.(1966) *For Marx*, Harmondsworth: Penguin
—— (1971) *Lenin and Philosophy*, London: Verso
—— and Balibar, E. (1970) *Reading Capital*, London: Verso
Arato, A. and Gebhardt, E. (eds) (1978) *The Essential Frankfurt School Reader*, Oxford: Basil Blackwell
Bell, D. (1974) *The Coming of Post-Industrial Society*, London: Heinemann
Belsey, C. (1991) 'Afterword: a Future for Materialist Feminist Criticism? in Valerie Wayne (ed) *The Matter of Difference: materialist feminist criticism of Shakespeare*, Hemel Hempstead: Harvester-Wheatsheaf
Best, S. and Kellner, D. (1991) *Postmodern Theory: Critical Interrogations*, London: Macmillan Press Ltd.
Bourdieu, P. (1984) *Distinction*, London: Routledge & Kegan Paul
Callinicos, A. (1989) *Against Postmodernism*, Cambridge: Polity
—— (1995) *Theories and Narratives*, Cambridge: Polity
Clarke, J. and Saunders, C. (1991) 'Who are you and so what?', *Sociology Review*, Vol. 1, No. 1, September

Connor, S. (1989) *Postmodernist Culture*, Oxford: Blackwell

Craib, I. (1992) *Modern Social Theory*, 2nd edn, Hemel Hempstead: Harvester-Wheatsheaf

Derrida, J. (1976) *On Grammatology*, Baltimore: John Hopkins Press

Eagleton, T. (1986) 'Capitalism, modernism and postmodernism' in *Against the Grain: Essays*, London: Verso

Foucault, M. (1970) *The Order of Things*, London: Tavistock

—— (1972) *The Archaeology of Knowledge*, London: Tavistock

—— (1979–86) *History of Sexuality*, 3 vols), London: Allen Lane

—— (1980) *Power/Knowledge*, ed. C. Gordon, New York: Pantheon

Goldthorpe, J.H. and Marshall, G. (1992) 'The promising future of class analysis: a response to recent critique' *Sociology*, Vol 26, No. 3, pp 381–400

Gramsci, A. (1971) *Selections from Prison Notebooks*, London: Lawrence & Wishart

Habermas, J. (1984, 1987) *The Theory of Communicative Action*, Vols 1 & 2, London: Heinemann

Hall, S. and Jefferson, T. (eds) (1976) *Resistance Through Rituals*, London: Hutchinson

Hall, S. and Jacques, M. (eds) (1989) *New Times*, London: Lawrence & Wishart

Harvey, D. (1989) *The Condition of Postmodernity*, Oxford: Basil Blackwell

Hebdidge, D. (1989) 'After the Masses', *Marxism Today*, January

Held, D. (1980) *Introduction to Critical Theory*, London: Hutchinson

Henry, I. (1993) *The Politics of Leisure Policy*, London: Macmillan

Hirst, P. (1989) 'After Henry', in Hall and Jacques (1989)

Jones, P. (1993) *Studying Society: Sociological Theories and Research Practices*, London: Collins Educational

Lash, S. and Urry, J. (1987) *The End of Organized Capitalism*, Cambridge: Polity

—— (1994) *Economies of Signs and Space*, London: Sage

Lyotard, J.P. (1984) *The Postmodern Condition*, Minneapolis, MN: University of Minnesota Press

Manning, P. (1993) 'Consumption, production and popular culture', *Sociology Review*, Vol. 2, No. 3, February

McRobbie, A. (1992) 'How to cope when class and nation aren't everything', *Guardian*, 22 August

Norris, C. (1990) 'Baudrillard and the politics of Postmodernism' in R. Boyne and A Rattansi (eds), *Postmodernism and Society*, London: Macmillan Press Ltd.

—— (1993) *The Truth about Postmodernism*, Oxford: Blackwell

Pahl, R. E. (1989) 'Is the emperor naked? Some questions on the adequacy of sociological theory in urban and regional studies', *International Urban and Regional Studies*, Vol 13, No. 4, pp 711–20

Poster, M. (ed.) (1988) *Jean Baudrillard: Selected Writings*, Cambridge: Polity

Saussure, F. de (1974) *Course in General Linguistics*, London: Fontana

Tomlinson, Alan (1991) 'Buying time: consumption and leisure', *Social Studies Review*, Vol. 6, No. 3, pp. 98–101

Trowler, P. (1991) *Investigating the Media*, London: Collins Educational

Turner, B. (1988) *Status*, Milton Keynes: Open University Press

Urry, J. (1990) *The Tourist Gaze*, London: Sage

Globalization and the future of work and leisure

We at Ford Motor Company look at the world map without any boundaries. We don't consider ourselves basically an American company. We are a multinational company, and when we approach a government that does not like the US, we always say, 'Who do you like? Britain? Germany?' We carry a lot of flags.

Robert Stevenson, Ford executive

Banking is rapidly becoming different to the constraints of time, place and currency . . . an Englisb buyer can get a Japanese mortgage, an American can tap his New York bank account through a cash machine in Hong Kong and a Japanese investor can buy shares in a London-based Scandinavian bank whose stock is denominated in sterling, dollars, Deutsche Marks and Swiss francs.

Financial Times, 8.5.87 quoted in M. Waters (1995) p. 88

The extreme globalization theorists paint a picture of a world set free for business to serve customers . . . Such a world free for trade has been the dream of classical economic liberalism since its inception. It is also an illusion. Markets and companies cannot exist without the protection of the public power. The open international economy depends ultimately on Western (particularly US) force and upon active public regulation backed by legal enforcement.

P. Hirst and G. Thompson (1995) p. 427

Recently sociologists have begun to consider the implications of a very important process: globalization. The suggestion behind this term is that it is no longer feasible to talk about the world as a set of linked but independent entities, normally identified as nation-states:

> The world has become in important respects a single social system, as a result of growing ties of interdependence which now affect virtually everyone. The global system is not just an environment within which particular societies – like Britain – develop and change. The social, political and economic connections which cross-cut borders between countries decisively condition the fate of those living within each of them. The general term

for this increasing interdependence of world society is globalization. [Giddens 1994, p. 528]

Before you read any further into this chapter, try to think up as many examples as you can of 'social, political and economic connections which cross-cut borders'. Work in small groups. Once you have finished your list, compare it with the lists produced by other groups. See if you can find any connection between the list you have prepared and those of other groups.

This process is held to be the result of a succession of changes in economic and social ties across countries that have cumulatively produced qualitative changes in the way we experience our lives. Our experience can no longer be understood within a strictly national context. This has important implications for the ways in which we think about work and leisure.

One example of such interconnections is provided by the European Space Agency, which developed the Ariane space rocket. As the Figure 9.1 shows, there are over fifteen countries involved in the various activities undertaken by this organization. The economic and social relations required for this sort of project are enormously complex. Projects like the ESA's have an increasingly important impact on work prospects in the

Figure 9.1 The European Space Agency's millions.

Source: *Observer*, 23 October 1994

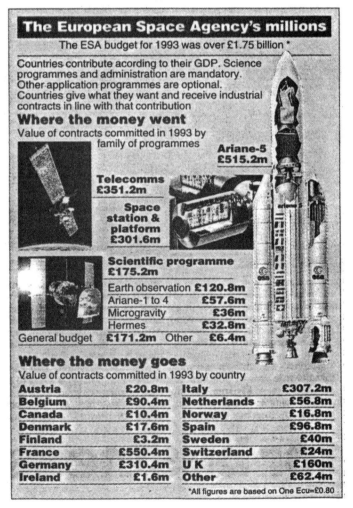

The European Space Agency's millions

The ESA budget for 1993 was over £1.75 billion *

Countries contribute acording to their GDP. Science programmes and administration are mandatory. Other application programmes are optional. Countries give what they want and receive industrial contracts in line with that contribution

Where the money went
Value of contracts committed in 1993 by family of programmes

Ariane-5 £515.2m

Telecomms £351.2m

Space station & platform £301.6m

Scientific programme £175.2m

Earth observation	£120.8m
Ariane-1 to 4	£57.6m
Microgravity	£36m
Hermes	£32.8m
General budget £171.2m	Other £6.4m

Where the money goes
Value of contracts committed in 1993 by country

Austria	£20.8m	Italy	£307.2m
Belgium	£90.4m	Netherlands	£56.8m
Canada	£10.4m	Norway	£16.8m
Denmark	£17.6m	Spain	£96.8m
Finland	£3.2m	Sweden	£40m
France	£550.4m	Switzerland	£24m
Germany	£310.4m	U K	£160m
Ireland	£1.6m	Other	£62.4m

*All figures are based on One Ecu=£0.80

UK. Information technology and telecommunications companies in the UK are now competing with enterprises in all these other countries for contracts worth millions of pounds, and the jobs of thousands of workers depend on the outcome.

> *Find out which British companies are involved in work for the European Space Agency.*

The example of Ariane is a reminder that one of the biggest changes in the sphere of leisure in recent years has been the introduction of satellite television. This technology needs satellites to be launched into space, which in turn creates a need for rockets. An innovation in TV viewing thus requires a whole network of global connections or at least an expansion of older connections.

Even without satellite TV it is possible to catch a glimpse of a world beyond the shores of Britain. The schedule for terrestrial TV reproduced in Figure 9.2 reveals several cross-national links. A number of programmes, such as *LA Law* and *NYPD Blue*, originate in the USA. Other series focus on activities taking place in countries such as Peru, Spain and Ecuador. Others show events happening in Britain but involving people from around the world; *Sportsnight*, for example, features a Zimbabwean boxer. The connections spanning the world that bring these images to our screens have an impact on our lives. Through the importation of series from America, phrases and cultural forms that did not originate here become part of our lives.

> *Look at Figure 9.2 in detail and see if you can identify any other international links that must exist for this schedule to be written.*

One phrase imported from America with which we are now familiar is the TV dinner – and it is not only the language we have adopted. The packaging of food and the ability to cook in microwaves means we can now synchronize our evening meal and watching TV (such meals are also useful when you are rushing to finish a book!). The social rituals surrounding the eating of food appear to have changed in this respect.

The food we eat has changed too. For example, we are now quite used to the wide variety of foods on offer, both in supermarkets and in fast-food retail outlets. Pizza, hamburger and kebab shops compete with a whole variety of cuisines from China and the Indian subcontinent, Mexico and more recently Thailand, Indonesia, Malaysia and Japan. In the local supermarket it is usually possible to buy prepared dishes or the ingredients to make meals from all or most of these countries, alongside Cajun and Creole dishes.

The variety of choice available in relation to this particular leisure activity has increased considerably in recent times. The implications, however, go much further than that. Think of how the soy sauce or tabouleh or lemon grass came to be in your local supermarket, and the connections and social relations that are involved. Think of the implications for the producers of foodstuffs in Britain. If a larger proportion of our food is coming from abroad, what does this mean for the agricultural and food processing industries in this country?

> *1) Make a list of all the different types of food outlets in your town or city.*
> *2) Investigate the extent to which the range of material available in supermarkets reflects the diversity of international food styles.*

Just by sitting watching TV and eating your TV dinner you are part of this fantastically

Figure 9.2 TV schedule for 26 October 1994

The Guide 22–28 October 1994, *Guardian*, 22 October 1994

WEDNESDAY

BBC1 6.0 News; **(T)** weather *133* **6.30 Regional News Magazines** *713* **7.0 FILM Innerspace** (Joe Dante, 1987) **(T) (S)** Science fiction adventure starring Martin Short, Meg Ryan and Dennis Quaid. See Movie Preview. *8591 4065* **8.55 Party Political Broadcast (T) (S)** Liberal Democrats *329626* **9.0 News**; **(T)** weather *1084* **9.30 PREVIEW Between The Lines (T) (S)** Things start to go wrong after a job falls into Clark's lap with suspicious ease. *122713* **10.25 Sportsnight (S)** Desmond Lynam introduces Commonwealth super-middleweight action as Henry Wharton defends his title against Zimbabwean challenger Supho Mayo at Leeds Town Hall. *3857317* **11.45 FILM Duel At Diablo** (Ralph Nelson, 1966) Western starring James Garner, Sidney Poitier and Bibi Andersson. See Movie Preview. *165959* **1.30 Weather** *4626379* **1.35 Close** *11112824* **4.0 BBC Select:** *TV Edits – French 3 TV1 5625824* **4.45 Close** *30195*

BBC2 6.00 Star Trek: The Next Generation (T) (S) A terribly shy crew member becomes dangerous when an alien probe endows him with super-human intelligence. *192959* **6.45 The Big Trip (T) (S)** Followed by Black Tracks. *686133* **7.30 All Black (S)** Black men express their views on love, marriage and bringing up baby. Last in the series. *539* **8.0 A Feast Of Floyd (T) (S)** Keith Floyd is in Spain *7423* **8.30 University Challenge** *6930* **9.0 Grace Under Fire (T) (S)** Grace is worried and nervous when she seems to be falling for Ryan Sparks. Followed by Mr Crabtree cartoon. *9626* **9.30 PREVIEW Video Diaries.** An expedition to an unexplored part of the Peruvian rainforest. Followed by Bard On The Box: Essential Shakespeare. *76268* **10.30 Party Political Broadcast (T) (S)** Liberal Democrats *712355* **10.35 Newsnight (T)** *956152* **11.20 The Late Show (S)** Melvyn Bragg and guests discuss the National Lottery. *457591* **12.0 Weatherview** *8901669* **12.05 FILM L'Atlante** (Jean Vigo, 1934) See Movie Preview *8918621* **2.0** Night School: Personal Health and Social Education *33447* **4.0** BBC Select: Benefits Agency today **(R)** *61021602* **4.15** Close *39466*

Carlton 6.0 Home and Away (T) (R) Alf attempts to talk sense into Luke and Nick concerning their proposed investment in the boat-shed. *201* **6.30 London Tonight (T)** *881* **7.0 Take Your Pick (T) (S)** Hosted by Des O'Connor. *5201* **7.30 Coronation Street (T)** It's beginning to look suspiciously like Mavis and Roger's relationship may be more than what it originally appeared. *715* **8.0 Back To School, Mr Bean (S)** That supremely strange man, Mr Bean, takes a trip to an Adult Education College Open Day. *1249* **8.30 Ellington (T) (S)** An all-action drama about Ellington, an honest sports promoter who seems to be one in a million. *71152* **10.0 Party Political Broadcast (T) (S)** Liberal Democrats *755572* **10.05 News; (T)** weather *808978* **10.45 Carlton Sport** *5400713* **12.0 FILM Cactus Jack** (Hal Needham, 1979) Western starring Kirk Douglas and Arnold Schwarzenegger. *44553* **1.30** Hollywood Report **(S)** *12756* **2.0** The Beat **(S)** *34737* **3.0** The Album Show **(S)** *50824* **4.0** Beyond Reality *24195* **4.30** The Chrystal Rose Show **(S) (R)** *73379* **5.0** America's Top Ten **(S) (R)** *52398* **5.30** News *64224*

Channel 4 6.0 Mork and Mindy (R) Mork and his son, Mearth, acidentally transfer minds. *171* **6.30 Boy Meets World (T) (S)** When Cory loses a birthday gift from his father he doesn't realise the sentimental meaning behind the present. *423* **7.0 News; (T)** weather *592355* **7.50 The Slot** *749065* **8.0 Brookside (T) (S)** *2591* **8.30 The Lonely Planet (T) (S)** Justine Shapiro travels from the Ecuadorian port of Guyaquil by train to the Andes and the active Cotopaxi volcano, enjoying the local delicacy of guinea pig. *1626* **9.0 PREVIEW Dispatches (T)** *141607* **9.45 PREVIEW Counter Culture: Body Business (T) (S)** *283510* **10.0 NYPD Blue (T)** A search is on to find a male killer who dresses as a woman. *4046* **11.0 Rory Bremner – Who Else? (S) (R)** *462423* **11.40 Nightingales (S) (R)** *486666* **12.10 LA Law (S)** *5480640* **1.05 FILM Let's Be Famous** (Walter Forde, 1939) Comedy of an Irish singer who thinks he is hitting the big time when signed up by the BBC, only to find he is to appear on a spelling quiz. *5236824* **2.35 Mission Eureka (R)** *9945737* **3.30** Close *93224*

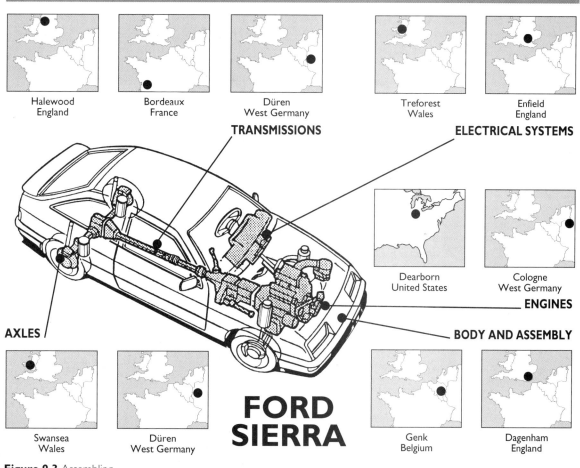

Halewood
England

Bordeaux
France

Düren
West Germany

TRANSMISSIONS

Treforest
Wales

Enfield
England

ELECTRICAL SYSTEMS

Dearborn
United States

Cologne
West Germany

ENGINES

AXLES

Swansea
Wales

Düren
West Germany

FORD SIERRA

Genk
Belgium

Dagenham
England

BODY AND ASSEMBLY

Figure 9.3 Assembling the Ford Sierra

Source: *Sunday Times*, 22 January 1989.

complex series of social and economic relationships. From a sociological standpoint, however, the important questions are how far such connections have increased in recent years, and the implications of the changes that have taken place.

The global economy

The idea that production and other economic processes are now fundamentally organized at a global level is most often explained by reference to the emergence of transnational corporations (TNCs). This phrase refers to companies that operate both within many different countries and across national boundaries. An example is Ford. This company certainly operates in more than one country, and the production processes involved in manufacturing its cars span national boundaries, as Figure 9.3 shows.

> *How many countries were involved in the production of Ford Sierras?*
> *According to Anthony Giddens, it is possible to distinguish between ethnocentric multinationals in which policy is determined in the country of origin, polycentric companies in which the HQ establishes broad outlines but local subsidiaries have some autonomy and local management, and geocentric transnationals which are international in their management structure. He states of Ford: 'In the late 1960s, Ford transformed the whole of its European operations, previously centred separately in several countries, into a single organization, Ford Europe' (Giddens 1994, p. 547).*

Answer the following questions:

1) *If Ford were an ethnocentric transnational, where would most power lie?*
2) *What does the information in the quote above suggest Ford is becoming?*
3) *What are the implications for control of the car industry?*

Gill and Law explain the importance of the TNCs as follows:

> Because of their often immense size, decisions about the location of invest-
> ment, production and technology by transnational firms influence not
> only the distribution of power resources between states and classes, but
> also the level of aggregate welfare in various nations and throughout the
> world. The growth in the size and extent of transnational corporations is
> the essence of the 'transnational stage' in the development of capitalism.
> [Gill and Law 1988, p. 191]

Attempts to capture world markets have also motivated a large increase in
international mergers, often financed by companies investing overseas, as evidenced
by a large rise in overseas investment: 'the stock of foreign direct investment rose
from US$14.3bn in 1914 to US$386.2bn in 1978. Of this, the most rapid growth, a
six-fold increase, took place between 1960 and 1978' (Gill and Law 1988, p. 193).
Chris Harman (1991) provides more recent figures showing that the value of US
companies acquired by non-American owners rose from $10.9 billion in 1985 to
$40.4 billion in 1987.

The promotion of free-market economics and the removal of controls on the
movement of capital around the globe as part of the process of deregulation
favoured by New Right governments in the 1980s has made it easier for globalization
to occur. In the field of finance, $600 billion worth of foreign exchange passes
through London every day (Lash and Urry 1994, p. 289); in 1961 about 100 foreign
banks were represented in London, but by the late 1980s that number had grown to
450. This feeds the growth of multinational capital.

According to Giddens (1994), the revenues of the top 200 transnational
corporations rose tenfold between the mid–1970s and the 1990s. Crum and Davies
(1990, p. 1) also underline their power and importance: 'it is estimated that the 200
very largest of these firms have combined sales equivalent to about one-third of the
gross domestic product (GDP) of the entire world'.

*Why has the growth of these companies been so spectacular in the 1980s and
1990s? What is it about the political and economic environment of the time that
has encouraged such growth?*

Many sociologists believe that the concentration of such enormous power in the
hands of a few companies is drastically altering the economic, social and political
landscape and transforming all our lives.

Globalization of production: the implications for work

There are effectively two variations of the globalization thesis in relation to its effect
on work. These will be outlined in turn.

The new international division of labour thesis

Taking as their starting point the increased mobility of capital around the globe, proponents of this view argue that as capitalists can now relatively easily disinvest in one country and invest in another, workers in each country may now be placed in competition with workers from other countries. The phenomenon of the division of labour has reached a new stage. This idea is best exemplified in the work of Frobel *et al.* (1980), in their book *The New International Division of Labour*.

Of particular importance for this idea is the transfer of capital from the advanced industrial countries in the North to less industrialized or newly industrializing countries in the South. The key reason for this movement is the much cheaper rates of pay that prevail in the South. The *Economist* (1 October 1994) estimated the hourly cost of production labour in various countries as follows: Germany, $35; USA, $16; South Korea, $5; Mexico, $2.40; Poland, $1.40; China, Indonesia and India, $0.50. Labour-intensive forms of economic activity (those that require large amounts of labour) are moved to countries in the southern hemisphere to reduce costs.

This theory is often used to explain shifts in manufacturing industry. For example, the UK shipbuilding industry is now all but defunct; meanwhile there has been a major increase in shipbuilding in South Korea. Economic growth in East Asia averaged 7.5 per cent between 1974 and 1993, compared to only 2.9 per cent in the developed world. To illustrate the scale of the East Asian economic miracle, the *Economist* notes that after 1780 it took Britain 58 years to double production, something South Korea achieved in 11 years from 1966.

In place of manufacturing, the service industries have assumed greater importance in the advanced countries. These are not so labour intensive, however, so new jobs in service industries will not be enough to compensate for the loss of manufacturing employment. According to proponents of the international division of labour thesis, unless the flow of jobs to the South can be reversed, workers in the North will face persistent mass unemployment. The implications of trying to keep mobile capital in advanced industries in the North are spelled out by James Fulcher (1991, p. 4):

> National economies have become increasingly dependent on their capacity to attract and retain this increasingly mobile capital, which prefers countries where wage costs are low, unions are weak, state regulations, whether concerned with health and safety, pollution, or arms control, are minimal, and tax-rates are low. Such typical features of Thatcherism as deregulation, reduced taxation and anti-unionism have long been a feature of the export processing zones, set up to attract capital to Third World societies during the 1970s.

The central thrust of this argument is that, in order to stop capital going to Third World or less advanced countries, the advanced industrialized countries must drive down their tax and pay rates to the levels prevalent in the Third World. So, briefly stated, the advent of the new international division of labour is said to offer workers a choice between lower wages and unemployment.

The global production variant

Very similar prospects flow from the idea of the rise of global production. The crucial difference is that the proponents of this variant, such as Bennett Harrison (1987),

Piore and Sabel (1984) and the United Nations Centre on Transcontinental Corporations, claim that production is becoming increasingly decentralized and fragmented around the world as a whole; they place less emphasis on capital flows from the advanced North to the less advanced South since they believe that it moves around the world in both directions.

Global production theorists also place heavy emphasis on the rise of the TNCs and the enormous power concentrated in their hands, marginalizing other decision-making bodies such as trade unions and even governments. The power of the TNCs rests on their ability to elude any form of governmental economic regulation. They are said to achieve this in a number of ways.

First, they practise entirely legal forms of tax avoidance via a procedure known as transfer pricing. Artificial prices can be set for components being transferred between branch plants of TNCs located in different countries. The ability to manipulate costs in this way gives TNCs control over the levels of profit they declare for each company; since taxation rates vary from one country to another, they can minimize their tax liability. The amount of tax revenue collected by governments overall is reduced, and state power is thus weakened overall since states are dependent on tax revenues to fund their expenditure.

Second, if a company is owned by people beyond the national boundaries in which it operates, its profits will flow out of the country. This reduces the amount of money available to the country to purchase imports, so either imports will have to be reduced or money must be transferred from other areas of government expenditure to pay for them.

Third, if these companies can flit about the globe at will, as the globalization thesis suggests, there is always the danger that they will shut down production in a particular country and relocate elsewhere. The effect would be to reduce the amount of investment, the amount of employment and therefore the amount of economic production (GDP) in the first country. All of this would reduce the tax revenue the government receives, and indeed increase its costs, due to the increased cost of unemployment benefits.

In order to avoid these undesirable effects, governments must keep the TNCs happy. This means imposing tax cuts, weakening the unions, exerting downward pressure on wages and promoting foreign investment – in other words, the whole collection of free-market economics implemented by New Right governments in the 1980s.

A further implication of the hypermobility of capital concerns the Welfare State. If governments are required to keep taxes low in order to stop the TNCs disinvesting, the amount of money available for expenditure on the Welfare State is drastically reduced. Governments cannot therefore assist workers affected by unemployment or low wages as much as they might otherwise wish to do.

Divide the class into two groups.
One group should investigate the new international division of labour thesis. This issue links up with the sociology of development. Look up recent figures on the proportion of manufacturing industry in various sectors that is now based in the Southern Hemisphere or the Third World. Write a report on this phenomenon and its implications. Remember to include any material you come across that is critical of this thesis.

The other group should investigate the globalization of production thesis. Look up recent figures for the proportion of manufacturing industry in various sectors that is now controlled by transnational corporations. Try to identify some examples. Write a report on this phenomenon and its implications. Remember to include any material you come across that is critical of this thesis.

Produce a report on these ideas and a summary of your findings in the form of a map of the world with your notes included.

Produce a map showing the operations of one of the transnational companies.

Political implications of the globalization thesis

The globalization thesis has come to play an important part in political debate. For instance, the Conservative government in the UK has opted out of the Social Chapter of the Maastricht Treaty, arguing that foreign investment is an important element of the British economy, and that the provisions of the Social Chapter for a minimum wage and consultation rights for workers would impose costs on business, which would lead investors to look elsewhere for attractive returns. The same argument is deployed against the setting of a minimum wage, which would lead to higher unemployment, according to the Conservatives. The only thing to do is to let the market fix wage rates.

This is the classic New Right position, of course. However, similar arguments can be heard from bodies close to the Labour Party. For example, the 1994 report of the Commission on Social Justice, set up by the late Labour leader John Smith, refers explicitly to globalization as an economic revolution that has sapped the independence of the nation-state and destroyed the notion of a job for life. It goes on to argue that, although unemployment should be tackled, the objective of a return to the full employment of the 1950s and 1960s is no longer appropriate since economic demand for labour now operates internationally and national governments cannot control the level of employment as they could in the past. It also argues that the level of a minimum wage must be reduced from £4.10 per hour (Labour's position at the time the report was published) to around £3.50 per hour. The overall theme of the document is that the ideas that inspired Beveridge to create the Welfare State no longer apply and therefore any Welfare State of the future will look radically different. The globalization of the world economy is cited as a key factor in support of this argument.

1) *Use newspaper and magazine reports (with the help of a CD-ROM if available) on the Social Chapter of the Treaty of Maastricht. Make a list of the arguments for and against the Chapter and explain how it fits into debates about globalization.*
2) *Obtain newspaper reports about the report of the Commission on Social Justice. Consider the extent to which the notion of globalization influenced its proposals.*

Thinking about the effects of globalization

There are a variety of sociological interpretations of these economic processes. We have already considered some of the implications; this section will look in more detail at how sociologists have sought to devise theories that present a developed analysis of these developments.

'New Times'

One of the most influential theories which is certainly influenced by, but also goes beyond, notions of globalization is the collection of idea that have been called 'New Times'. These ideas were developed by a group of neo-Marxist, and later post-Marxist, writers around the Communist Party journal, *Marxism Today*.

A central tenet of this group is the need to move away from reliance on forms of analysis and action centred on social class and economic struggle. Such ideas have been influential in moving many neo-Marxists towards post-Marxism and radical pluralism. One of the reasons they adduce in arguing that it is no longer possible to analyse or indeed bring about change in terms of social class, as Marxists do, is their interpretation of globalization.

One of the fundamental elements of the Fordist system of production, according to the 'New Times' writers, was the need for mass consumption to sustain the mass production that was at the heart of the system. This required full employment, which was achieved by government intervention in the economy to stimulate demand. This approach went under the name of Keynesianism. In the present, post-Fordist era the emergence of giant multinationals has undermined the ability of governments to regulate their own economies and therefore to achieve the level of employment required to sustain mass consumption. Therefore one of the main props of Fordism begins to break down:

> The growing trend towards internationalization and globalization . . . is not new. It has been a persistent tendency since the 1950s, as evidenced by the growth of the international firm. But the capitalist crisis in the 1970s gave it a new meaning and momentum. It accelerated the trend towards global markets . . . it paved the way towards a far more global monetary system. These developments have greatly enhanced the economic interdependence of national economies such that it is no longer possible for the average European nation state to pursue national economic policies in the old way. [Jacques 1989, pp. 236–7]

Adherents of this view not surprisingly place great emphasis on striving for a degree of coordination of economic policy through the European Community, a view which for a time became very popular inside the Labour Party.

From organized to disorganized capitalism

A related view is presented by Scott Lash and John Urry in their book *The End of Organized Capitalism* (1987). Whereas the 'New Times' argument largely rests on the changes denoted by the move from Fordism to post-Fordism and the rise of Thatcherism, Lash and Urry take a more comparative approach and focus on the effects of globalization on social and cultural life.

They argue that the characteristic of the organized period of capitalism was the central importance of social class; the organization of the economy classically involved trade unions and employers' organizations alongside the state. Parties organized along social class lines were predominant. Taking the notion of 'organized capitalism' as an ideal type, Lash and Urry believe it was approached most closely in Germany, slightly less so in Britain, and even less so in France and the USA.

Organized capitalism sank into crisis in the 1970s for several reasons, including the increasing globalization of capital, but also because employers adopted new attitudes which induced workers to identify with them rather than with their class-based organizations; social and cultural life was also no longer organized around social class, especially with the rise of popular culture.

Lash and Urry argue that these developments have provided the basis both for the free-market New Right and for a new brand of politics with a small 'p', meaning loosely organized new social movements and lifestyle politics. The old structures of organized capitalism have melted away and have been replaced by a pluralist, disorganized brand of capitalism. The labour movement and the reformist strategy of capturing governmental power to make changes in society are no longer the only forms of opposition to capitalism; they have been weakened by globalization and the divisions generated by social and cultural change, and there has been increasing disenchantment with both. New forms of identity have arisen.

From the workers' point of view the implication of this model is once again that they face economic instability, but they should not place their reliance in the state; they should recognize that their problems have been partly caused by the structures championed by the labour movement itself, and therefore they need to develop new identities and forms of involvement. What differentiates this model from the 'New Times' one is the greater number of variables seen as contributing to the transformation. Disorganized capitalism is both post-Fordist and postmodern, that is, it reflects both economic and cultural changes.

In their follow-up book, *Economies of Signs and Space* (1994), Lash and Urry argue that much postmodern thinking leads to pessimism. They reject the extreme postmodernist position that proclaims the end of truth and falsehood entailed in much postmodernism; rather they reason that 'another set of radically divergent processes is simultaneously taking place. These processes may open up possibilities for the recasting of meaning in work and leisure, for the reconstitution of community and the particular, . . . and for heterogenization . . . of everyday life' (Lash and Urry 1994, p. 3). These possibilities are based on the growth of reflexive individuals in an environment dominated by information and communication structures:

> The modernization and postmodernization of contemporary political economies produce, not just a flattening, but a deepening of the self. Such a growing reflexivity of subjects that accompanies the end of organized capitalism opens up many positive possibilities for social relations, for intimate relations, for friendship, for work relations, for leisure and for consumption. [Lash and Urry 1994, p. 31]

There is thus hope that the transformations we are witnessing may be positive, and the pessimism of most analyses of globalization is avoided.

Globalization and leisure

The effects of globalization on the world of leisure and culture are generally viewed much more optimistically than the predicted impacts on the field of work.

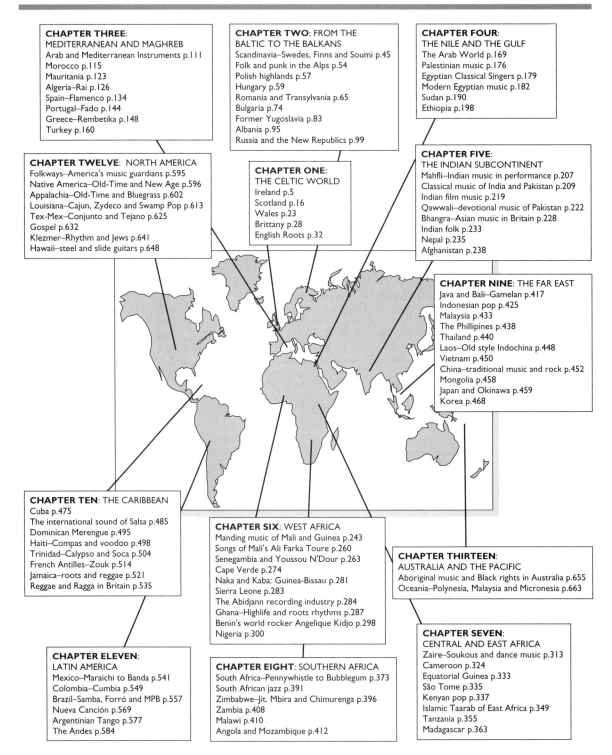

CHAPTER THREE:
MEDITERRANEAN AND MAGHREB
Arab and Mediterranean Instruments p.111
Morocco p.115
Mauritania p.123
Algeria–Rai p.126
Spain–Flamenco p.134
Portugal–Fado p.144
Greece–Rembetika p.148
Turkey p.160

CHAPTER TWO: FROM THE
BALTIC TO THE BALKANS
Scandinavia–Swedes, Finns and Soumi p.45
Folk and punk in the Alps p.54
Polish highlands p.57
Hungary p.59
Romania and Transylvania p.65
Bulgaria p.74
Former Yugoslavia p.83
Albania p.95
Russia and the New Republics p.99

CHAPTER FOUR:
THE NILE AND THE GULF
The Arab World p.169
Palestinian music p.176
Egyptian Classical Singers p.179
Modern Egyptian music p.182
Sudan p.190
Ethiopia p.198

CHAPTER TWELVE: NORTH AMERICA
Folkways–America's music guardians p.595
Native America–Old-Time and New Age p.596
Appalachia–Old-Time and Bluegrass p.602
Louisiana–Cajun, Zydeco and Swamp Pop p.613
Tex-Mex–Conjunto and Tejano p.625
Gospel p.632
Klezmer–Rhythm and Jews p.641
Hawaii–steel and slide guitars p.648

CHAPTER ONE:
THE CELTIC WORLD
Ireland p.5
Scotland p.16
Wales p.23
Brittany p.28
English Roots p.32

CHAPTER FIVE:
THE INDIAN SUBCONTINENT
Mahfli–Indian music in performance p.207
Classical music of India and Pakistan p.209
Indian film music p.219
Qawwali–devotional music of Pakistan p.222
Bhangra–Asian music in Britain p.228
Indian folk p.233
Nepal p.235
Afghanistan p.238

CHAPTER NINE: THE FAR EAST
Java and Bali–Gamelan p.417
Indonesian pop p.425
Malaysia p.433
The Phillipines p.438
Thailand p.440
Laos–Old style Indochina p.448
Vietnam p.450
China–traditional music and rock p.452
Mongolia p.458
Japan and Okinawa p.459
Korea p.468

CHAPTER TEN: THE CARIBBEAN
Cuba p.475
The international sound of Salsa p.485
Dominican Merengue p.495
Haiti–Compas and voodoo p.498
Trinidad–Calypso and Soca p.504
French Antilles–Zouk p.514
Jamaica–roots and reggae p.521
Reggae and Ragga in Britain p.535

CHAPTER SIX: WEST AFRICA
Manding music of Mali and Guinea p.243
Songs of Mali's Ali Farka Toure p.260
Senegambia and Youssou N'Dour p.263
Cape Verde p.274
Naka and Kaba: Guinea-Bissau p.281
Sierra Leone p.283
The Abidjann recording industry p.284
Ghana–Highlife and roots rhythms p.287
Benin's world rocker Angelique Kidjo p.298
Nigeria p.300

CHAPTER THIRTEEN:
AUSTRALIA AND THE PACIFIC
Aboriginal music and Black rights in Australia p.655
Oceania–Polynesia, Malaysia and Micronesia p.663

CHAPTER ELEVEN:
LATIN AMERICA
Mexico–Maraichi to Banda p.541
Colombia–Cumbia p.549
Brazil–Samba, Forró and MPB p.557
Nueva Canción p.569
Argentinian Tango p.577
The Andes p.584

CHAPTER EIGHT: SOUTHERN AFRICA
South Africa–Pennywhistle to Bubblegum p.373
South African jazz p.391
Zimbabwe–Jit. Mbira and Chimurenga p.396
Zambia p.408
Malawi p.410
Angola and Mozambique p.412

CHAPTER SEVEN:
CENTRAL AND EAST AFRICA
Zaire–Soukous and dance music p.313
Cameroon p.324
Equatorial Guinea p.333
São Tome p.335
Kenyan pop p.337
Islamic Taarab of East Africa p.349
Tanzania p.355
Madagascar p.363

Figure 9.4 World music

Source: Broughton *et al.* (1994)

The increased interconnectedness of the world has made the products of other cultures much more accessible. This is true of food, music, the cinema and television, but of course there has also been a dramatic expansion of travel and tourism.

In 1987 a new category of music, World Music, first appeared; since then it has been the fastest growth area in record stores. Figure 9.4 gives some idea of the scope and breadth of the cultural styles now becoming available to us. The editors of the 700-page *Rough Guide to World Music* comment:

> When we started work on this book, some four years back, the task seemed relatively simple . . . We would write about those diverse and wonderful musics emerging on the new crop of labels: zouk, soukous, cajun and zydeco, rai, qawwali, rembetika, taarab, gypsy bands from Transylvania: that sort of thing . . . it wasn't long, however, before we realized such modest aims were unrealistic. If we were going to feature salsa and merengue, then we'd have to include samba, forro, tango, cumbia and vallenato; if we had Bulgarian singers and Hungarian dancehall bands then why not flamenco or fado? [Broughton *et al.* 1994]

Does your local record shop have a section for World Music? What sort of music does it contain?

Figure 9.4 provides a list of the different styles of music categorized as World Music. In what ways does the map identify music in Britain as influenced by World Music? Use your knowledge of contemporary musical trends to write a report on any other influences you are aware of.

The involvement of Peter Gabriel in promoting WOMAD and the participation of black South African musicians on Paul Simon's *Graceland* album have helped to stimulate this growing market for global music.

It is debatable, however, whether World Music is really an example of globalization, since globalization in the economic sense means operating and producing in more than one country (as in the case of the Ford car example quoted earlier). The result is something which is the product of many countries. Although World Music is consumed in many countries, its authenticity derives from its local roots. Perhaps we should consider World Music to be a plurality of local musics rather than a manifestation of globalization. The same points can be made in relation to food, films and television programmes.

It seems likely that, even if the boundaries and divisions between national cultures are not breaking down as fast as the boundaries between national economies, the increasing availability of global cultures is leading to multicultural productions. However, we should not overlook the fact that one cultural reaction to globalization has been a reassertion of national cultures. This response may give people pleasure and a sense of authenticity, but it can also lead to the destructive phenomena of racism and xenophobia.

Globalization, production and consumption

In this chapter we have considered separately the effects of globalization on work (production) and consumption (leisure) but it is important to notice that there are links between the two. The effects may not be the same in both areas, as we have seen, but changes in one sphere affect the other.

In his analysis of tourism, Urry (1990) suggests that the globalization of that industry has created an international division of labour. For instance, Spain specializes in cheap access to the sun, Switzerland in skiing, Kenya in 'game tourism' and Mexico in 'ethnic tourism'. Britain offers historical and heritage tourism. Since most of the mansions and castles of interest are located away from the coast, the economics of the UK tourist industry have meant a shift away from a base in seaside resorts such as Blackpool towards inland locations. This has had implications not only for jobs, but also for the kind of facilities available for British tourists in their own country. These changes are linked to the processes of globalization.

> *To what extent do the brochures available in high street travel agents reflect an*
> *international division of labour? Where do other countries fit into this scheme?*
> *Use brochures from travel agencies to investigate and produce a map showing*
> *the international division of labour in the tourist industry.*
>   *Investigate the employment implications of the changes identified here for*
> *the area you live in.*

There is, of course, a negative global effect of the rise in tourism and indeed of the rise of globalization more generally, namely the global impact of environmental change and environmental damage. A second problem arises for less advanced countries, which are under pressure from the International Monetary Fund to earn foreign currency through tourism and exports more generally, often at the expense of meeting the basic needs of their indigenous populations.

Critical perspectives on globalization

Not all sociologists accept the globalization thesis. Their views are not often heard, for 'globalization' is a fashionable buzz-word. Nevertheless they have two basic points to make:

- The extent of the changes is overstated, particularly when it is implied that the whole world is involved.

- Long-standing changes that result from larger historical trends are wrongly identified as being products of the 1980s and 1990s.

On the second point, Ralph Miliband, for instance, remarked that although internationalism had reached new dimensions, 'As long ago as 1848, Marx and Engels noted in the *Communist Manifesto* the relentlessly international drives of capitalism and its compulsive disregard for national boundaries' (Miliband 1973, p. 14).

The conclusion of both these lines of criticism is not that there have been no changes in the level of international economic relations but that these changes are often misinterpreted and do not necessarily merit talking about a new stage of capitalism.

We will now look in more detail at some of the challenges to the concept of globalization.

How global is global?

The most common criticism is that 'globalization' is a misnomer because the flows of investment that lie at the heart of the process stay well within certain areas and do not encompass the whole globe. The new international division of labour thesis, in particular, invokes the idea of poorly paid workers in Third World countries acting as a form of competition to First World workers for the attentions of investment managers in charge of transnational corporations. The evidence suggests that this is not the case:

> the share of foreign capital received by the developing countries has steadily fallen from a peak of around 30 per cent in 1967 . . . Of the developed countries, Canada, the US, UK and West Germany are the leading host countries to the affiliates of foreign multinational enterprises; in the late 1970s they accounted for nearly two-thirds of all FDI [foreign direct investment] in developed countries and nearly half of all FDI. [Gill and Law 1988, pp. 195–6]

 Investigate more recent figures for foreign direct investment. A special issue of New Internationalist *on the subject of globalization, published in August 1993, gave detailed consideration to this issue.*

Apparently, therefore, we are witnessing not so much globalization as increasingly intense competition among a few advanced industrial economies. The spectre that workers in the advanced countries face competition from the low-wage Third World seems to be somewhat overdrawn.

The demand for a low-wage economy?

The idea that TNCs flit around the globe at will searching for low-wage situations has come under attack: 'In a study of FDI to 54 LDCs, Friedrich Schneider and Bruno S. Fey have found that labour-force wages and skill-level characteristics were by far the least important among factors affecting FDI from the period from 1976 to 1980' (Gordon 1988).

Political stability and the size of the market are far more important determinants of location, and these are most likely to be found in the advanced economies. Since the assumption that TNCs search restlessly for low wages is at the heart of the pessimistic prognosis for workers in advanced countries, this is an important issue.

Transnational corporations have feelings too!

Gordon (1988) accepts that the kinds of instability mentioned in theories of globalization exist, but he maintains that they also adversely affect the TNCs themselves. Some theories of globalization seem to imply that they can withstand any amount of buffeting, but this is not the case:

> It may appear . . . that I am belittling the power of capital, especially the mammoth transnational corporations . . . Quite to the contrary, I yield to few in my apprehension of the global power of capitalists and their corporate juggernauts. I shall argue, nonetheless, that we have all been staggering from the blows of economic crisis, including the multinationals. [Gordon 1988, p. 25]

Gordon makes a detailed analysis of the trends in the internationalization of capital and concludes that the phenomena that are being highlighted today are reflections of

Table 9.1 The global distribution of industrial production (%)

Country or grouping	1870	1896–1900	1913	1926–1929	1938	1948	1966	1973	1979	1984
United Kingdom	32	20	14	9	10.2	6.7	4.8	3.8	3.4	3.0
European Economic Community					27.5	15.4	18.8	17.2	15.5	14.1
France	10	7	7	7	7.7	5.4	5.3	5.0	4.8	4.4
Germany	13	17	14	12	12.3	4.6	8.1	7.4	6.4	5.8
Rest of EEC					7.5	5.3	5.4	4.8	4.3	3.9
United States	23	30	36	42	28.1	44.4	35.2	29.5	28.3	28.4
Japan		1	1	3	5.7	1.6	5.3	7.8	7.4	8.2
Other advanced economies	15	17	20	19	10.9	9.4	7.1	8.2	7.3	7.3
Centrally planned economies					7.2	8.4	16.7	19.5	23.5	23.4
USSR	4	5	4	4	4.9	6.3	11.1	12.4	14.2	14.7
Other CPEs					2.3	2.2	5.6	7.1	9.3	10.7
Less developed economies	3	3	4	3	10.4	14.0	12.2	14.0	14.6	13.9
European NICs					2.9	1.9	2.1	2.8	3.0	2.9
Latin America					2.2	4.3	4.1	6.7	6.7	6.3
Latin America NICs					1.3	2.9	3.2	3.6	4.2	4.3
Other Asia					2.7	2.5	3.1	2.8	3.1	2.9
Other Asian NICs					0.2	0.1	0.4	0.7	1.3	1.3
Other LDCs					2.5	5.3	2.9	1.7	1.7	1.8

Source: Gordon 1988 pp32–3

more general long-term trends. The reduction of the share of world output taken by the advanced economies of the West is not due to a rise in the proportion taken by the Third World, but in fact represents the post-Second World War growth in the share appropriated by Japan and the centrally planned economies of Eastern Europe. Table 9.1 provides some figures to illustrate the point.

Use these figures to create graphs showing the share of global industrial production taken during the period 1938 to 1984 by (1) the UK, (2) the EEC, (3) the USA, (4) Japan, (5) the centrally planned economies, (6) less developed economies.

You can obtain updates of these figures from the annual United Nations Yearbook of Industrial Statistics *which you should be able to find in a reference library. Use this to update your graphs. Write a report outlining the key movements identified in your graphs.*

Gordon concludes that what we are seeing is best understood 'not as a symptom of structural transformation but rather as a consequence of the erosion of the social structure of accumulation which conditioned international capitalist prosperity during the 1950s and 1960s. We are still experiencing the decay of the older order and not yet the inauguration of a new' (p. 25).

Nation-states and the military

The Second World War did witness a significant shift of production to the Third World. In 1948 the share of world production taken by less developed countries had reached 14.0 per cent – higher than the 13.9 per cent reached in 1984, supposedly in the high point of global integration. This points to an important factor often not considered by theorists of globalization, namely the state and the military.

As Paul Hirst (1993) among others has pointed out, the USA may no longer be economically dominant but it still wields the greatest military might; this power guarantees the operations of the MNCs and TNCs if difficulties arise. During the Gulf War the interests of the major oil companies were at stake, but the war was fought not by Esso and Shell but by armies organized by nation-states, which are very far from being impotent. Lash and Urry make no mention of military expenditure, and their picture of disorganized capitalism with a weakened state seems to ignore this important contemporary aspect of social life.

> *A related area is the growth in international arms sales. John Pilger has estimated that 20 per cent of world arms sales are from the UK.*
>
> *Governments are involved in arms exports, if only because export certificates are needed. It has been alleged that aid for Third World countries has become entwined with the promotion of arms sales, as in the case of the Pergau dam in Malaysia and the Samarinda power station in Indonesia. A report by Michael Durham in the* Observer *(13 November 1994) stated: 'Since 1980, Britain's aid to Tanzania, the world's second poorest country, has remained at a constant low. Aid to Indonesia, which is far from impoverished, has shot up.'*
>
> *Use newspaper and magazine articles (*New Internationalist *had a special issue on the arms trade in November 1994) to investigate the growth of the world arms trade. To what extent are national governments involved in this business? What are the implications for the notion of globalization?*

Alex Callinicos (1989) also argues that the vision of states that are impotent in the face of all-powerful TNCs massively overstates the power that individual states had in the era of 'organized capitalism'. Only on the basis of this overstated contrast can the state today be portrayed as weak.

The implication of this analysis for the future of work and leisure is that we are not at the mercy of hypermobile TNCs that hold the state to ransom. The state retains the power to intervene in the economy and thereby affect the future of work and leisure, contrary to the more extreme versions of the globalization thesis.

The protection that TNCs need from the state may explain why they are actually relatively immobile. *Business Week* (14 May 1990) identified forty-seven TNCs; all of them had the majority of their shares held in their home country, and only fourteen had a majority of their assets outside that country. Thus the TNCs do seem to retain links with particular countries (quoted in Harman 1991, p. 32).

Fixed capital

A final criticism made of theories of globalization is that they sometimes seem to imply that all capital is whizzing around the globe at a rate of knots. This is not the case.

Although the ownership of industries such as gas, electricity and water may now be partially international in character, the services and the work itself cannot be moved around the globe. Heathrow Airport may link Britain to the World, but it remains in Britain. Even potentially mobile industries cannot be shifted without expense and the loss of the original investment. Hypermobility is not painless.

> *Write a report outlining the criticisms of the globalization thesis and investigate current figures in each of these areas. This could be done by splitting your class up into groups and allocating one topic to each group.*
>
> *Use the information you have gathered together with information from this chapter and previous exercises to arrange a debate on the extent and importance of globalization. Try to incorporate references to other areas of sociology outside work and leisure into the debate.*

Conclusion

It is clear that something is happening in the international economic environment and that this something will have repercussions on work and leisure, and indeed on politics and the Welfare State, as we move towards the twenty-first century.

However, there are disagreements about the extent of these changes and about whether they represent the latest phase in a long-running development or a new stage or type of capitalism with very different methods and consequences. The position you take on this question will determine how important you think these processes are and how much influence they will have on the work and leisure prospects you are likely to encounter in the future.

Structured question

Item A

Eighty of the top 200 transnational corporations in the world are based in the United States, contributing just over half the total sales. The share of American companies has, however, fallen significantly since 1960, a period in which Japanese companies have grown dramatically: only five Japanese corporations were in the top 200 in 1960, as compared to twenty-eight in 1991. Contrary to common belief, most of the investment by transnational companies is within the industrialized world: three-quarters of all foreign direct investment is within the industrialized world. Nevertheless, the involvement of transnationals in Third World countries is very extensive, with Brazil, Mexico and India showing the highest levels of foreign investment. since 1970 the most rapid rate of increase in corporate investment by far has been in the Asian newly industrializing countries of Singapore, Hong Kong, South Korea and Malaysia.

Source: Giddens (1994), p. 543

Item B

The first source of globalization research is the world-system model, inspired by the work of Immanuel Wallerstein . . .

In some senses, Wallerstein and his school could rightly claim to have been global all along – after all, what could be more global than the 'world-system'? However, there is no specific concept of the 'global' in world-system literature . . .

The economics of the world-system model rests on the international division of labour that distinguishes core, semi-periphery and periphery countries . . .

But many sociologists are not convinced that the

world-system model, usually considered to be 'economistic' (that is, too locked into economic factors) can deal with cultural issues adequately. . .

A second model of globalization derives specifically from research on the 'globalization of culture' . . .

Although these researchers cannot be identified as a school in the same way as world-system researchers can be, there are some common themes running through their works.

First and foremost, they are all interested in the question of how individual and/or national identity can survive in the face of an emerging 'global culture'. Second, they tend to prioritize the cultural over the political and/or the economic.

A distinctive feature of this model is that it poses the existence of 'global society' and/or 'global culture', either as a possibility or a reality . . .

A third model of globalization is my own attempt to lay the foundations of a sociology of the global system based on transnational practices. The point here is to develop a concept of the 'global' that involves more than the relations between states . . .

Transnational practices are practices that originate with non-state actors and cross state borders . . . The transnational corporation (TNC) is the most important institution for economic transnational practices; the transnational capitalist class (TCC) for political transnational practices; and the culture-ideology of consumerism for transnational cultural-ideological practices . . .

While the world-system model tends to be economistic (minimizing the importance of cultural factors), and the globalization of culture model tends to be culturalist (minimizing economic factors), the global system model attempts to analyse how the economic, the political and culture-ideology are systematically connected and organized in terms of economic interests.

Source: Adapted from Sklair (1993)

Item C

It is now virtually a commonplace among left

observers and activists that we have recently witnessed the emergence of a New International Division of Labour and the Globalization of Production. For many these twin tendencies manifest such deep structural transformations in the world economy that group or government efforts to swim against the currents are becoming increasingly ineffectual, if not futile. The power of labour, community and the state has seemed to wither as multinational corporations sweep irresistibly around the globe . . .

I argue in this essay that widespread perceptions about the NIDL and the GOP have been significantly distorted and that much of the conventional wisdom about recent changes in the global economy requires substantial revision. These changes are best understood not as a symptom of structural transformation but rather as a consequence of the erosion of the social structure of accumulation which conditioned international capitalist prosperity during the 1950s and 1960s. We are still experiencing the decay of the older order and not yet the inauguration of a new . . . We have been witnessing the decay of the postwar global economy rather than the construction of a fundamentally new and enduring system of production and exchange . . .

First, I would argue that we have not witnessed movement towards an increasingly 'open' international economy, with productive capital buzzing around the globe . . . The international economy . . . has witnessed declining rather than increasing mobility of productive capital.

Second, and correspondingly, the role of the state has grown substantially since the early 1970s; state policies have become increasingly decisive on the international front, not more futile . . .

But why the fuss? . . . The NIDL/GOP perspectives have helped foster, in my view, a spreading political fatalism in the advanced countries. If we struggle to extend the frontiers of subsistence and security at home, one gathers, we shall stare balefully at capital's behind, strutting across the continents and seas, leaving us to amuse ourselves with our unrealized dreams of progress . . .

I disagree with these political inferences. The TNCs are neither all-powerful nor fully equipped to shape a new world economy by themselves. They require workers and they require consumers.

Source: Adapted from Gordon (1988)

1) What percentage of the top 200 transnational corporations is based in the United States, according to Item A? **(1 mark)**

2) Explain the meaning of the terms 'economistic' and 'culturalist' (Item B).

(4 marks)

3) Using material from the items and elsewhere, assess the extent to which sociological evidence supports the argument that 'we have been witnessing the decay of the postwar global economy rather than the construction of a fundamentally new and enduring system of production and exchange' (Item C).

(12 marks)

4) Assess the relative usefulness of the three models of globalization outlined in Item B for sociological analysis of work and leisure in a global context. **(8 marks)**

Coursework suggestions

Investigate whether the processes identified as globalization have had an effect on the area in which you live. Investigate the changes in the employment market in the last 30 years using material from the reference library or by interviewing careers officers or job centre workers. Investigate whether there is any evidence of any of the changes identified as being linked to globalization. You will need to read up about globalization and criticisms of it.

Alternatively you could investigate the extent to which there is any evidence of leisure activities in your area being affected by globalization. If you live in a tourist resort you could conduct a case study to test the ideas developed by John Urry in relation to the rise of a new international division of labour in the tourist industry.

In either case, you will need to assess the relative usefulness of the models sociologists have developed to analyse and describe these phenomena.

Bibliography

Broughton, S., Ellingham, M., Muddyman, D. and Trillo, R. (1994) *World Music: The Rough Guide,* London: Rough Guides

Callinicos, A. (1989) *Against Postmodernism,* Cambridge: Polity

Crum and Davies (1990) *The Multinationals,* London: Heinemann

Frobel, F., Heinrichs, J. and Kreye, O. (1980) *The New International Division of Labour*, Cambridge: Cambridge University Press

Fulcher, J. (1991) 'A new stage in the development of capitalist society?', *Sociology Review,* November

Giddens, A. (1994) *Sociology,* 2nd edn, Cambridge: Polity

Gill, S. and Law, D. (1988) *The Global Political Economy,* Hemel Hempstead: Harvester-Wheatsheaf

Gordon, D.M. (1988) 'The global economy: new edifice or crumbling foundations', *New Left Review,* No. 168

Harman, C. (1991) 'The state and capitalism today', *International Socialism Journal,* Summer

Harrison, B. (1987) 'Cold bath or restructuring?', *Science and Society*, Spring, pp. 72–81

Hirst, P. (1993) 'Globalisation is fashionable but is it a myth?', *Guardian,* 22 March

Hirst, P and Thompson, G. (1995) 'Globalization and the future of the nation state', *Economy and Society*, Vol. 24, No. 3 August, pp. 408–42.

Jacques, M. (1989) 'Britain and Europe', in Jacques, M. and Hall, S. (eds) *New Times,* London: Lawrence & Wishart

Lash, S. and Urry, J. (1987) *The End of Organized Capitalism,* Cambridge: Polity

—— (1994) *Economies of Signs and Space,* London: Sage

Miliband, R. (1973) *The State in Capitalist Society*, London: Quartet

Piore, J. and Sabel, C.F. (1984) *The Second Industrial Divide: Possibilities for Prosperity*, New York: Basic Books

Sklair, L. (1993) 'Going global: competing models of globalization', *Sociology Review,* November

Urry, J. (1990) *The Tourist Gaze,* London: Sage

Waters, M. (1990) *Globalization*, London: Routledge

Index